Ease The squeeze

Develop a Life Plan, a Giving Plan, and a Financial Plan

A Blueprint for a Solid Financial Foundation

Practical & Spiritual Approaches to Money and Life

Doug Hagedorn

Ease the Squeeze
by Doug Hagedorn

Printed in the United States of America

Library of Congress Control Number: 2002109296
ISBN 1-591601-71-1

Xulon Press
11350 Random Hills Road
Suite 800
Fairfax, VA 22030
(703) 279-6511
XulonPress.com

To order additional copies, call 1-866-909-BOOK (2665).

Acknowledgements

To God be the Glory. Without YOU, I am nothing. I love you. If any blessing results from this book, may Jesus Christ receive all the praise.

To my wife Dana. You are my rock and my encourager, not to mention a wonderful wife and mother. Thanks for allowing me to do this work. I love you.

To Emily, Jacob, and Justin. You are our investment in the future. Be a light for Jesus. We love you.

To Mom and Dad. Thanks for the firm foundation. I love you.

To Shelley and Joggers. Love ya! Thanks for putting up with me all those years. You could each write a book about obstinate, obnoxious brothers.

To Pastor Tracy. For encouraging me to take a risk! (I'm a 7.4 now.)

To Dan White. It will be said one day, "Well done, good and faithful servant!"

To Larry Burkett. You are an inspiration!

To the G.R. posse + 1—Andy, Howie, Ken, Oosse, and Quimby—Who'da thunk it?

To my early manuscript editing servants—Keith Barber, Nancy Bratcher, Steve Diemer, Georgia Emry, Joy Engelsmann, Jeff & Dawn Kregel, Cathy Oosse, Andy Postema, Aunt Arlene, Steve Roemerman, Dan White, Cheryl Winger, and of course Dana, Dad, and Mom—your brutal honesty and valuable inputs made this a better book. Thanks for the sharpening!

To Jack Stewart and Pastor Clint Bratcher. Thanks for believing in me!

To Len. Thanks for the title!

To Dennis Peterson.[1] May your editing gifts continue to be used for the kingdom of God. You were truly a divine appointment! Thanks for keeping me humble!

Contents

SECTION 3—THE BRICK & MORTAR: "A FINANCIAL PLAN"

An Opening Word

Writing a book was not at all what I expected. The easy part was actually getting my *initial* thoughts on paper. The five-plus years of research and study preparing for financial seminars and teachings on giving had helped me formulate material for topics I wanted to address. I can honestly say that the most *difficult* part of the entire process was trying to *effectively* communicate those *initial* thoughts that were staggering around in my head. After completing the third or fourth rewrite (I lost track), I happened upon a quotation that really summarized it all:

"The difficulty in literature is not to write, but to write what you mean: not to affect your reader, but to affect him precisely as you wish"
—Robert Louis Stevenson

I am thankful for those who read the early manuscripts, provided feedback early on, and helped bring some clarity to my thoughts. A few surprises have also occurred along the journey. One surprise was the length of the book. My initial goal was a seventy- to eighty-page document. You can quickly tell that I underscoped the effort! The second surprise was the topic on which I planned to write. When I initially thought about writing a book, I surmised that the sole purpose was to share my financial-freedom story and help others walk the same path. In fact, the mission statement for my financial seminars is "To free people from the slavery of debt and release them into the liberty of true, biblical financial freedom." Although that is also a primary purpose of this book, I quickly discovered that this really cannot be accomplished without a proper "life plan." Our priorities, choices, and life goals significantly impact our financial plans, so for me simply to discuss debt, budgets, and savings glosses over many important issues that need to be dealt with. Thus, I ended up writing a portion of the book on these foundational issues.

My initial thought was to include a chapter on giving, but when I looked up I realized that I had written eight chapters on varied subjects such as giving, blessings, tithing, voluntary giving, and the importance of the condition of the heart relating to these matters. I also touch on a few other hot-potato issues just for fun. In my studies on the area of giving, I have been careful to avoid "cherry picking" Scriptures out of context, and I hope to provide you with some thought-provoking insights with a balanced, biblical perspective. Once we have a "life plan" and a "giving plan," then we are ready for a "financial plan." Thus, *Ease the Squeeze* is organized into three major sections to help individuals deal with three specific areas: (1) a life plan, (2) a giving plan, and (3) a financial plan.

Why the book? Do we need another financial self-help book? When I set out to write this book, I wanted a book that would give biblical counsel coupled with practical application. My desire was to mix teaching with *immediate* opportunities to put learning into practice. *Ease the Squeeze* attempts to address the symptoms of our debt, shifting life priorities, decreased giving, and a lack of financial planning, and then it provides practical solutions for financial freedom; goal setting; budgeting; saving money; simplifying our lives; and responsible, biblical giving. My hope is that God will use it to influence some area of your life.

For some people, my financial testimony might provide a much-needed dose of faith and hope. For others it might be a tool to assist them in getting out from under a mountain of debt or to help set up a budget. For still others, it might provide insight into the subject of giving. For yet others, it might challenge them to step back and set some family or personal goals. It might also be a tool in the toolbox of a pastor, teacher, or church board member.

My prayer is that by the time you have finished reading this book, you will at least be better equipped to handle finances from a biblical viewpoint. However, my real heart's desire is that this book and your resulting actions will lead to a life-changing testimony that will influence your world and others around you so that others will see the difference that God has made in your life.

It is really quite stunning that we are more prosperous as a nation than ever but also more stressed, more counseled, more divorced, and more in debt than any other generation. On top of the financial and personal challenges, our charitable giving has been on a gradual decline since 1968.

What is Your Financial IQ?

On a recent test administered by the National Council on Economic Education regarding financial matters, 49 percent of adults received an F, and only 6 percent received an A.[1] Our *lack of knowledge,* coupled with a *lack of action,* has left us financially and personally "squeezed." Only 3 percent of Americans actually have a financial plan. Only 9 percent of pastors thought that they had adequate training about financial issues at the seminary level.[2] Debt has become a way of life for many individuals as well as our nation. A recent case in point is the fact that 57 percent of credit-card users now hold a balance of greater than $8000 from month to month.[3] The following quotation summarizes part of the dilemma: "First we are manipulated into buying what we don't need. Then we can't pay for it. Then we don't even have a place to put it. Then we don't have time to use it!"

Stirring and Stopping

Nothing irks me more than spending multiple hours reading a book that I then put quickly back on the shelf without its having challenged me or assisted me in making a positive change in my life. I will be up front with you—my goal is to *stir you to action.* You will see that this book encourages your participation. Past research shows that we learn and retain more when we *participate!* I have attempted to provide a number of participation opportunities along the way.

The word *selah* is used seventy-one times in the Psalms and could have possibly indicated a moment when the worshipers were to "pause and act." It could have been an opportunity to meditate, or it could have been an opportunity to praise the Lord in a particular manner. I have provided numerous "Selah Stops" along the way in the hope that you will slow down or pause to pray or act if a section of the book is stirring you. If you wait too long, that stirring might go away. Obviously, you might not opt to participate at each "Selah Stop" or "Action Point," but I hope that you will at least yield or come to a rolling stop at a few of them!

> *"The great aim of education is not knowledge, but action."*
> **—Herbert Spencer**

My prayer is that my testimony of financial freedom and the "how-to's" and tools that I offer will assist you in paving the way to your own testimony. I have rolled up my sleeves and shared not only some valuable research but also some of the lessons learned—both successes and failures—along the financial journey. My hope is that if you are married or have children, you will work through portions of the book with your spouse and children to bring more unity to your financial and life goals.

> WARNING! The author is not you! Noting the obvious, each of us is a unique being. Me, too! Some of us might have a personality type that chokes on worksheets. Some of us might wish that every page had a chart or a graph. Some of you might wish that I would get right to the solutions rather than ask you to take a look in the mirror regarding your current situation. My personality type is not the same as yours. So, if a worksheet, Selah Stop, Action Point, or chapter does not fit well with your personality type or approach preference, I hope that you will move on.

> *Chew it all, but swallow and digest what works for you!*

One last observation: I never purchase a book without first reading the back cover, the table of contents, and the introduction. It always humors me to read the back cover before I start the book and then to read it again after I've finished the book to see if it met my expectations. The back cover is a marketing individual's dream and a realist's funny page. Although I really believe everything written on the back cover of *this book* (or it would never have made it there), it really would have been much funnier if I had included some of the quotations from my closest friends and family from my *early* manuscript efforts. One of my close friends wrote, "You *are* getting an editor aren't you?" One of my family members said, "I am not an editor, and I could tell quickly I was in over my head." My favorite was, "I am not sure who has the comma problem, me or you!" Yes, there were also both many humbling, complimentary comments and many helpful suggestions, but my hope is that the back cover marketing will turn into a real-life testimony for you, your family, and your church.

How to Get Your Money out of this Book!

1. Mark it up!
2. Make some *specific* action points at the end of each chapter, both long and short term.
3. After completing the book, summarize your *key* action points for the entire book on one page of paper, print it out and carry it in your Bible or daily planner, where you can look at it weekly and check things off as you act. The key phrase in this point is *one page*. Anything more, and you will probably ignore it. Chapter 24 might be of some assistance if you are not a great note taker.
4. Go back through the book a few weeks after you finish reading it and skim the highlighted areas. We never comprehend everything in one reading.
5. Apply its principles! The best way to do this is *SELAH!* Participate at the Selah Stops, and apply something that you have read or tailor it appropriately to your situation.

Sample Selah Stop!

6. Keep a Bible handy!
7. Share the principles with a spouse, friend, or family member.

Research also shows that we learn and retain so much more when we teach what we have learned to others.

John Knox commented in a sermon to King Henry in the 1500s that "so much is written, and yet so little is well observed."[4] May you read, absorb, observe, observe well, and *then* be moved to action as you *Ease the Squeeze* in your finances and your life!

Section 1

Laying the Foundation

"A Life Plan"

CHAPTER 1

Modern-Day Pharaoh

═══════════════════════════════

As I pen the very first words of my first draft, it is not at all how I pictured it. I was surprised that I actually had a little idealistic imagery, white-picket-fence American dreaming tucked away somewhere deep down. Much of that actually sickens me, but in respect to writing a book, I actually found the thought of it rather appealing to my natural senses. A scene from an old film came to mind as to how I would proceed with this massive undertaking of putting my thoughts and experiences—and *hopefully* some godly wisdom—on paper.

As I replay the movie scene in my mind, the author sits peacefully in his farmhouse in a quiet, serene, country setting and gazes out the window at beautiful, old oak trees three times his age; the leaves rustling gently in the wind; and a backdrop of lush pastures and gardens. The writer hums along with the chirping of the morning songbirds on a sunny day. Squirrels and rabbits scamper and chase each other just a few feet away. His typewriter sets patiently waiting, poised as his partner and best friend "to be" for weeks and months to come. This is the point where I would edit the scene to include a cup of coffee, a large piece of coffeecake or cinnamon roll, and a backrub from my wife. I would also probably replace the typewriter with a laptop because the thought of white out makes my skin crawl. I would also add numerous therapeutic walks in the crisp, autumn mornings as a daily mandatory item on my schedule.

Sound idealistic? Yep. But a little jolt of air turbulence brings me back to reality as I sit here on a crowded plane and I am reminded of the wrestling that my stomach is doing with the fine appetizer (the same one I had a few weeks ago, I think) that I enjoyed before our battle with cloud cover enroute from Dallas to Los Angeles. The view out the window is utter darkness. I stare longingly at the laptop screen of the man seated next to me while I write with a church pen (and a dandy it is) on the back of an old tattered 8 -1/2 x 11 e-mail sent to my boss, the content of which is a bitter reminder of the previous month's shortcomings and challenges. I have no coffee, no backrub, no songbirds, no country setting, and no artificial tranquility. However, I *do* know that God's timing is perfect, that His ways are, in fact, higher than mine,[1] and that I am extremely grateful for His patience, His mercy, and His blessings. I'll describe later why I am thankful for the trials and tribulations through which He allowed me to grow. Without them, there would be no book and no financial testimony.

I am not aware of the severity of your financial, spiritual, or even physical situation—how much debt you have or how it has affected your marriage and family. I do not know the struggles through which you have gone as a pastor, church member, parent, spouse, child, family member, or employee. But I *do* know that I can testify that nothing is impossible with Him. NOTHING! I do know that I was at one time in the spiritual ICU, the financial ICU, and nearly the hospital ICU—but God's grace was sufficient for me. It is sufficient for you, too. He has plenty of grace to go around. He is no respecter of persons. Regardless of how deep your life hole or financial hole is, He is ready and waiting to help you! He is ready to start working alongside you to help fill the hole. His arm is not too short.[2] He is not too distant. He is not shortsighted. He has not forgotten you. All things are possible; only believe!

Time for an "About Face"

I remember an old song that Mother used to sing to me. Although my memory is usually poor, its words are burned into my heart, and they still ring in my ears today.

Turn your eyes upon Jesus
Look full in His wonderful face
And the things of earth will grow strangely dim
In the light of His glory and grace.[3]

The only reason I joined the ranks of those having a testimony of financial liberty is because I did an "about face." I turned my eyes *from* myself and my circumstances and *toward* Jesus. Let's face it: we all make mistakes. We all learn from the school of hard knocks and go through a certain amount of "on the job training." It is critical that we admit our mistakes, ask forgiveness, and get beyond our guilt. No doubt, you have made some mistakes with your finances. No doubt in the early chapters of this book you will be further challenged to come to grips with *why* you are in your current situation. May it be nothing more than a call for you to move forward, to stop wallowing in the guilt in which the enemy wants to keep you mired.

SELAH 1-1

My desire is that you harvest what *God* desires for you to harvest from this book. Before moving forward, take thirty seconds to pray, asking God for wisdom and that the power of the Holy Spirit would speak to your mind, your emotions, and your will as you read this book. If you do not know how to pray, feel free to pray something like this: "God, you know me better than anyone else. You know what I need to get from this book. I ask that *You* help me, that *You* teach me, and that *You* speak to me as I read it. Please wash away the guilt that would attack my thoughts, and forgive me for my past mistakes and sins. In Jesus' name. Amen."

Those who know me the best know that this book is a way of life for me and my family. It is not a prepackaged, target-marketed, write-to-sell effort. It is *me!* For those of you who *really* know me, I am certain that you will roll your eyes as you read certain parts of the book and laugh out loud at other parts of it because you know it is *me* writing, not a ghostwriter!

Although I joked earlier about the "idealistic" view that I had about writing a book, I think in some respects it parallels how we often put God in a box with our views about how He *should* act or how He *should* "lead" us or speak to us. God is a God of variety, and He works in different ways at different times through different people. To be honest, I questioned Him for a few years about why we needed another book on priorities, finances, giving, and money from a biblical perspective. However, the more I questioned, the more He seemed to clarify that we are all unique and that a different perspective might help an individual whereas a different book might not affect them.

Amazed!

Coincidentally (or not!), the very day on which I started writing this book was the day when our family became completely and totally debt free—no more credit card debt, no more vehicle notes, and no more mortgage!

Before

Before that day, our situation was as follows.
- We had thirteen credit cards with total debts of $6,000.
- We had two vehicle notes with total debts of $22,000.
- We had one repossessed mobile home with a $15,000 debt.
- We had one house mortgage of $58,000.
- My wife was forced to work a second job over the holidays to scrape together enough money to stave off the bill collectors and barely make the minimum payments on our credit cards.
- The thought of having children was a major stress point because of our lack of finances.
- We were giving nothing to the church, missions, or other ministries.

After

Six and a half years later, here's how we stand.

- We have *no* credit cards and $0 debt.
- Our two vehicle notes are paid off, and we bought two different vehicles with cash, and we have $0 debt.
- The one mobile home debt was totally forgiven through a miracle, so we owe $0 on it!
- Our one home mortgage ($58,000) is totally paid off.
- We sold the house, bought a new house, and paid it off two years later, so now we owe $0.
- My wife stays at home with our three children.
- We are investing 10 percent of our income in 401k, Individual Retirement Accounts (IRA), and a fund for our children's education.
- We are giving 30 percent of our income to the church, missions, and other vital ministries.

Wow! I'm still amazed! As I look back on these "before-and-after" statistics, I realize that it was not because I won the lottery or doubled my income that this radical transformation in our finances occurred. It was because our eyes were opened and we made the decision to do an "about face" in our lives and in our finances. Yes, God blessed us with a few miracles along the way, but I truly believe that it was because we were faithful, disciplined, and obedient.

I cannot explain adequately the joy and freedom that I feel as a result of owing no man anything. My debt is only to the Lord, and we feel unchained from the heavy burden of debt. It has been a long and winding six-and-a-half-year journey to freedom from *all* debt, but it has been so rewarding!

A Stubborn Student

Was I always faithful, disciplined, and obedient? Far from it! I am thankful that God was patient with this modern-day Pharaoh, a selfish, independent, hard-headed, and selectively deaf person.

I heard what *I wanted* to hear and did what *I wanted* to do. I learned that both God and my wife Dana have to practice the "Rule of Seven" with me rather consistently: I need to hear something seven times before I actually *get it,* kind of like a modern Pharaoh. It sticks after seven times—*sometimes!* Dana could probably confirm that the seven is obviously an average, and that more often than not God probably gets most of those on the "less than" side of seven whereas she ends up on the "more than" side of seven with me.

I was raised in a household that ran a fairly tight financial ship. Unfortunately, I chose to venture off on my own spending sprees. For about ten years after moving from the nest, I frittered away untold thousands of dollars. I saved nothing. I gave little. I spent recklessly and frivolously. I lived for myself and no one else. I was taught some financial lessons at home, but few elsewhere. It would pain me deeply to calculate how much money I wasted during that time. One would think that I should have stayed on the straight and narrow financial path as a result of the potent combination of Dutch ancestry (penny pinchers), a minister father, a banker grandfather, and eight years of paper routes! Nope. I had to learn from my own failings. Some of it was ignorance and some of it was laziness, but much of it was Pharaohitis.

If we could only squeeze a little more "life priority" management, money management 101, and basic biblical financial principles into our children's education, I believe that we would be much better off as individuals, as a society, and as Christians. That was not the case for many of us as we grew up, and it is still not the case for kids today. But it is our *parental responsibility* to train our children in the way they should go, and when they are old they will not turn from it.[4] Thankfully, my Christian parents believed in the truth of a statement by sociologist Neil Postman:

> *"Children are the living messages we send to a time that we will not see."*

They invested in me and taught me. May we never sacrifice our children or our marriages on the altar of idolatry, selfishness, and temporal things!

> *"In a house where the adults are consumed with satisfying their lusts, a child becomes a victim."*
> —**Dennis Rainey**, *One Home at a Time*[5]

Even most pastors wish that they had more financial training. In a survey conducted by "The Stewardship Project" as noted in *Behind the Stained Glass Windows—Money Dynamics in the Church,* 73 percent of pastors strongly agree that they would like more education opportunities in effectively challenging their church members about their financial stewardship. Only 9 percent thought that they had adequate training about stewardship at the seminary level. [6]

Delay of Game

I was taught. I heard, but I *delayed* before I obeyed. One of the worst diseases infecting the American church is that we are too often hearers but not often doers.

Hold on. Before I pick on the general Christian population, let me shift the log from my own eye so I can see a little better. Jesus seems to have described me fairly well in the story of the wise builder and the foolish builder.

> Therefore everyone who hears these words of mine and puts them into practice is like a wise man who built his house on the rock. The rain came down, the streams rose, and the winds blew and beat against that house: yet it did not fall, because it had its foundation on the rock. <u>But everyone who hears these words of mine and does not put them into practice is like a foolish man who built his house on sand</u>. The rain came down, the streams rose, and the winds blew and beat against that house, and it fell with a great crash.[7]

I was a great hearer, but a lousy doer. Actually, if she was honest, Dana could vouch that my self-assessment of "great hearer" isn't totally accurate either. I am thankful that although I was stubborn, spiritually deaf, and financially inept, I never totally crashed and God never gave up on me! He was patient with me. It does not matter how much the winds and rains of this world have stormed against your finances, you *will* survive if you put God's Word into practice. He promised!

Strong Voices and Humble Servants

I stand amazed that God uses ordinary men and women to influence our lives. It happened in the New Testament days (Peter and John were unschooled, *ordinary*[8] men), and it happens today. That gives me hope that this ordinary book, written by a very *ordinary* man will affect someone's life the way two men affected mine. I do not view them as ordinary because of their extraordinary touch on my life, but if you asked both of them, they would say that they are nothing special—just men serving and obeying God's timeless principles.

No matter how heedless, insensate, materialistic, selfish, unjust and greedy a society may be, if there can be found in it a few clear and powerful voices that speak out against its corruptions, the spirit and the hope of reform can persist.

—John Adams, second President of the United States

That truth still applies today. The clear and powerful voices of two ordinary men had an extraordinary impact on my life. A godly, humble, and faithful servant named Dan White offered a ten-week "Financial/Budgeting" class. I thought that ten weeks seemed like a heavy commitment for a pretty simple subject, and based on the turnout for the class, others must have thought the same thing. But Dana and I knew that we had to pay the price to invest our time to lay the proper financial foundation early in our marriage.

To be honest, I do not remember 90 percent of the content of the class, but the principles and financial tools spurred me to action. Three specific things, however, did stick with me. The first thing was a somber comment by the instructor that most people who went through the class (or one like it) would *not* make the necessary changes to affect their financial future. It was sort of like the parable of the foolish man building on the sand again.[9] The second thing was that "financial freedom," "budgeting," and "giving principles" really can be dressed up, gussied up, and dolled up only so much. The third thing was the width of the instructor's tie. Wow! The video series was obviously taped in the 1970s when brown was in and the wider the tie the more fashionable it was. (I still have a few of those ties because I know they will be back.)

All of this just goes to show again that God can use the foolish things to confound the wise, and it also shows that correct biblical principles are timeless. The methods might change—from parchments to videos—but the message remains the same. We often ignore the simple things, the basics, at our own peril, or we simply forget or lose them amid the shouts and noise of modern voices, most of which tell us what we *want* to hear, not what we *need* to hear. I am thankful that God uses ordinary men. I am thankful God used Dan White to offer a financial class that radically changed my life.

Extraordinary Men

The second voice in my financial life was Larry Burkett. I am so thankful for how God used him as a powerful catalyst to transform my financial thinking and actions. His solid, biblical, common-sense approach was a refreshing, challenging voice in my materialistic wilderness.

The video series was nothing showy. It was just the basics. Just the meat. Hold the milk please. Financial and spiritual junk food looks good, tastes good, and sounds good. It has a pleasing short-term impact. But it does not last, and it surely does not have a lasting impact; it affects only our emotional taste buds. But Dan White and Larry Burkett—two ordinary men—showed me the path to financial freedom and the path to being more like Jesus.

People stumble or lose focus with the "get-rich-quick" opportunities, the "get-out-of-debt next week" plans. It is the "lose-fifty-pounds-in-thirty-days" mentality. It has even infiltrated the church with advertising that reeks of manipulation and "quick" fortunes. We now hear about new methods to "increase your church giving by 200 percent in two months."

You can get dressed up for the one-hour wedding, but a one-hour wedding does not a marriage make. Falling in love sounds great, but staying in love, serving our spouses, and living with weaknesses and shortfalls is *work*. A marriage does not succeed or grow on autopilot. So it is with money and finances. A financial planner or a two-day seminar can give you great ideas, options, and alternatives and even help you begin to construct the framework of a plan, but *nothing happens unless you do something.* Hearing and doing are two very different things. One is hard, and the other is harder.

"Planning to do is NOT doing."

Tough Words

I commend you for reading this book. Some people will not even attempt to learn or hear. But hearing is just preparation for the battle; it is not the war itself. "Faith without deeds is dead (James 2:25)." It seems so obvious. But, oh the obedience!

"A man of words and not of deeds is like a garden full of weeds."
—Nursery Rhyme

I look back and realize that my financial principles were grounded firmly in what *the media* and *man* taught me, and very little of them were what God had to say. I avoided His "tough words." I was king of the littles:

> Little *self-control*
> Little *discipline*
> Little *obedience*
> Little *sacrifice*
> Little *accountability*
> Little *responsibility*
> Little *patience*

These "tough words" were foreign to me, so I practiced them very seldom. I guess I had latched on to that great American expectation of *results with no action*. Quick freedom. Quick riches. Quick happiness. I wanted instant results without change or sacrifice. Why should I be surprised that *my lack of action was leading to lack of result*? Only in the last few years, after seeing the progress of our financial journey, do I realize that we must master these tough words to understand biblical money management specifically and biblical Christianity generally. The problem is that these words and the modeling of this behavior is rarely taught and even more rarely heeded.

> *"What you're doing thunders above your head so loudly, I can't*
> *hear what you're saying."*
> **—Ralph Waldo Emerson**

Little did I know (no pun intended) that my ignorance and disdain for these tough words resulted in *little* results! My little inputs gave me little outputs. It's kind of like that "reap what you sow" thing! I was king of the littles and had a kingdom of littles:

Little *blessing*
Little *freedom*
Little *contentment*
Little *unity*
Little *joy*
Little *faith*

I wanted big results with little change. I mention the "tough words" now because they are foundational to moving forward with your finances. Fortunately, God works on us gradually (in small steps rather than by giant leaps). We often *learn* gradually because we are slow or hardheaded. (That was me—the "Rule of Seven"). So, don't throw down the book because the challenge is too steep or if the squeeze is not eased overnight. It will happen! Start challenging yourself with the "tough words." Make the choice and act! Set high but realistic expectations for your journey to freedom. God will be faithful to help you complete what you start.

Get Out of the Box!

In response to my questioning the Lord about writing this book, I believe that the Lord's answer was as simple and as basic as His Word, which we often make too difficult.

1. Focus on the basics.
2. Use the Bible as your foundation.
3. Listen to God, not to men (Gal. 1:10).
4. Be yourself.

I think that these four items can apply to most of the human race today, whether you are a Bible school student, a pastor, a teacher, an employee, a manager, a housewife, or an author.

I would *like to* tell you of the overnight miracle regarding our finances in the areas of both debt and giving. I'm sorry to disappoint the "Microwave Minions" out there in Christian La-la Land. I know God *can* do an overnight miracle. I know that He is God and that I am not. That is why I will not put Him in a box. My testimony, *however*, is *not* an overnight testimony. I did not start giving immediately. I did not begin sacrificing immediately. I did not change immediately. I did not get out of debt immediately. Some of this was my plan; some of it was God's. Some of it was disobedience; some of it was to teach me patience. Do not put God in a black-and-white box. Yes, His laws are black and white, and His Word is black and white. But His actions, modes of operation, means, and sovereignty are beyond our little boxes, traditions, and experiences—denominationally, doctrinally, and personally. I love the words of Wayne Watson's song:

They've got it all figured out, little room for mystery, little room for doubt, got no time for questions, everything is black and white.

If you ain't heard our version, brother, you ain't really heard, everything is crystal clear, nothing left to learn.

Lord have mercy on our arrogant souls, before we were us, it was You alone.

God ain't gonna stay in the little box I put him in. He won't be contained by some shiny, wrapped-up view of him.[10]

—Wayne Watson, "A Beautiful Place," Word Records, 1993

Just because God did it for me one way does not mean that He will do it for you the same way. In fact, I can guarantee that *He won't!* I humbly believe that God has given me some wisdom in the area of biblical finance. But my way is not the only way, and God will not be contained by Doug's catechism of seven steps, five ways, or three keys to financial freedom.

A football team can score a touchdown in many different ways. Kick-off returns for touchdowns are great, but that steady, ninety-nine-yard, fifteen-play drive is just as sweet and as rewarding when you see the result. God will honor His Word. He will never leave you nor forsake you,[11] and nothing is impossible for Him! He will do it His way, but He needs your *participation!*

ACTION POINTS

1. Ordinary and not-so-ordinary people have touched your life. Make a list of the most influential people in your life and explain briefly how they influenced you.

   _____
   _____
   _____
   _____
   _____

2. Write or call one of those people to tell them the impact that they've had on you. Share with them how their investment in you has resulted in fruit in your life or that of others.

   _____
   _____

3. Review the "tough words" discussed earlier. On which ones do you need work? Maybe God will want you to focus on one particular word so that you can become a "doer."

   _____
   _____
   _____
   _____
   _____
   _____

4. How have you put God in a box: (a) in your life? (b) in your spiritual journey? (c) in your finances?

   _____
   _____
   _____
   _____
   _____

CHAPTER 2

Foundational Blueprints

B efore we submerge ourselves in your current financial situation, I want to touch on some foundational issues that will affect your checkbook balance or your credit card statement as much as will implementing the tools that we cover later. It is often difficult to assess our current situation without rewinding the tape and looking at our past and the path that we're traveling. We should not dwell on the past, but we should understand it so that we can assess the changes that we must make. It is humbling and challenging to share our weaknesses and personal lessons learned. But Paul did it. He wrote that he was, "the worst of sinners."[1] He also wrote, "For what I want to do I do not do, but what I hate I do."[2] And James said that we are to "confess your sins to each other."[3]

We who call ourselves Christians must guard against wearing hypocritical masks and having "holier-than-thou" attitudes. We must not be like the teachers of Jesus' day who resembled a cup that was clean on the outside but that was actually not dealing with the dirty inside of the cup.[4] I will spend a considerable amount of time talking about the condition of the heart when it comes to finances. I believe that the heart's condition is foundational to having successful finances. It is also critical that you make a commitment to "confess your faults" in the area of finances first to Jesus and then to another person. The topics of money and politically charged issues are almost taboos in the church today, but Jesus did not run from them. Neither should we.

The Real Thing

Generally, I think that many people have a difficult time being vulnerable, open, "real," and letting others into their world—because they're afraid of what people will think. Although Jesus is the one who forgives us of our sins, I think it would be a most refreshing change in our Christian lives and a radical shift toward biblical Christianity to heed James's challenge to "confess your sins to each other."[5] I am not advocating a move toward constructing a confessional in every garage or stationing a pastor or a priest at your job site. However, we need to move out of our Christian cocoons of isolation and live real Christianity. Becoming vulnerable enough to share our financial faults with one another might open the door for us to learn from each other or to realize that other people are dealing with similar issues. This act of vulnerability could lead quickly to a fulfillment of the next portion of James 5:16—"and pray for each other." People have seen enough phoniness and "dressed-up" Christianity. May we move closer to the real Jesus by opening ourselves up as real, ordinary people.

Admit your shortcomings and failures and then roll up your sleeves! It does not matter if you have too much debt, too little income, no budget, no plan, have been too selfish, or too disobedient. *It is time to be real and move forward!*

"What? Roll up My Sleeves?"

I have counseled couples regarding their financial situations, and a thread of commonality is evident in the outcomes of these meetings. I see some successes, but I also see many failures. Some couples will give it a short-term try, but when they realize that I will not *legislate* self-control, planning or the discipline necessary to implement a plan, most of them drift slowly away.

I realized that the responsibility to change was *mine* after I attended that financial class many years ago, but it did not change the fact that I felt as though I had been whacked on the side of my head with a watermelon. The work and responsibility belonged to *me! I* helped create our mess, and *I* would have to be the one to clean it up. If only counselors could do the counseling *and* the changing for us it would be so much easier!

To be honest, I did not feel like rolling up my sleeves. I wanted to dig out of my financial situation overnight, although it had taken years for me to slide down the deep hole. I am so excited to see some of those whom I counsel make major changes and add new disciplines or habits that will influence their families for generations to come. Unfortunately, many couples want to do little or nothing after they realize that the book, the seminar, the worksheet, or the Scripture does not transmit to them some magical discipline or that it offers no self-control pill that they can pop once to make their problems go away.

> ### *"God is a gradual God."*
> ### —Tracy Jantz, 2000

I really believe that if we *act* as much as we plan and pray and if we obey when we hear, we could turn this world upside down for Jesus![6] We need a proper mixture of prayer, planning, and acting! Acting without prayer can be just as dangerous as inaction.

I am so thankful that as I sat through that financial class, the Holy Spirit was convicting me. He was challenging me to change. He was not condemning me or laying a guilt trip on me. He wanted to partner with me. He wanted to act in conjunction with me. That conviction meant that God was working on me. He had not given up on me. If the Holy Spirit is not convicting us, either of two things has occurred: (1) God has given up on us (which *we* know is not true), or (2) we have achieved perfection (which *our spouses and families* know is not true).

If you think you have arrived, you need to take a few steps back.

I Hate that Word!

Richard Foster wrote a heavy but excellent book titled *Celebration of the Disciplines*.[7] In it, he mentions a number of "disciplines" and discusses both the challenges and the rewards of exercising them. Most of us do not enjoy "disciplines." See if you enjoy them as little as I did!

SELAH 2-1

Give yourself a little "disciplines" test to remind yourself what you probably already know! Circle the number of the enjoyment level of each of the disciplines listed in the left column. Draw a square around the number to indicate the enjoyment level of the "fun stuff" listed in the right column. (Consider 1 to be "least enjoyable" and 5 to be "greatest enjoyment." The first discipline, prayer, and the first "fun stuff," movies, is done as a sample; your assessment might differ.)

Disciplines		Enjoyment Level				The Fun Stuff
Prayer	1	2	(3)	4	[5]	Movies
Fasting	1	2	3	4	5	Sports
Study	1	2	3	4	5	Shopping
Church	1	2	3	4	5	Reading
Meditation	1	2	3	4	5	Travel
Simplicity	1	2	3	4	5	Vacation
Solitude	1	2	3	4	5	Eating out
Service	1	2	3	4	5	Recreation

Confession	1	2	3	4	5	Napping
Worship	1	2	3	4	5	TV

Now how about a few financial disciplines?

Budgeting	1	2	3	4	5	Spending
Balance checkbook	1	2	3	4	5	Hobbies
Cutting my spending	1	2	3	4	5	Fellowship
Setting financial goals	1	2	3	4	5	Entertainment
Giving	1	2	3	4	5	Sleeping

I have found two very useful personal disciplines that help me keep my priorities straight and track the progress in my financial mountain climbing: planning and goal setting. Some people enjoy these tasks more than do other people, but it is biblical to have goals. Paul probably had the best goal when he said, "I want to know Christ."[8] He also admitted a little later that he had not yet attained the goals in that verse, but "I press on toward the goal to win the prize for which God has called me heavenward in Christ Jesus."[9]

Your plans are your dreams with deadlines. Without plans, you will have no direction.

DISCIPLINE 1: A Life Foundation

A survey by pollster George Barna found that *"an astounding proportion of adults—43%—admit that they are still trying to figure out the meaning and purpose of [their] life.*"[10] Before you attempt to develop a budget or any sort of financial plan, I highly recommend that you take some time to get away by yourself and meditate on the question "What is the purpose of my life?" The answer to that question should be the foundation on which your personal goals and your financial plan are built. Some people call it a "Mission Statement"; I call it my "Life Foundation."

Before one constructs a home, he creates a plan and then follows it. The first task of actual construction is to lay the foundation. How ludicrous it would be to set up your queen-size bed before the cement is poured or the carpet is laid. Your "Life Foundation" is the concrete on which your personal and financial goals will be built. My personal "Life Foundation" is simple, and it is appropriate for me. Yours might be totally different. It might be two lines or a full page. It might be spiritual, practical, or a mixture. It also will change over the years. Ten years ago, mine had nothing to do with family or children. The main thing is that it be *yours!* Be yourself!

Creating this plan deserves some careful thought and prayer. It might take you a number of weeks before you are comfortable with it. Consider your purpose and values, what is most important to you, what you desire to be or do, etc. Writing it will force you to analyze your priorities and beliefs and hopefully to live a more purposeful life. If you are purposeful in planning your life, then you will live it more productively and efficiently. You will focus on the things that are the most important. Analyze the things that you are doing, how you spend your time, and your financial expenditures and income to see if they line up with your "Life Foundation."

Every minute spent planning will save two minutes in execution.
—Henry Kaiser

My Life Foundation

⇨ **"Abandoned to God, serving my family, loving the lost"** ⇦

SELAH 2-2

On a clean sheet of paper write your "Life Foundation." Then sleep on it. Review it the next day. Then leave it be for another week and then review it again. You might start working on it now and then set it aside until after you finish reading this book. You might have to revise it several times, so be patient.

DISCIPLINE 2: The Goal Cards

Now that you have the bull's eye (your Life Foundation) defined, put some more specific rings (your goals) around the target. Your plans and goals should be specific, attainable, and realistic but still challenge you to move beyond where you are today.

I do two things every January. First, I list all of God's blessings that I've enjoyed during the previous year. That exercise allows me to review His faithfulness and goodness to me. I share the list with my family so that they can add some items that I might have forgotten. I keep each year's list, and someday I hope to give them to my children and grandchildren as a testament to God's goodness.

Second, I set annual goals to keep my priorities straight and to track my progress in my financial mountain climbing. This is one of the best personal disciplines I have initiated. I set goals for the upcoming year in specific areas of my life: spiritual, financial, family, ministerial, physical, and vocational. Some people might consider creating a "report card" for yourself a little elementary. Other people might be disgusted and turned off by it. If it is too much for you, then I suggest that you list five or six priorities for the next year. Maybe list one item from each of the areas listed in the following "goal chart." Then type your list and post it in a highly visible place. I have one taped to my computer and another copy in my daily planner.

My chart lists six priority categories for the year to help me achieve my "Life Foundation." Although I try to look at my goals at least weekly, I "grade" myself only every quarter (every three months) because, frankly, I cannot stomach seeing some of my grades more often than that. Because I tend to be very detailed with my goals, I set in bold-faced type the goals that are the most important to me so that I can prioritize my time and energy. You might end up with a much smaller, more focused list than mine. If your list of goals is too long, you might throw in the towel when you get too many low grades. Tailor your list for *you*. Be honest. The key is to help you focus and readjust when you mess up, not to lay a guilt trip on yourself.

Figure 2-1
Annual Goal Card

SPIRITUAL	Start Date	1Q	2Q	3Q	4Q	Entire Year	Accountable
Read my Bible daily	NOW	B-	C	B+	B-	B-	Men's Group
Pray with my wife daily	Feb.	-	F	D+	C	C-	Wife
Attend church	NOW	A	A	A	A	A	Wife
Memorize one verse a week	NOW	D+	C-	C+	C-	C-	Wife
FINANCIAL/PERSONAL							
No new debt	NOW	A-	B	B+	A	A-	Family
Complete and stay on a budget	Mar.	-	B-	B-	C	B-	Fin. Advisor
Pay off *all* credit cards	2 yrs.	D	C	B	B+	B-	Spouse
Begin giving	NOW	B-	A	A	A	A	Pastor
Support two missionaries	NOW	D+	A	A	A	A	Spouse
Pay off cars and other debt	4 yrs.	D-	D-	D	C-	D+	Spouse

FAMILY							
Date night with wife (monthly)	NOW	C	C+	B-	C-	C+	Wife
Family Fun Night (weekly)	NOW	C	C+	B	B+	B-	Family
Date night with kids (weekly)	Mar.	-	C	B-	A-	B+	Family
Read/pray with kids (daily)	NOW	A	A	A	A	A	Family
MINISTERIAL							
Attend men's meeting monthly	NOW	C-	C	C+	B	B-	Pastor
Start men's Bible study	1 yr.	-	-	-	-	-	Friend
Teach a class	2 yrs.	-	-	-	-	-	?
VOCATIONAL							
Complete Project A	1 yr.	-	-	-	-	-	Boss
PHYSICAL							
Exercise 3 times a week	NOW	B	B-	C+	C-	C	Wife

SELAH 2-3

Now it's bookmark time, time to put into practice what you have read. *Your* goals, not mine, are what God cares about right now. *Your* financial problems and *your* eventual financial testimony are what matter.

1. On a clean piece of paper, list all of the blessings that you have enjoyed over the past twelve months. Consider financial, personal, family, job, church, health, leisure, education, and spiritual areas of life. Have your family add to your list. Then pray, thanking the Lord for His blessings.
2. On a different piece of paper, list some goals for yourself and your family. Consider the example in Figure 2-2. Next, share it with your spouse, kids, and pastor or friend. Then put your PLAN into ACTION! Post it on the refrigerator. Get someone to hold you accountable! If you do not have the energy or personality style to do a "report card," then list a handful of priorities for the next year that will help you achieve your "Life Foundation."

If you have never set goals before, then this might have been a painful section of the book. Then again, it might be very fruitful. If we do not set goals, we are like a sailboat without sails. We must analyze our current situation, but then we must *act* to make a difference.

"The prudent see danger and take refuge, but the simple keep going and suffer for it."[11]

After you have a Life Foundation and goals for the coming year, it is time to set some long-term goals for the next ten years. You might choose to keep the same items under the goals, but this also might be a good time to set some *very specific* financial goals.

Figure 2-2
Long-Term Goal Card

FINANCIAL GOALS	6 months	1 year	5 years	10 years	Grade Now	Grade in 6 months	Grade in 12 months
Reduce credit-card debt- $	6000	3500	0	0	D-		
Pay off vehicle debt- $	12000	11500	0	0	D		
Pay off house- $	75000	74000	60000	0	D		
Giving	10%	12%	15%	15%	C-		
Support missionaries	2	3	5	10	C		
No new credit-card debt	X	X	X	X	A		
College investment accounts	500	1000	5000	15000	B-		
SPIRITUAL GOALS	6 months	1 year	5 years	10 years	Grade Now	Grade in 6 months	Grade in 12 months
Read my Bible daily	X	X	X	X	B+		
Memorize one verse/week	-	X	X	X	C		
Involved in men/women group	-	X	X	X	C-		
Begin ministry_____	-	X	X	X	D+		
Help ministry_____	-	X	X	X	A-		
Pray with kids/wife daily	X	X	X	X	B-		
Attend church	X	X	X	X	A		
FAMILY GOALS	6 months	1 year	5 years	10 years	Grade Now	Grade in 6 months	Grade in 12 months
Date night with wife-monthly	X	X	X	X	C		
Family night-weekly	-	X	X	X	B-		
Reduce hobby_____	-	X	X	X	D+		
Date night with kids-weekly	X	X	X	X	A-		
Family vacation_____	-	X	X	X	B+		
Family ministry_____	-	X	X	X	C-		
MINISTRY GOALS	6 months	1 year	5 years	10 years	Grade Now	Grade in 6 months	Grade in 12 months
Etc.							
PHYSICAL GOALS	6 months	1 year	5 years	10 years	Grade Now	Grade in 6 months	Grade in 12 months
Etc.							

A Word of Warning

Do not file the goals and then never look at them again. Review them regularly to assess your progress. *Do not feel guilty and trash these goals!* Rather, let them guide you in areas where you need to improve. Guess what? I still get some D's and F's! That's okay. I do better the next three months after I refocus a bit. Goals are not meant to constrain us but rather to keep us focused on our priorities and direction. We might occasionally veer off the straight and narrow financial and personal paths, but if you have goals, you at least have a path to which you can come back.

Later in the book, we will see how your spending decisions line up with your goals. Remember, we are still laying the foundation!

> *"Be doers of the word, and not hearers only,*
> *deceiving yourselves."*
> **—James 1:22**

<u>ACTION POINTS</u>

1. Consider and pray about any Christian masks or phoniness with which you might need to deal. Do you need to confess anything regarding your finances?

   _____
   _____
   _____
   _____
   _____
   _____
   _____

2. Share your list of blessings with someone. Get your family to add to it.

3. List a discipline or two on which you will work *this week*. List one or two disciplines on which to work *this year*.

   _____
   _____
   _____
   _____
   _____
   _____

4. Take a first attempt at writing your a "Life Foundation."

   _____
   _____
   _____
   _____
   _____
   _____
   _____

5. Take a stab at fulfilling some of your short-term and long-term goals. Establish at least five or six priorities for the upcoming year. Print and post your list somewhere highly visible!

CHAPTER 3

Choices and Priorities

A plan without action is good fireplace fodder. Creating a list does nothing except decrease the supply of ink and paper. *Doing something* with the list is what matters. Many people have good intentions when they set out to improve their finances, but after easing their conscience by thinking about it more, even reading a book or making a list, they feel better for a while but then slip back into old habits. They take no action and have no accountability.

Procrastination in dealing with your finances is deadly. I challenge you to take that next step! The road to freedom and liberty is not far off. I believe that God is a God of small steps more than of giant leaps. Conduct a word study of how many times the words *steps* and *leaps* is used in the Bible and see which word is used more often. I will save you some time—God wants to order your *steps.*[1]

He wants you to be diligent and make plans, but He wants to be involved in those plans. And He doesn't want to be a rubber stamp or a co-pilot; rather, He wants to be the pilot and the teacher. Involve God early in your financial and life plans, and then you will not have to wonder where He is down the road or beg Him to rescue you or get you back on track.

We must plan, but we must also pray. The easy kind of prayer is "talking" prayer, but we also need "listening prayer" and "praying the Word." We should saturate our plans with prayer and *fasting*.

Ouch! (Splash of cold water!) *Fasting.* We don't hear that word much anymore. Now would be an opportune time to remember my earlier statement: "chew it all, but only digest what is for you!" If you question the need to fast and pray, or if you need more insight, I would suggest that you conduct a Bible word study on fasting and read the following books so you can see the results of fasting!

> ➤ *God's Chosen Fast*—by Arthur Wallis[2]
> ➤ *The Coming Revival—America's Call to Fast, Pray and Seek God's Face*—by Bill Bright[3]
> ➤ *Rees Howells, Intercessor*—by Norman Grubb[4]
> ➤ *The Complete Works of E.M. Bounds on Prayer*[5]

Individuals and churches make too many decisions and take too many steps without bathing them in prayer and fasting. I am not talking about bathing them until they are soggy but until they are clean and pure. You will know when to get the decisions out of the water because you have been with Jesus!

Walking with Jesus means surrendering to Him. Surrendering *everything*—our time, our money, our desires, our purpose! If you trust in the Lord with *all* of your heart and don't lean unto your own understanding, and if you acknowledge Him in *all* of your ways, then He will direct your paths.[6] Wow! Great promise. Do you believe it? It applies to your finances, too. And, oh the joy when you apply this principle! I do believe that God can do miracles and rescue you, but He also might have a greater plan to teach you, grow you, and train you through slow, methodical, disciplined steps. You might not benefit as much with an overnight "financial miracle" as you will by His gradual methods. Remember small steps, not giant leaps.

The Speech—and the Reaction

When I counsel couples with financial problems, I open our first meeting with a brief speech that goes something like this.

I cannot do the work for you. Moving forward will require some disciplined actions and changes over the next six months. You have heard it said that it takes twenty-one days to make a habit—so the next month or so is critical. I know you understand that, but some people think that *I* will do all the work and that *I* will make the changes for them."

On a few occasions, I receive a blank stare or a pale, puppy-dog look or two that indicate that some people yearn for the "take-two-aspirin-and-call-me-in-the-morning" answer to their problems. If we are honest, we would all like the quick solution. I have discovered that I often do not make the difficult and correct choices until I am desperate.

How Desperate Are You?

Many pastors and counselors give good, solid, biblical advice and then when the follow-up meeting occurs, guess what? Their advice has not been heeded and the action plans have not been accomplished. Perhaps the counselees have had their consciences eased, but no changes have been made in their lives.

Perhaps now is a good time to ask the following soul-searching questions.
- How badly do you want God's will?
- How badly do you want to be free financially?
- How desperate are you?
- Are you desperate enough to give up your hobby for a period of time?
- Are you desperate enough to serve your spouse before yourself?
- Are you desperate enough to make a change in your lifestyle if necessary?
- Are you willing to change some of your priorities?

Fixing one's finances without fixing one's spiritual condition is similar to rotating your tires but ignoring the slipping transmission, the scraping brakes, and the smoking engine!

A man's treatment of money is the most decisive test of his character—how he makes it and how he spends it.
—Moffat

Hear me out. I promise that I will get to the solutions, but knowing that you have a financial wound or injury is only part of the journey. We must understand how the injury came about so that you can avoid it the next time. I have met too many individuals who declare bankruptcy or consolidate their debts only to go back to their old habits because they never analyzed their problems deeply enough.

SELAH 3-1

Read the parable of the sower in Matthew 13:1–23.

Knowing the condition of the soil is paramount for a farmer who wants to ensure a productive harvest. Similarly, analyzing your financial "soil condition" is essential. You can fertilize, prune, and water, but if you don't deal with the root damage, the results will not be longlasting. The bottom line is that *your spiritual condition influences your financial condition.*

"When material things are under spiritual control, they fulfill their proper subordinate role."[7]
—Watchman Nee

Jesus said it best: "I am the vine; you are the branches. If a man remains in me and I in him, he will bear much fruit; apart from me you can do nothing."[8] I want you to bear fruit, but first we need to ensure that all of the seeds are planted and the soil is good.

Technology—A Blessing (and a Curse?)

In the age in which we live, I believe that the greatest difficulty with making our choices and establishing priorities is the sheer number of them. One of the best books I have read in the last few years focused on the unexpected pains of progress. In his book *Margin,*[9] Richard A. Swenson forces a very introspective look at the blessings and curses of our modern society. According to

Swenson, "If we are overloaded we have no Margin." No margin in our time, our finances, our peace of mind, our relationships, etc. Almost everyone seems to be suffering from "overload." Margin is the opposite of overload. It is the space that once existed between our load and our limits. It is our breathing room. So, with all of our technological advancements, why don't we have more margin?

❖ The car is loaded with extras.

❖ The paycheck is bigger than that of our parents.

❖ We have more technological "labor-saving help" (e.g., washing machines, dryers, car washes, dishwashers, vacuum cleaners) than did the previous generation.

❖ We can multitask easier than ever, as the following examples illustrate:
We can talk on the phone while we walk or drive!
We can eat and talk at the same time (Internet chat).
We begin driving to the place which we want to go without even knowing where it is thanks to global positioning systems (GPS).
We can go to Japan without physically going there thanks to videoconferencing, and we can get on a plane and be in another country on the same day!

❖ We can order our medicine, pay bills, buy groceries, or attempt to diagnose our illness online.

❖ We can shop for Christmas gifts while sitting in our easy chairs.

❖ We do not have to dry our clothes on a line, communicate by letter, mail a large proposal by three-day mail, use white-out liquid, or sing out of hymnals.

❖ We have fast food and faster food (I miss the leisurely rump roast and mashed potato days!).

❖ We can eat and drive at the same time thanks to drive-throughs (eating chicken wings or fish sticks while driving could be dangerous to one's health).

❖ We can now be stalked and tracked anywhere (faxes/pagers/voice mail/cell phones/laptops!).

❖ We have one-stop Super Store shopping (groceries, soccer balls, videos, and technology toys all under one roof!).

❖ We can be grumpy and the teller doesn't even know it- auto-

mated teller machines (ATMs).
- ❖ We don't even have to read ourselves anymore (books on tape).
- ❖ We can pay at the pump.
- ❖ We have Palm Pilots and DSL connections.

The list goes on. Modern technology has indeed provided us with many benefits. In some cases, our technology choices give us more margin, but in other cases they take it away. We are accessible anywhere, or we can choose to ignore the rings, beeps, blips, or voice that says, "You've got mail." Ironically, we are now actually *creating new technology to baby-sit old technology* that we only *partially want.* We have answering machines to answer our telephones. We have caller ID to keep the telemarketers from telling us that we need something else.

More . . . and Less

Technology has indeed been a blessing in many respects, but progress also has its side effects. In spite of all of this technology, we are more stressed, more divorced, more counseled, and more in debt than any other generation. *If we have ten times more material abundance than our ancestors did, why are we not ten times more content and more fulfilled? Most importantly, why don't we have* more *time on our hands?*

We have unprecedented prosperity in our land and all of the fringe benefits that are coupled with it: entertainment, recreation, technology, comforts, and conveniences. Yet, despair and frustration can possibly be joined at the hip of some of these benefits.

Our "progress" has adversely affected extended family cohesiveness and all but eliminated that neighborhood community feeling as the average American moves seven times during his or her lifetime because of job changes, many of which are to different cities and states. We are often guilty of focusing more on external progress—money, technology, education, careers, health, material items, etc.—rather than on internal progress—social, emotional, family, and spiritual successes. Although both external and internal progress are important, quite possibly we have given improper weight to external progress.

Some of the best (and perhaps the most difficult to apply) advice that I was ever given was that of my father: "Bloom where you are planted." We can get so caught up in the external trappings of success that the very progress we pursue externally, when achieved, can adversely affect our internal progress and success. I have had opportunities to move from my current positions, both secular and ministerial, but it was critical to ensure that I analyzed my motives in each case. God has honored my patience and has allowed me to bloom in my sixteenth year with the same corporation, in the same state. The day might come when it's time to move on, but my task is to ensure that I am in step with God's plan, and not just pursuing my plan and the external benefits that might go along with a change.

The Yardstick

What if we measured success solely according to the Bible? What would God's yardstick look like? I'll bet that love, joy, peace, patience, kindness, goodness, faithfulness, gentleness, and self-control[10] would rank pretty high. Some of our important technology acronyms (e.g., DVD, PDA, ISP) might not show up on His top-ten list. Unfortunately, many people get trapped still using "the Joneses" or "the TV sitcom" as the measure of their success. It has even crept (or leapt in some cases) into the church, as many churches choose their leaders based on their external successes—financial influence, community stature, career advancements, and educational attainments. Many of these things are not bad in themselves, but they should not be weighted heavier than an individual's internal characteristics—his or her heart's condition and passion for eternal things. We must guard against using temporal measurement systems.

How are we doing as a country? As individuals? Are we really making the kind of progress that is healthy? Our progress and technology obviously has pros and cons. I would have had a much more difficult time writing portions of this book without the Internet. I am also thankful for the spell-check feature! However, much of our external progress has led to internal back-pedaling. Examine the following list and see for yourself if we are doing better or worse than previous generations. (You might also want to poll some members of the previous generation.)

SELAH 3-2

Technology and Progress. They have made our choices more numerous and priorities more difficult to juggle. How are we doing compared with generations that have gone before us? The following exercise is a quick soul-searcher. Offer your assessment of each category by circling either "Better" or "Worse."

Category	Assessment		
Marriages	Better	or	Worse
Parenting	Better	or	Worse
Family unity	Better	or	Worse
Real communication	Better	or	Worse
Church commitment	Better	or	Worse
Church unity	Better	or	Worse
Personal debt	Better	or	Worse
Corporate debt	Better	or	Worse
Political virtue	Better	or	Worse
Value of life	Better	or	Worse
Sense of community	Better	or	Worse
Wealth	Better	or	Worse
Technology	Better	or	Worse
Productivity	Better	or	Worse
Inner peace	Better	or	Worse
Material things	Better	or	Worse
Contentment	Better	or	Worse
Violence	Better	or	Worse
Values/morals	Better	or	Worse
Knowledge	Better	or	Worse
Education	Better	or	Worse
Health	Better	or	Worse
Stress	Better	or	Worse

A Solution

One choice might be to simplify! You can do it with Christ's strength. Jesus had a great impact in His three-and-a-half years of ministry, but the Bible does not record His having had the latest technology toys or that He was ever stressed-out with no time for rest or peace. It doesn't even say that He healed all, ministered to all, visited all, taught all, had unlimited temporal resources, or worked twenty-hour ministry days every day. He also did not sit on the couch for hours every day being entertained. He was sensitive to His Father's priorities for each day.

Prioritize your life with God's help, and stick to your priorities. If life were a pinball game and you were the pinball, you would have many people and things trying to chart your course. The bottom line is that only *you and God* should choose your priorities. Learn to say no. Learn to focus on the majors. Do what will produce *eternal* results. Set goals, and track your progress against them.

If you can practice these disciplines, they will also begin to flow easily into your financial choices and priorities. Learning to say "no" or "not now" in spending is also very difficult and takes *practice.*

How are your choices influencing your life's goals? Are your priorities aligned with your Life Foundation? How can your spending choices affect your financial goals. If your goal is "to get out of debt in five years," how does that purchase of a new sailboat affect that goal? Our choices should be linked to our goals. An admirable goal might be "to spend quality time with my family this year." What priorities do you need to change to accomplish that goal? What difficult choices do you need to make to turn that goal into a reality?

Sometimes we need to ask ourselves the tough questions. No one will do it for us! If your work ethic, career aspirations, or spending habits are adversely affecting your family, your church commitment, or your time with the Lord, maybe you should reevaluate your priorities in light of God's priorities.

"Well, I can make 10 percent more money if I move eight states away," you argue. How does that choice affect your fulfillment of God's priorities? Your decision-making process should include God's priorities and some of the internal priorities about which we have talked.

I recall an interview recently with individuals over the age of sixty-five. The question posed was "If you could live your life over, what would you change?" The responses were overwhelmingly unanimous: "I would have spent more time and money investing in things that would outlive me and impact generations to come!" Wow, if we could *understand and live* that truth before it is too late!

Hit the Road, Jack!

If you are struggling to know what God's priorities are for your life, you might try a getaway. My once-a-year goal is to take a weekend and go off by myself to a hotel or a cabin with my Bible, a note pad, and a pen. Try fasting and praying. We often have "people overload," and it is necessary to get away from the pinball game of life once in a while. Control your own destiny.

"I would rather sit on a pumpkin and have it all to myself, than be crowded on a velvet cushion."
—Thoreau

Debt, stress, overload, and media suffocate us. The disease of busyness has crippled us all. It is good to get away and breathe, think, pray, study, meditate, and listen. If you do so, allow your spouse to do the same! Because I spend a lot of time in the car, another thing that I have done is to play praise-and-worship music while driving to allow my mind to declutter and to allow God to soothe my overloaded life with His presence while I worship Him. Some days I will turn off the radio and just sit in peace and quiet.

Following are some crazy ideas of ways to simplify, slow down, and seek peace. The beauty is that they will also save you money! Instead of rushing right past this section or merely skimming it, circle the ideas that you might put into practice. (We will discuss specific money-saving ideas in more detail later.)

Figure 3-1
Simplify and Prioritize!

- Turn off the TV.
- Skip the newspaper for a week.
- Have a family night when the entire family reads or plays games or sports together.
- Take a walk.
- Take a sabbatical.
- Go to church.
- Get to know a neighbor.
- Go camping or hiking.
- Go to a museum.
- Sit on the porch or in the yard, drink lemonade, and talk to passersby.
- Start a daily/weekly planner to regain control.
- Volunteer for a local ministry.
- Sit and talk with your spouse or kids.
- Read the Bible to your kids.
- Do a craft.
- Read and meditate upon the Bible.
- Be available to meet the needs of others.
- Reflect on priorities or your Life Foundation.
- Mute advertisements and the TV or radio.
- Sell some of your stuff.
- Reject fashion; embrace usefulness.
- Say no!
- Listen or sing worship music in the car and at home.
- Write an old-fashioned letter.
- Fast regularly from media, TV, food, and activities.
- Work in the garden.
- "Simplify, simplify" (Thoreau).
- Avoid some of the modern gadgetry.
- Enjoy without owning by visiting the library, the beach, or museums.
- Reduce your work hours (check out the lyrics to "Cats in the Cradle").
- Begin a hobby that the whole family can enjoy (e.g., hiking or

camping).
• Get involved with neighborhood activities.

Our lives can become so consumed by acquiring, consuming, and climbing to the next level. We must aggressively pursuing simplification. Many of the "items of technology or progress" we have talked about are obviously not SIN, but if they get in the way of our relationships with Jesus, family and others, they have the potential of becoming detrimental to our priorities at best, and modern day idols at worse. Richard Swenson notes:

> *"Our Margin has been stolen away, and progress was the thief."*[11]

The thief of progress has stolen our emotional energy, spiritual energy, time, and finances. Swenson mentions that our health is found in "contentment, simplicity, balance, and rest."[12] I would add a relationship with Jesus Christ.

Simplifying also forces us to take a rather introspective look at our priorities. I know that one time in my life, just after marrying, that my focus was on doing things that were important to *me*. My focus was not on serving my wife and children first. My goal was to meet *my* needs. Although I was involved in a ministry teaching and touching the lives of hundreds of children weekly, I was sacrificing my own family on the altar of "ministry." God dealt with me patiently and gently, but the conviction was deep, and it took me two years until I obeyed. One of the hardest things I ever did in my life was to "sacrifice my Isaac," laying aside that ministry to focus on my family first. Fortunately, the Lord has allowed me to stay involved with ministry and touching lives, and my priorities are now back in order.

Some people might be on the other end of the spectrum. They are so focused on themselves and their family that they are not touching the lives of *anyone* else. Ensure that your foundation of priorities is built on what *God* desires, not on what *you* desire! His plan is different for each of us.

SELAH 3-3

The following exercise might be too depressing for some people, but it's impact on me was dramatic, so I will share it. I read of an individual who performs the following exercise to keep his priorities in order. Every now and again, he forces himself to imagine what it would be like to attend his own funeral as a spectator.

Imagine your own funeral. Where will it be? Who will attend? What will be inscribed on your grave? What will your obituary say? Who will give your eulogy, and what will they say? What will your spouse say? What will your children say? What will your parents say? What will your boss say? Your pastor? What will other speakers say? Could your family describe meaningful times that you and they spent together or only things that you bought them? What would you have left behind that would be carried on throughout future generations although you are gone? Your spouse and children will now represent you to a world that you will no longer see. What will they have? Your wealth? Your love? Your servanthood? Your commitment and example of following Jesus Christ above all else?

What legacy are you leaving behind? This is pretty heavy stuff, but it was a challenging exercise for me. Take a few minutes to ponder this situation for yourself. One day it will be a *reality!*

SELAH 3-4

List the things that you commit to do in the next thirty days to *simplify*. Use the list in Figure 3-1 as a starting point. Share the list with your spouse, another family member, or a friend, and add to the list according to their input. I challenge you to meditate on this activity rather than just skimming through the list. This exercise is really critical to developing a solid foundation for biblical finances.

It is sad that we even have to consider such a list. But it is your life. *If you do not take control of it, someone else will.* The marketing folks, your boss, your career, the culture, or the latest fashions will dictate it for you. It is your money, and it is your time.

I liked D.L. Moody's response to a reporter who asked him which people gave him the most trouble. He answered unhesitatingly,

> *"I've had more trouble with D.L. Moody than any man alive."*
> **—D.L. Moody**

It is easy to play "the blame game," passing the buck to the media, the culture, the pastor, the boss, or the spouse. But this life is *yours*. God gives you a free will to choose how you will live it. You must take ownership of and responsibility for how you live your life.

ACTION POINTS

1. Consider fasting. Start with one meal. Fast from the media. Fast from technology or a hobby. If you are considering a food fast, you might read the books by Arthur Wallis or Bill Bright that were referenced earlier for some sound advice on some of the basics (purpose, length, kinds, etc.).

2. Read John 15:1–8. Do you need to do some pruning in your lifestyle?

   _____
   _____
   _____

3. How has technology impeded progress in your family, finances, spiritual walk, inner peace, etc? Which items in Figure 3-1 can you begin doing immediately?

   _____
   _____
   _____
   _____
   _____
   _____

4. How did the funeral exercise (Selah 3-3) make you feel? What immediate changes do you need to make after considering the funeral exercise?

   _____
   _____
   _____
   _____
   _____
   _____

5. Schedule a date for a sabbatical/getaway. _____

CHAPTER 4

A Time to Diet and a Time to Get Mad!

One of the questions that I needed to answer for myself was, "Why do we make the choices and priorities that we do?"

How you use your time is really the core of who you are, and it also greatly affects your finances. I reprint the following statistics from Richard Swenson's book *Margin*[1] to help put our societal ills in perspective.

In a lifetime, the average American will

- spend six months sitting at traffic lights waiting for them to change;
- spend one year searching through desk clutter looking for misplaced objects;
- spend eight months opening junk mail;
- spend two years trying to call people who aren't in or whose lines are busy;
- spend five years waiting in lines;
- spend three years in meetings (I think I've surpassed this by far already);
- learn how to operate 22,000 different things;

- commute forty-five minutes every day;
- be interrupted seventy-three times every day;
- receive six hundred advertising messages every day (TV, newspaper, magazine, radio, billboards);
- travel seventy-seven hundred miles every year;
- watch seventeen hundred hours of television every year; and
- open six hundred pieces of mail every year (I think that this amount is monthly for us)

We are overheating as a society, which means that we are overheating as individuals.

We can go faster ....But we have more places to go.
We have more room.........................But we have more junk to store.
We have more light.........................But we work more and sleep less.
We have more income ....But we give less.
We have more religion....................But we are less moral.
We talk and hear more from the media than we do from our own families.
We average four minutes a day in meaningful communication with our spouse.

Wow! The choices that we make greatly influence both our finances and our purpose in life. One of the benefits of simplifying our lifestyles is that we will have both *time and money* to respond to unforeseen needs.

"When others need help, they don't need it two days from now. We must be ready to allow ourselves to be interrupted by God."
—Dietrich Bonhoeffer

Our closets are full. We need three-car garages and temporary storage facilities for all of our "stuff"—and our things are really *not even ours* if we are in debt. If you stop a minute and really think about all of this, it should begin to stir up some anger and discontent with our lifestyles, hopefully enough to move you to action.

A SCARY REVELATION

Here is a scary revelation:

First, we are manipulated into buying what we don't need.
　　Then we cannot pay for it.
　　　　Then we do not even have a place to put it.
　　　　　　Then we do not have time to use it!
　　　　　　　　Something is wrong!

We have less time and money for church and beneficial ministries, less time for prayer and meditation, and less energy and interest to invest in other people. We have been duped, folks! When our spouse "calls" or God "calls" or the children "call," do they get a busy signal?

The Big "D"

I hate to bring up the *D* word, but we need a different kind of *diet*. But most of us are on one kind of diet or another anyway. We need a diet of temporal things. Not just food. We all struggle with human lusts and passions, whether it is "stuff", food, power, or anything else. Food is not evil, but the *love* of it can get a grip on us. Similarly, money is not evil, but "the *love* of money is the root of all kinds of evil."[2] It, too, can get a grip on us.

The *Dallas Morning News*[3] quoted a government report that stated that 61 percent of American adults are now considered overweight; 26 percent are considered obese, or grossly overweight, up from 23 percent during the period from 1988–1994; and 25 to 50 percent of all Americans are on a physical diet at any given time. Other statistics reveal that "we spend $33 billion annually on weight loss products and services."[4] John Kenneth Galbraith observes, "More die in the United States of too much food than of too little."[5] I am not trying to encourage you to go on a physical diet but rather making a case that we can be "too full." We can be "too blessed" (i.e., spoiled).

We are a blessed country, but the blessings are suffocating us. We need a diet from the material things and the temporal priorities! We are an overfed society; we're overfed with stuff, media, noise, and credit.

> *"Many people have had to learn in their private lives, and nations have had to learn in their historical experience, that perhaps the worst form of tragedy is wanting something badly, getting it, and finding it empty."*
> **—Henry Kissinger**

The people of the United States spend more money on eating out than the individual gross national products of 200 of the 210 nations of the world. Is our land's prosperity the blessing of God or the iced-over highway that is causing us to slide toward spiritual and financial ruin? Our financial prosperity and independence have resulted in an independence from God. Many people act and live as though they didn't need Him. We forget to thank Him. When was the last time you heard a politician attribute our blessings and prosperity to God himself? We will usually attribute success to a political party, the Chairman of the Federal Reserve System, or an event. But what about Almighty God? We should "Remember the Lord your God, for it is He who gives you the ability to produce wealth."[6]

Warning!

> *"Within the human heart 'things' have taken over. God's gifts now take the place of God, and the whole course of nature is upset by the monstrous substitution."*
> **—A.W. Tozer**

SELAH 4-1

Take thirty seconds to ask forgiveness if you have not thanked the Lord for all with which He has blessed you. Then thank Him!

Marketers and Needs

It is difficult to "diet" financially when the advertisers dangle in front of us all of the "junk food" and "must have" items. We must beware of the influence that marketing and advertising can have upon us.

Marketing can be one of two things. It can be getting the word out about your product or service, or it can be "need creation." William D. Perreault Jr. defined *marketing* as "creation and delivery of a standard of living."[7] Note the definition. It "*creates* a standard of living." Yes, marketing begins with an attempt to meet people's needs, but it has now shifted much to "persuading." *Needs* are the basics that we require to live. *Wants* are *learned* during our lifetimes and are influenced by advertising, peers, neighbors, etc.

Obviously, the marketing businesses and marketers have learned that advertising is an effective means for promoting a product, and it also has been very productive at "creating a perceived need." If we hear something about a product many times, we soon start to believe that it is a "must have," especially if our neighbor, coworker, or friend has one. The advertising blitz is upon us[8] (see Figure 4-1)!

Figure 4-1
The Advertising Blitz

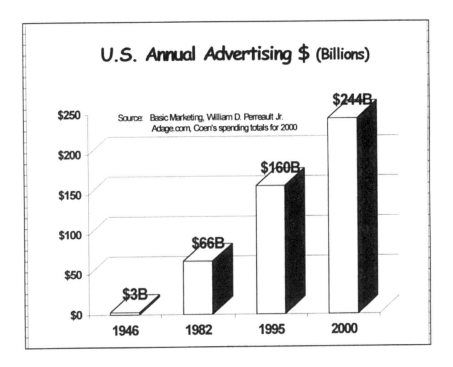

Perreault also notes[9], "All other nations <u>combined</u> spend only about 25% more than the U.S. alone" on advertising! Although some advertising might be helpful or informative for making our consumer decisions, the marketers know that we respond to advertising like sheep being led to the slaughter. The sad part is that they are targeting our kids in massive efforts. According to the Center for a New American Dream, "children are exhibiting extraordinary influence over their parents' spending. Fifteen years ago, children aged four to 12 influenced about $50 billion of their parents' purchases. By 1997, that figure had more than tripled to $188 billion. Marketers call this influence the 'nag factor'." Why the change? "Children watch between 50 and 100 TV commercials per day. That's 20,000 to 40,000, TV ads annually."[10] *Protect your children!*

The marketing gurus target our "discretionary income." They do a fabulous job of convincing us that we *need* something. This is not a problem that has been around for just a few years, as the following quotation reveals.

"Surely it is right to supply our necessities. But what are necessities? Advancing civilization multiplies them. Friction matches were a luxury once, a necessity now. And may we allow ourselves nothing for the comforts and luxuries of life? Where shall we draw the line between justifiable and unjustifiable expenditure?"
—Josiah Strong, 1885

Living in America, it is difficult, if not impossible, to isolate ourselves from the media. Our definition of *necessity* has been skewed because of the land of prosperity in which we live and the blitz of advertising upon us. Ninety-nine percent of us now own a television. [11] Would we consider it a necessity? Most likely. Is it really? How about some of the other constant "upgrades" that we are convinced we need? This tug of war for our dollars and time is not an area of our lives that will be conquered just once; it's a *daily struggle. The barrage hits us daily.* We have gone from a saving land to a consuming land. We spend what we do not have to satisfy our wants and desires, and we have convinced ourselves that many of these desires are, in fact, needs.

"Our economy is based upon people wanting more—
their happiness on wanting less."
—Frank A. Clark

The Good Ol' Days

Living a content life in the 1800–1900s meant the basic needs: health, education, a warm home in the winter, safe food, clean water, a good team of horses, and good seed. Our "needs" have matured. But are the new "needs" of today really helping us, or are they hurting our peace of mind, family unity, and budgets? I read a great article in *Money Magazine*[12] that illustrated a shifting of our "needs" over the years. The article asked, "What has defined success through the decades?" The following items were considered *status symbols* during the various decades mentioned:

1900s—Model T cars, radio
1910s—Electric clocks, Kodak camera
1920s—Vacuum cleaner, washing machine
1930s—Baseball tickets, canned food, indoor plumbing
1940s—Television, air travel, college degree, refrigerator
1950s—Color TV, credit card, Disneyland trip
1960s—Stereo sound system, 35-mm camera
1970s—Designer jeans, VCR
1980s—Microwave, personal computer
1990s—Internet stocks, Palm Pilot, cell phones, SUVs
2000s—Internet cell phone, flat-screen TV

How many of yesteryear's status symbols are today's needs? The issue is no longer about meeting our basic needs or about being content. We have turned inward. Fifty-one percent of Christians and 54 percent of non-Christians believe that no matter how they feel about money, it is still the main symbol of success in life.[13] In that regard, little difference exists between a believer and a nonbeliever.

We have even come up with creative new words to mask our culture's sickness. Covetousness is now called *ambition*, greed is called *initiative*, and hoarding is called *prudent planning*. We have watered down our wants and desires and call them *needs*. I saw a sign of the times recently on a billboard that read, "Needs, Wants, <u>Deserve</u>". That sums it up. You deserve the best today. Reward yourself. You earned it.

SELAH 4-2

Jot down a few things that you own because you have "fallen prey" to the advertisers, technology toy sellers, or "keeping up with the Joneses," helping to "convince" you that you needed something when maybe you really did not.

We ought to reject things that cause an addiction in us—whether it be a hobby, a drink, or an expenditure. Refuse to be a slave to anything but Jesus. Paul did. *Simplicity is freedom, not lack.* We do not have much lack in this great country of ours, but we do lack simplicity.

"Give a man everything he wants, and at that moment, everything will not be everything."
—Immanuel Kant

Tape Measures

Nineteen percent of Christians and 20 percent of non-Christians believe that you can usually tell how successful a person is by examining what they own.[14] How do we measure success? If we are honest, we will admit that it is extremely difficult for us to measure ourselves by God's tape measure. If we are not careful, we tend to measure ourselves by our "stuff" and by our "stature."

Stuff	Stature
Vehicles	Salary
Houses	Social standing
Clothes	Degrees and titles
Toys	Neighborhoods
Jewelry	Education and reputation
Technology	Appearance
Vacations and leisure activity	Portfolio

It might be healthful for us to look internally instead of externally to see if some reshuffling of priorities or lifestyle is appropriate. An example of some of the daily "needs-versus-wants" battles that we face follows. Obviously, we also face many others. Our simplification challenge is not easy in this country.

Needs	Wants	Like-to's (Desires)
Clothes that fit and look nice	New clothes	Latest brand, fashion
Bread and water	Sandwich and salad	Lobster and prime rib
Used car, bus, or train	New model car	Luxury car, loaded

SELAH 4-3

Take a few minutes to list some of the "needs," "wants," and "like-to" purchases that you will face in the coming months and years. This exercise will provide a framework for some of the practical financial applications later in the book that will have a positive influence on your life. You might have your spouse participate in this activity as well. Consider the basic need items such as vehicles and housing, but also include vacations, education, furniture, hobbies, and "toys."

SHORT TERM (next six months to one year)

Needs	Wants	Like-to's

LONG TERM (one to five years)

Needs	Wants	Like-to's

With the growing number of voices screaming that you "need"

something, *you* must aggressively pursue "anticulture" strategies—whether that means turning off the television ads or simplifying your lifestyle—to quiet those voices. Some of the voices that are shouting at you are saying,

- ❖ Debt is okay; it's normal.
- ❖ Debt is an asset if used correctly.
- ❖ Use other people's money.
- ❖ You need a larger size than you now have.
- ❖ You need it faster.
- ❖ You need the latest.
- ❖ You deserve it.
- ❖ You need it.
- ❖ Hollywood has it.
- ❖ Go ahead, spoil yourself.

You only go around once in life. Be a *counterculturist*! Try some of the following options:

SLOW	*not*	*FAST*
WAIT	*not*	*NOW*
SIMPLIFY	*not*	*CONSUME*
PEACE	*not*	*NOISE*
SERVE	*not*	*SELF*
PLAN	*not*	*FLY BY THE SEAT...*
PRAY	*not*	*DO IT ON YOUR OWN*
FAMILY	*not*	*CAREER*
SACRIFICE	*not*	*HOARD*
DO	*not*	*JUST HEAR*
GIVE	*not*	*GET*
ENOUGH	*not*	*MORE*
LAST	*not*	*FIRST*
CONTENT	*not*	*ACQUIRE*

Richard J. Foster states that "conformity to a sick society is to be sick."[15] Jesus said, "It is not the healthy who need a doctor, but the sick." [16] First, we must admit that we are sick. The sickness begins on the inside and manifests itself on the outside—sneezing, coughing, etc. We take medicines for a cold; we see doctors for our health issues. We need to take a similar initiative for our cultural financial sickness. The "myth of more" is intoxicating. More, however, is never enough.

"There are two ways to get enough, one is to continue to accumulate more and more. The other is to desire less."
—G.K. Chesterton

Our society and culture have a strong pull on us. Our "stuff and stature" have a grip on many an individual, both Christian and non-Christian alike. It is time to regain the grip instead of being gripped. It is time to go on the offensive for the sake of your finances, your family, and your future. An offensive posture, full of self-control, will lead to results. The Greek word for self-control means "to grip," or "to take hold of."

SELAH 4-4

1. List five areas of your finances that lack self-control or that could use some improvement (e.g., impulse spending, hobby, recreation, giving, etc.).

   _____

   _____

   _____

   _____

   _____

2. Now rank them from 1 to 5. The first item is the most important and the highest priority, etc...
3. Set a date when you are going to "regain your grip" of each one.
4. Talk to someone who has modeled this behavior and ask for his or her advice.
5. Ask someone to hold you accountable.
6. Do it!

These areas do not need to be hidden or avoided but rather dealt with for you to move forward. Begin a game plan today for dealing with them. If not, you will continue to tread water at best or sink at worst.

Selah Sermonette

Yes, I know that I have a lot of "Selahs" in this chapter. I am getting you warmed up for the *doing* yet to come in the book so you can move toward financial freedom. When are you most challenged by a pastor's words or a difficult Bible study that you have completed? Ten minutes after hearing it or three days after hearing? Enough lecturing and sermonizing! Please do yourself a favor and decide to act now. Participate in a Selah or two!

SELAH 4-5

Remember our discussion of the "disciplines" (Selah 2-1) called meditation and prayer? I would highly recommend taking a few minutes to ponder and *talk to God* (and listen!) about each of the areas you listed in Selah 4-4. The most astounding results will come in your finances when interaction with God occurs and you begin to make changes in your choices and priorities. This potent mixture will ignite radical and transforming change in every area of your life! It gets me excited just thinking about your testimony to come!

ACTION POINTS

1. Thank the Lord for His blessings in your life. List the blessings that you've enjoyed during the past year (if you have not done so already).

   _____
   _____
   _____
   _____
   _____

2. Consider the "stuff" and "stature" that have influenced you more than they should have. Make some corrections. Identify two specific areas on which you need to work.

   _____
   _____
   _____
   _____
   _____

3. _Do something_ with your needs, wants, and desires list. Get your spouse or a family member to do the same exercise. Use it to begin setting some long-term goals. Look back at Figures 2-1 and 2-2 and your report card to determine if they should be updated.

4. Identify a few "counterculture" practices from the list or some of your own ideas on which you will begin to act today!

   _____
   _____
   _____
   _____
   _____
   _____

5. Begin a "self-control" plan for items listed in Selah 4-4.

CHAPTER 5

My Financial Foundation— and Then Some

I want to share some of the positive and negative lessons learned from my background. Although I was raised in a Christian home and had a father who was in the ministry and a stay-at-home mother, I rebelled and went my own way. As I consider *why* I rebelled, I believe that I can narrow it to a few issues. I recall from my childhood a heavy emphasis on the "thou shalt nots" without much emphasis on understanding the "why nots."

It is extremely easy for me to say no to my children. In fact, I am well versed in doing so. However, it is more difficult for me to sit and explain *"why* not" and have a discussion with them about it. Again, it is easier for me as a parent to focus on the external than on an "inside-out" change. The shepherding of a child's *heart* is most critical. Tedd Tripp comments in his fantastic book *Shepherding a Child's Heart* that "the more you talk with your children, helping them to understand themselves, their temptations, fears and doubts, the more you prepare them to understand life in the world."[1]

Where Was the Beef?

I have learned that my "school education" about financial

responsibility and my "real-life education" were two very different things. When I was growing up, the best responsibility—and the one about which I griped most—was the three paper routes that I had for nearly ten years of my life. I kept the records, collected dues, managed overdue notices, and delivered the newspapers. My parents then gave me a portion of the money to spend and banked the rest for college. Now I am not certain of the entire motivation of my parents because they, too, have some Dutch (frugal) heritage in them. Could their motives have been to

- teach Doug financial responsibility?
- give Doug some extra spending money?
- teach Doug financial principles so that he can write a book about them some day?
- keep Doug and his friend, Andy out of trouble?
- or have Doug save some money to ease the college education burden on Ma and Pa?

Actually, I am certain that my parents intended a mixture of "teaching" and "saving for college." Regardless of their entire motivation, it was the *best* schooling in financial management that I was ever "taught." My parents encouraged me and assisted me, but it was on-the-job training (OJT). We *learn* what we *do!*

Similarly, my "Christian education" when I was growing up did not make me a Christian. It, too, was OJT. Keith Green said it best: "Going to church doesn't make you a Christian any more than going to McDonald's makes you a hamburger." Education is part of each of our foundations. Unfortunately, my early Christian education and church upbringing did not provide me with a solid foundation because the focus was primarily on man's opinions rather than on biblical opinions. Doctrines, dogmas, and rules are all fine—if they line up with the Word of God and if the Word of God is taught first and foremost. Such was not the case in my upbringing other than what I got from my parents. They had a great impact on me (much more than did my "school education"), and, thankfully, they gave me a foundation, both financially and spiritually. I believe it to be true that those with whom you spend the most time will have the greatest impact on your life. I am thankful for their investment in me early in life.

After much prayer and research, Dana and I decided to educate our children initially at home. Although it is a year-to-year decision, we are in our third year of this challenging and rewarding endeavor. It is not easy. It is a challenge and a heavy load for my wife, but we have felt strongly impressed to do this at least in their early years. We did it not to isolate them but to train them, prepare them, and invest in them before sending them onto the battlefield of life. We want them to be soldiers who know their enemy (Satan, the world, the flesh), their battle plan and maps (the Word) and who are grounded and strong as Christians. We are thankful for the opportunity to home school and pray that our investment will bear fruit in future years. As parents, we must assist and lead in the training and education of our children financially and spiritually, regardless of whether they are in a public school, a private school, or a home school.

Ah . . . Me!

I chose in my "dependent" years to focus mostly on myself, rather than on God. It set the tone for my "independent" (code word for "rebellious") years. We Americans are so blessed that we often do not think that we really "need" God. Yes, we know that we are supposed to need Him, and, yes, we might believe in Him. But do we really lean on Him? Do we really surrender every area of our lives to Him? We tend to be quite self-sufficient and trust in our careers, our wisdom, etc. I know that I was guilty. Even some of the good financial things with which we are blessed in this country—IRAs, 401k, pensions, insurance, etc.—help us lean more on ourselves and hinder us from trusting in the Lord with all of our heart. We are to lean not on our own understanding, but in all our ways acknowledge Him and He will make our paths straight.[2]

That was not me! I was fresh out of school, "doing it my way," as the old song says. I was awakened from my self-focused "me!" slumber when an external situation helped take my eyes off *my* needs and *my* circumstances. Desert Storm was my wake-up call. I began to fear that the "end of times" was near, and Jesus was coming back soon. I knew that I was not ready and that I really never had given my everything to Jesus. I finally made a good choice—complete surrender! "You can have it *all* Lord—my career, my life, my earthly things—I will do whatever You want.

You are Lord of all."

Until that time, He had been Lord of *most* but not Lord of *all*. I went to church every week. I read the Bible. I prayed. I had my devotions. I even knew that I was a sinner. I knew that Jesus died for me. I believed in Him. I believed in heaven and hell. I believed that man is destined to die once, and after that the judgment.[3] I knew all of that, and I believed it all. But I had not made Him King. *I* still had control. I would not surrender certain areas—my partying, my career, my desire to be married. They were my idols.

Thankfully, He never gave up on me. He was asking me to surrender my heart, to give it to Him. Not just a part but the whole.

Why did I deny God certain areas? Fear. Fear of giving up total control. Fear of being called to the mission field. Fear of being poor. I was not trusting Him with the lordship and ownership of my entire life. Thankfully, the seeds sown by my parents and others— seeds that had long been dormant—were not dead. After hearing the gospel message of salvation hundreds of times, after sitting in pew after pew living in lukewarmness and eternal insecurity, *finally*, on February 10, 1991, I decided to surrender all—myself, my future, my idols—and repent of my sins. I became a new person in Christ Jesus! I was free! The old really passed away, and the new came in!

I am so thankful that God was patient in waiting on me! Although I do believe that people can make *some* improvements in their financial situations without improving their spiritual conditions, I also believe that focusing on spiritual things (i.e., God's plans and priorities) *first* will have a much greater impact on your finances than any spreadsheet or tool we will talk about later in this book. Why? Because if we put everything in proper perspective (i.e., God first and me second), everything else almost naturally falls into place. If we love the Lord our God with *all* of our heart, *all* of our soul, *all* of our minds, and *all* of our strength, our money and finances will take their proper subordinate place.

> *If a person gets his attitude toward money straight, it will help straighten out almost every other area in his life.*
> **—Billy Graham**

Tricked?

"Well," you might be saying, "I thought that this book was about finances. You tricked me!"

No. It *is* about finances. But finances and spirituality go hand in hand.

"True biblical spirituality touches all of life, including things of government and law, not just religious things."
—Francis Schaeffer

Yes, the Bible talks about money, finances, and giving more than any other subject—sixteen of thirty-eight parables, more than 2,300 times—but it is almost always discussed with warnings, addressing a heart condition or an improper motive. The spiritual and the financial cannot be separated. Our walk with the Lord should affect *every* area of our lives. God does not dwell just in our churches or religious institutions on Sundays and Wednesdays; rather, He lives in our "temples" every day, every hour, and every minute.

We are the temples of the Holy Spirit if we are believers. My spending patterns should be affected by that fact. My giving should be affected. My work ethic should be affected. My family relationships, what comes out of my mouth, what goes into my body, what goes into my ears, what I view with my eyes, and where I go should all be affected. Christ changes us from the inside out!

Just a Normal Feller

I was a typical American back in the early 1990s when we began our debt-free journey. I was making a good salary ($35,000). Yet, I had no budget, no long-term financial plan, no short- or long-term goals for my life, family, or finances. I also had massive credit card debt (at least it was massive to me), two car loans, and a brand spanking new thirty-year mortgage. My giving to the Lord was a portion of what I had in my pocket on Sunday morning or a twenty-dollar check every now and then.

- If a major disaster had occurred, I would not have been prepared.

- If I had lost my job, I would not have been prepared.
- If my wife or parents had fallen sick, I would not have been prepared.
- If God had called me to the mission field, I could not have gone.
- If . . . If . . . If. . . .

I was not ready. My financial house was built on the sand. I was truly bound financially, and that led to my spiritual bondage as well. I equate it to being free from jail but with the handcuffs still on my wrists. That is not saying that one cannot be born again, or saved, and in financial bondage; it is just that such an individual cannot have *total* freedom. Most of us do not even realize that we are in bondage because we get caught in the trap of comparing ourselves with others. It is engrained in the American Dream. A wise man once said,

"People buy things they don't need, with money they don't have to impress people they don't even like."

I know that my motives for buying and acquiring were not to impress, but I also know that my peers, neighbors, and the marketers all had an influence on me. One of those comparative influences was the belief that debt was okay. It is normal. Well, I discovered from reading Christian authors, attending a Larry Burkett seminar, and studying the Word that "normal" is not always okay. In fact, the only references to debt in the Bible are warnings. Of the more than fifty passages that speak directly about debt and the more than twenty passages that refer indirectly to debt, none of them is positive or even neutral. They are all extremely negative. I knew that the Bible contains no commands against debt, but warnings are everywhere in it! One such warning is in Romans 13:8, which says, "Let no debt remain outstanding, except the continuing debt to love one another."

We started our journey toward financial liberty when we committed ourselves to the Larry Burkett budgeting class, but that was only the first baby step. *We* took a series of actions that brought us to where we are today. *God* took a series of actions that allowed us to be where we are today. The journey *was* and *is* a mixture of God's action and our action. I will talk about each of these roles later.

ACTION POINTS

1. Think about your foundation (e.g., childhood, religious upbringing, financial training). Was it solid? What aspects of your life need to be rebuilt?

_____

_____

_____

_____

_____

_____

_____

2. Think about your foundation and how you can make some changes for the better for *your* children.

_____

_____

_____

_____

_____

3. Thank someone—your parents or someone else—who influenced you and helped you build a positive foundation for your life.

_____

_____

_____

_____

4. Consider your relationship with Jesus Christ. Have you surrendered *all* to Him? Who is the king of your life, your future, and your "stuff?"

_____

_____

_____

_____

_____

CHAPTER 6

Cocaine and the Plastic Plunge

I referred to some of my financial woes in the preceding chapter, and I do not believe that I am alone in not having a firm financial foundation on which to build. In addition to minimal education and training (both at home and in school), we have been heavily influenced by the media and our culture and have been lulled to sleep with cushy lifestyles and live-for-today attitudes. Before covering some startling statistics, I would like to begin this chapter by having you ask yourself a few difficult questions that I had to confront myself before we began our financial journey. This exercise helped me develop a sense of urgency and purpose, and I hope that it will stir the same reaction in you. Answer the following questions aloud as you read them. It might help press you into duty a little more quickly.

SELAH 6-1

1. Who really owns your material things? Does the way you live reflect that?
2. How badly do you want to be financially free? Are you willing to make some radical changes to reach that goal?

3. What if the stock market crashed today? Would you still be financially free?
4. What if fire destroyed all of your property? Are you prepared?
5. What if you lost your job today? Are you prepared?
6. What if your spouse/parents/family died today? Are you prepared?
7. What if God called you to the ministry or mission field today? Could you go?
8. Do you still feel stressed or bound although you might be out of debt?
9. Does watching the stock market make you anxious?
10. If a major unexpected medical emergency arose, could you afford it?
11. What if a major energy crisis occurred and significantly affected your finances?
12. What if you had an unexpected child (or even a planned child for that matter)?
13. If you died today, would it put your family in financial turmoil? Have you left them with a plan and an inheritance? Do you have a will?
14. If you died today, what would your epitaph say? Have you left a legacy? What would your financial legacy be?
15. If you died today, would Jesus say, "Well done good and faithful servant. You took care of what I let you borrow during your short time on my earth"?

Please understand that I did not pose these questions to instill fear or guilt but rather to help you consider some potential realities and to challenge you to consider your readiness and current plan of action. Do not be too downcast if you could not answer these questions as you would like. Not many folks can. I know that I could not; in fact, I still cannot answer some of them as I would like. But I do remember the feeling of bondage and helplessness associated with not being ready.

> *"No one who is financially bound is spiritually free."* [1]
> —*Larry Burkett*

You might feel beyond help. The good news is that *nothing is too difficult for God! "All things are possible with God."*[2] "You have made the heavens and the earth by your great power and outstretched arm. *Nothing is too hard for you."*[3] God is for you, not against you. He will do His part if you do yours. It is a *promise!*

Powerless

Read Nehemiah 5:3–5. The passage describes the Jewish people and how they were mortgaging their fields, their vineyards, and their homes to get grain during the famine. Some people were forced to borrow money to pay the king's tax on their fields and vineyards. The passage then talks about slavery, and compares the principle of slavery with being "powerless." The people said, "[W]e are powerless, because our fields and our vineyards belong to others."

We must realize that our being in debt means that *someone else owns us* or our goods. When we have debt, we are not in a position of power but rather of slavery. Just as slavery meant being subject to another person, so we are subject to the lender when we are in debt. In fact, Proverbs 22:7 says,

"The rich rule over the poor, and the borrower is *servant* to the lender."

The word *servant* in the original language could actually be translated "slave." This principle of financial slavery is so simple, and we know it—but we do not want to face the fact that we really are slaves! The fact is that if we owe something on anything, then the true owner of the thing is the lender, and we are not even the "real" caretakers or stewards of that thing. If you have the most beautiful house in the neighborhood but still owe someone else for it, then it is really not yours. We have become a society of slaves to the lenders.

Drugs and Mind Control

Debt is like economic cocaine. We are hooked societally, govern-mentally, and individually. We are so programmed to believe that we *have* to borrow. Sales personnel nearly fall to the ground when I say that I am paying cash for furniture or a vehicle. They *assumed* that we are going to charge it. We always have. Everyone else does. We have an "assumed mind set" that debt is okay. It is normal.

But it has not *always* been normal. In the Great Depression era, people seldom borrowed. But today we borrow for our next meal, gas, braces, furniture, vacation, cars, etc. Therefore, people just *assume* that we need to be concerned about the following questions.

- What is our credit rating?
- What is the monthly payment?
- What is the interest rate?
- For how many months should the note be?

Instead, we should really start asking this question: How many months will I need to *save* so that I can purchase this item with cash?

Most people operate with a mind set of debt and credit. Credit ratings are overemphasized, overrated, and a necessary American evil. Only in the last three years have I not cared about my credit rating. I do not need to borrow! I really do not care what the monthly payment is. I pay cash! I really do not care what the interest rate is for borrowing purposes but only for *gaining* interest, not *paying* someone else interest. I no longer need to decide between a seventy-two-month note and a sixty-month note. I am saving monthly for my next purchase, for Christmas presents, etc.

We truly are being told (and we listen and heed) that debt can even be considered an asset when it is used correctly. I have seen numerous advertisements to that effect over the last few years. The last time I checked, a debt was a *liability*—a ball and chain, a handcuff, *not* an asset. The bankers and financial institutions really own most Americans. Credit cards are three times more profitable than other parts of their portfolios. In fact, car dealerships make much more money on the lending and credit than they do on the sale of the car.

Buy Now, Pay Later

The marketers and financial money machines are after your dollar. They know that the average American family will make between one and two million dollars in a lifetime, and they want your piece of the pie. Their marketing uses such phrases as "helping" you, "giving away money," "no interest for a year," and "buy now, pay later." *Always read the fine print!* Often, that *small* print can mean *big* headaches down the road.

My wife and I have a running joke: If it sounds too good to be true, each of us tells the other to go back and read the fine print. It usually *is* too good to be true. If you miss a payment, most likely, you will be charged interest and back payments. Also, that low interest rate might be low for only six months.

> ***"Consumers have to borrow to support a level of consumption***
> ***they have come to anticipate."***
> **—James Medof**

I call it an inability to delay gratification! A "gotta-have-it-now" syndrome has gripped us. We demand it now and hope that we can pay for it later. Too much. Too soon. The Bible calls it a lack of self-control or a lack of patience. Our grandparents survived with one car and without all of the modern gadgets that we have. They did not fill their houses with furniture in the first year of marriage. They paid cash for nearly everything.

Patience and discipline are not very exciting principles, but they are necessary to achieve our long-term goals. Ask any athlete or musician!

SELAH 6-2

Warning Signs Test

Following are some warning signs that indicate potential troubles on the horizon. Score yourself according to the following color scale:

- ❖ RED (describes me/us perfectly)
- ❖ YELLOW (I/we struggle some)
- ❖ GREEN (You must be talking about someone else)

Problem area	Assessment		
Considering debt consolidation	GREEN	YELLOW	RED
Making minimum payments only	GREEN	YELLOW	RED
Not paying off credit cards at the end of month	GREEN	YELLOW	RED
Paying bills late	GREEN	YELLOW	RED
Juggling bills	GREEN	YELLOW	RED
Creditor calling	GREEN	YELLOW	RED
Spending more than you make	GREEN	YELLOW	RED
Savings are minimal	GREEN	YELLOW	RED
Giving is less than 10 percent	GREEN	YELLOW	RED
Giving is not joyful	GREEN	YELLOW	RED
Anxious about the stock market	GREEN	YELLOW	RED
Charging everyday items	GREEN	YELLOW	RED
Checks are bouncing	GREEN	YELLOW	RED
Overtime or second job is necessary	GREEN	YELLOW	RED
Hiding charges from your spouse	GREEN	YELLOW	RED
Domestic disputes about finances	GREEN	YELLOW	RED
Daily concern over your investments	GREEN	YELLOW	RED
Time spent thinking about money/finances	GREEN	YELLOW	RED
Not able to invest in your 401k to the maximum	GREEN	YELLOW	RED

Scoring:

10 or more Red = Time to make some radical changes—a Financial Overhaul is needed.

5–9 Yellow or Red = Time to make some changes—too many warning signs.

0–4 Yellow or Red = Time to make some targeted changes— tuneup in certain areas.

The purpose for this little exercise was not to drag you down farther. Valid reasons might exist for the situation in which you find yourself, but we must *look up* to move forward. No one is beyond help. The Lord is here to carry your burdens. Read Matthew 11:28–30 and Psalm 68:19. His yoke is easy, and His burden is light. Come to me *all* who are heavy-laden and I will give you rest. *No one is excluded.*

We will cover in detail some practical steps to becoming debt-free later in the book, but a financial transformation begins with a heart that is committed to Jesus Christ and continues with financial discipline. Proverbs 13:18 states that poverty and shame will come to him who disdains correction. If we are disciplined and DO, change will occur. The Greek word for *discipline* is "gymnazo," from which we get the words *gymnastics* and *gymnasium*. Discipline is *daily and sustained* training. It is "sanctified sweating." Putting some discipline into your finances is not pleasant, just as that daily trip to the gym is not joy unspeakable and full of glory. On some days, you have to drag yourself. We must learn to say yes to God and His ways and no to self.

> **"Discipline yourself for the purpose of godliness."**
> **—1 Timothy 4:7**

SELAH 6-3

What disciplines can you begin immediately in your finances? A biblical work ethic? More careful time stewardship? Cut spending in specific areas? A debt repayment plan? Selling possessions? Making a commitment to No new debt? Consistent giving? Consistent saving? Refer to Selahs 6-1 and 6-2 for some specific disciplines that you can begin immediately, and list them.

_____

_____

_____

_____

_____

The Plastic Plunge

According to www.cardweb.com,[4] the average U.S. household pays $1000 per year in credit card *interest!* That is $104.7 Billion in interest annually for the entire country. [5] The credit card providers want you to take the plastic plunge. Why? They live off your interest. Revolving credit was not an issue until 1968, when credit cards became a large enough force in the economy that the government began keeping track of it. Revolving credit is now 42 percent of all outstanding consumer credit,[6]; it is even larger than automobile debt.

Just for fun, count how many credit card offers you get in a month. In 1990, 210 million Visas and MasterCards were in use. In 1995, that number had nearly doubled to 376 million (AP news). The latest numbers from Cardfacts.com[7] show 613 million Visas and MasterCards; 698 million credit cards are in use when you include American Express and Discover cards. The dollar volume in annual usage for the "big four" credit cards is *$824 billion!*[8] I actually received a credit card offer recently that deserves the "most ridiculous" award. It said that I was preapproved for a credit limit of five hundred dollars, and all *I* needed to do was simply to open an account with them for one hundred dollars. I needed to *send them a check* for one hundred dollars so I could have a credit line of five hundred dollars?! Huh? We have plunged into financial insanity!

Average number of credit cards per cardholder household[9]

Bank credit cards	6.0
Retail credit cards	8.3
Debit cards	2.4
Total	16.7

Have a Merry, Merry Christmas

"For the first time in history American consumers charged more than $121.4 billion to their major credit cards during the 2001 holiday season."[10] This amount was $28 billion in 1990. Between Thanksgiving and Christmas, Americans will use their major credit cards more than 1.3 billion times, and the average U.S. household will rack up nearly $1100 in credit card charges. "For the entire year of 2000 Americans, for the first time charged *more than $1.0 trillion* in purchases to major credit cards (not including store cards, gas cards, and debit cards)."[11]

Credit cards make you feel wealthier than you really are, and they make it easier for you to spend money you really do not have.

Figure 6-1
They Have More of Our Money

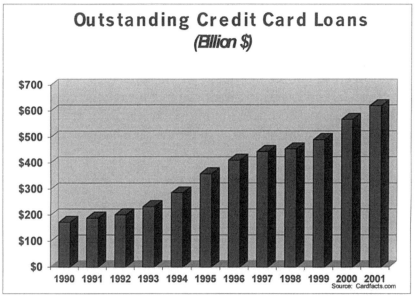

The credit card providers' sole desire is to make money off you, and they are succeeding (see Figure 6-1). [12] It is not to give you a bountiful "cash back bonus" of $2.43 at the end of the year. It is not to give you a picture of a pretty sports team on your card. They seem to be your best pal by sending you some "blank checks" just when you need them the most! But they have a motive: they want you to make the *minimum payment* and earn as much interest from you as they can. If you do not believe me, take a look at the numbers.

"The Heist"
Two Credit Card Scenarios

Scenario 1—$5000 in credit card debt, 18 percent interest, paying $110/month *every month.*

Time required to pay off card:	6 years
Interest paid:	$3353
Total cost of item plus interest:	$8353

This is *not* a good investment of the $3353 in interest by any stretch of the imaginatioin, but it could be worse.

Scenario 2—Same debt situation: $5000 in credit card debt, 18 percent interest, but the minimum payment decreases a little each month. You might pay $110/month the *first month*, then pay slightly lower amounts the following months. For the sake of simplicity, assume that the payment is $109 in month 2, $108 in month 3, etc.

Time to pay off card:	34 years
Interest paid:	$10,055
Total cost of item plus interest	$15,055!

Twenty-eight years longer and $7000 more! This is an expensive lesson for reducing your minimum payment by that $1/per month. The financial institutions and credit card companies would like you to think that they are there to help you. Do not kid yourself. They are in it for themselves.

Are credit cards bad in themselves? No. They are bad only when they get a grip on you. If you knew that you did not have a credit card on which to lean, only cash, how would you change your spending patterns? If credit cards were outlawed, could you make it to your next paycheck?

"Your credit card is not saving you from emergency, it is creating them."

I Am Here to Report a Drowning

The average family is increasingly drowning in credit card debt. In 1990, the average American family had two credit cards with $2985 in debt. In 1997, that average was above $6000 on four credit cards (AP), and, according to credit card tracker Cardweb.com,[13] the average U.S. household with at least one credit card carried a balance of *$8367* in the year 2001 (see Figure 6-2).

Figure 6-2
Drowning in Debt

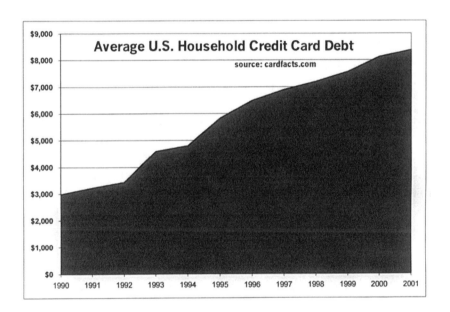

For some reason, we feel better because most of those around us are in the same boat. During our personal "debt days," I know that when I talked to others about our financial pressures I did not get too many blank stares. In fact, one survey showed that only 3 percent of Americans actually have a financial plan.

Nellie Mae,[14] a provider of federal and private education loans for college students, recently found that 78 percent of college students had credit cards in 2000 with an average debt of $2748, up from $1879 just two years earlier. The percentage of students with four or more credit cards rose from 27 percent in 1998 to 32 percent in 2000. Twenty-five percent of those students owed more than $3000. Ten percent of them owed more than $7000! They get a free T-shirt for signing up and then a year later have thousands of dollars of debt and are hooked on debt for life. They are barraged with free offers. It is similar to someone's offering them drugs or cigarettes free the first time. The credit card companies try to get them while they are young and hope that they will become "regulars" after they get a taste!

In 1999 alone, an estimated 461,000 Americans younger than 35 sought protection from their creditors in bankruptcy. [15] At one local Consumer Credit Counseling Service, *more than half* of all clients are 18 to 35 years old. What is sold as freedom is really chains. I recall the "rush" and "joy" that I felt when I bought something that I really wanted but knew that I could not afford. It felt as though it were free!

Who is kidding whom? It feels good until that first bill comes, and the second, and. . . .

Forty-four million households (57 percent of card users) carry card balances of an average of $8025 month to month. At an interest rate of 17 percent, that is, $114/month per household. If this amount were invested on behalf of your child's education or another worthy purpose at 8 percent for eighteen years, it would amount to $54,989. [16] The credit card companies want to milk you for all they can. Paying the minimum amounts on the following two examples for debts of $2000 and $5000 net you very little progress, often resulting in your *never* paying off your debt and quite often resulting in your paying more than *twice* what you thought you were paying after adding the interest. So that ten-dollar restaurant meal was really a twenty-dollar meal. That twenty-dollar tank of gas was really forty dollars. That $500 dining room table was really $1000.

Throwing Money to the Wind
The Truth about Interest and Payoffs

Card Balance	Monthly Payment	Interest Rate	Pay-off date	Interest Amt. $
$2000	$20	12%	*Never*	?
$2000	$30	18%	*Never*	?
$2000	$50	18%	5 yr, 2 mo	$1077
$2000	$20	10%	**18 yrs**	**$2318**
$5000	$50	12%	**Never**	?
$5000	$75	18%	**Never**	?
$5000	$100	18%	7 yr, 10 mo	**$4311**

The best investment you can make if you have credit card debt is to *pay them off* and not pay that 15–20 percent interest. The next thing you can do is to cut them up! When you get financially free, you will not have to worry about monthly payments or credit card transfers or what your credit rating is because you will not need to borrow again, and even if you do, it will be for only a short time.

I would highly recommend a *fast* from your credit cards for ninety days. See if it is an addiction. See if it is an economic drug. One way to start clean—and I recommend it only if one has made a firm commitment to *no new debt*—is to transfer all credit card debts to a low-interest card. Do so only after reading the fine print because many companies coax you to get the low introductory rate but then the rate balloons after six months and could actually cost you more than what you currently pay. Beware of the high annual fees on some cards. Bankrate.com can lead you to some low-interest-rate cards, but ensure that you get all details before making the change. Remember, almost everything is negotiable.

The first step on our financial journey was to commit to no more credit card use. We cut up all of our credit cards. We realized that the cards were controlling us rather than us controlling them. The most important commitment we made was that there would be *no new debt*, and the best, immediate action was to cut 'em up!

The drug of debt can adversely affect your family, marriage, or even church just as any other drug can affect you. Debt can hand-cuff a church from giving to missions or meeting the needs of a community that it desires to reach.

Are we victims? Are we irresponsible? Or are we innocent doves? I really think that the answer is a combination, but the victim mentality ends here. When you gain knowledge, you are responsible for what you *do* with that knowledge. God will hold us accountable. If we want the handcuffs off badly enough, we will make changes—even if they are small changes—to undo the handcuffs.

It has been said in both Christian and non-Christian circles that 80 percent of marital dissension and divorce stems from financial pressures. The number of families in debt counseling has tripled over the last decade. In Center for Financial Well-Being surveys, 37% of respondents admitted that financial concerns adversely affected their productivity in the past year. One survey also showed that personal financial issues were the number one source of stress. 49% of the respondents cited it as the number one issue. Only 22% cited relationships, and 17% cited work." [17] Although I do not agree with the last sentence of the following quotation, I do believe that you can no longer tell the difference between many Christian families' financial situations and those of a non-Christian family.

"He is both a fool and a rascal who has a quarter coming in, and on the strength of it spends five dollars which does not belong to him. . . . Scripture says, 'Owe no man anything,' which does not mean pay your debts, but never have any to pay. My opinion is, that those who break this law ought to be turned out of the Christian church."
—Charles Spurgeon

Spurgeon, the prince of preachers of old, would be tossed out of most churches with his radical stance on debt. We must be on guard against the disease of greed and materialism. We must "put to death the earthly nature,"[18] and the Bible includes greed in that list. We need to "Watch out! Be on your guard against all kinds of greed; A man's life does not consist in the abundance of his possessions."[19] We are not supposed to be normal. If we call ourselves Christians, we are supposed to come out from among them and be separate. We should not bow our knees to any creditor or financial institution but rather to Christ alone. When we are saddled and enslaved by debt, we are bowing to creditors. We are not to conform any longer to the pattern of this world.[20]

We need to escape the culture of debt and credit, of "easy" payment plans and lifestyles beyond our incomes, and be a light and a witness to those who are suffocating from the results of debt. I encourage you to begin your retreat from the plastic-plunge lifestyle today!

ACTION POINTS

1. What changes will you make based on your self-assessment of readiness from Selahs 6-1 and 6-2? Are you ready if . . . ?

   _____
   _____
   _____
   _____
   _____
   _____
   _____
   _____

2. What are some recent examples of "gotta have it now" in your household?

   _____
   _____
   _____
   _____
   _____
   _____
   _____
   _____

3. On how many credit cards do you owe?_____
   How much money do you owe on them?_____

4. How much debt does your church have?_____
   Do plans exist for paying it off early?_____

CHAPTER 7

Tricks, Traps, and Monsters

Escaping the culture of debt and credit is easier said than done. In addition to the blitz of advertising, media, and technology, the lenders also use slick tactics to woo us into the mesmerizing web of materialism.

The Monthly Payment Trap

One of the lenders' tricks is to try to change your thinking. The monthly payment trap is an attempt to get you to think about smaller numbers as opposed to the entire amount of debt into which you are about ready to sink. They want you to think monthly rather than yearly or over the life of the debt. Which of the following situations sounds best?

- a $900/month mortgage payment
- a $100,000 house (principal only)
- a $270,000 house (including your principal and interest to be paid)

If you answered $900/month, congratulations! The lowest number always sounds best! You will never hear a salesman or financial banker discuss the $270,000 number.

Tradeoffs

We were shopping for a van recently and were confronted with a choice. The brand new van with all of the options and features we wanted, as well as the color my wife really wanted, had a price tag of $23,000. We had also been looking at used vehicles and had located one for $15,000. It had 20,000 miles and fewer options, and it was not the color my wife desired. The monthly payment difference was only a little more than $100/month. That does not sound so bad. But what we often fail to think about in the heat of making a major purchase is the tradeoff for that extra *monthly* payment. For us, the tradeoff for having a few options and the right color was not worth the tradeoff of a nice vacation every year. That was really the choice we were making, not just $100 extra a month. Each of us has different priorities, so what is important to one might not be a priority to another person. Ensure that you are analyzing the tradeoffs of that monthly payment. Never rush into major purchasing decisions. Go slowly! Shop around! Know what a good price is! Consider all of the tradeoffs!

Add up those "Dollar-a-Day" Sales Pitches

I recently sat through one of the most convincing sales speeches I have ever heard. The salesman had been doing it for twenty-five years, and it showed. He used the "only-dollars-a-day" line most effectively. If you put it that way, it really does not sound like much—unless I have other debt! A couple of bucks a day can add up in a hurry if I have ten other "few-dollars-a-day" obligations. Always ask about the *total cost*.

The Enemy's Trap

The enemy does not have just one trick up his sleeve; he has a multifaceted game plan to lead to your destruction. I do not want to over spiritualize this, but money and "stuff" is as big a target as any. If Satan tried it during Jesus' temptation, he will try it on you. "All this I will give you . . . if you will bow down and worship me."[1] Obviously, none of us would fall down and worship Satan. However, his desire is to get us to wander or to stray from our faith because of an eagerness for money.[2]

The other interesting characteristic that we discover in this passage about Satan is that he tried the "instant gratification" approach. You can have it *all*, and you can have it *now*. It is a trap of the enemy!

Materialism is SIN!

I was driving home recently listening to a radio program. The speaker was warning against *self-sufficiency*, and he told a rather incredible story. A visiting evangelist was preaching in Mozambique. Half of the congregation exited during the middle of his message. A few minutes later, the same number of people (but different individuals) returned. Later, he asked what had happened. The naked villagers on the outskirts of town wanted to hear the gospel message but had no clothes, so the regular attendees gave them their clothes halfway through the message so that they, too, could hear the gospel! We find that difficult to relate to in our nation of blessing.

We are conditioned to be self-sufficient in this country. We think that we really do not even need God because of our false security in things. The similarities between the American church and the Laodicean church, mentioned in Revelation 3:14–17, are striking. It was a wealthy city, and they were unaware of their spiritual poverty and nakedness. They thought that they had it all together. They were rebuked in the Scripture because God loved them. No record exists of Paul ever visiting them, but he mentions them twice.

The enemy would like to lull us to sleep by luring us to put our trust in things. If we do, we are sinning. "If I have put my trust in gold or said to pure gold 'you are my *security*,' if I have rejoiced over my great wealth, the fortune my hands had gained, . . . then these also would be *sins* to be judged!"[3]

The Bait in the Trap

"People who want to get rich fall into temptation and a trap and into many foolish and harmful desires that plunge men into ruin and destruction. For the love of money is a root of all kinds of evil. Some people eager for money, have wandered from the faith

and pierced themselves with many griefs."
—1 Timothy 6:9-10

The enemy dangles the deceitfulness of wealth as bait. It chokes us and makes us unfruitful. I know of at least two former pastors who have succumbed to "get-rich-quick" schemes that led to an eagerness for money, and it plunged them into destruction. Would they admit that it plunged them into ruin and destruction? No, they were unaware of their spiritual poverty and nakedness.

The enemy baits the trap with the boasts of ease, comfort and satisfaction. The deceit is this: if we can just get that next promotion, one more raise, or a larger house, then we will be satisfied.

"Whoever loves money never has money enough; whoever loves wealth is never satisfied with his income.
This too is meaningless."
Ecclesiastes 5:10

"A faithful man will be richly blessed, but one eager to get rich will not go unpunished!"
—Proverbs 28:20

Idols?

Can we have a modern idol? I know I have. Anything that comes between me and my relationship with God is an idol. Anything that is more important than my time with Him or that consumes my passion, money, or thoughts more than my desire for Him has the potential to become an idol.

I remember two very specific instances when the Holy Spirit was dealing with me regarding idols in my life. I remember the day when my friend Andy and I trashed approximately $10,000 in CDs and tapes. Not only did my music have a grip on me but also the words did not glorify Jesus. I also remember the season when I felt that God wanted me to give up two of my favorite things—golf and reading the paper—so that I could spend more time with Him. Ouch! It was tough! Idols? How could they be idols? There was nothing wrong with golf and newspapers, but I was giving both of these things my most valuable time, the best part of my day. I was consumed with them but could not give Jesus ten minutes. These things were competing with Jesus, and Jesus was losing. So they were idols in my life. By my actions, I showed that they were more important to me than was my walk with Jesus. I was also consumed with sports on television during this same time. I fasted from TV for a season to reorder my priorities, and now they do not have a grip on me like they used to. In fact, I now spend very little time watching television and can spend time doing more productive things instead.

Am I telling you to give up your hobby or your paper? No. It might not have a grip on you or get in your way of worshipping Jesus and loving Him with all your heart. All that I ask is that you pray and ask God to point out to you any areas or "things" that need a "grip adjustment."

"The reason Jesus talked so much about money is that it competes with God for lordship of our lives."
—Howard Dayton, Crown Ministries

SELAH 7-1

Stop to pray for a few minutes, asking the Lord to point out to you any "idols" in your life that need to be laid down or "fasted from."

Watch Out!

This trap of idolatry is actually so serious that it is lumped with prostitution, homosexuality, thievery, and drunkenness.[4] Ephesians 5:5 says that "no . . . greedy person . . . has any inheritance in the kingdom of Christ." If Jesus mentions it, we had better take heed. "Watch out! Be on your guard against all kinds of greed; a man's life does not consist in the abundance of his possessions."[5] It is so easy to put our trust in things made by man. This is idolatry.[6]

We can have nothing and yet possess everything, or it is possible we can have everything yet possess nothing.[7]

Avoiding the Trap

1. We need to learn to be content. That does not happen overnight. In fact, there will never be an instant cure for this problem in America. Paul "learned the secret of being content in any and every situation."[8]
2. We need to "keep our lives free from the love of money."[9] This, too, will take work and *simplification!*
3. We must deny ourselves and take up our cross. What good will it be for a man if he gains the whole world, yet forfeits his soul?[10] This idea is radical! We are to "put to death whatever belongs to the earthly nature."[11] Greed and idolatry are listed among things that are identified as part of our earthly nature.
4. Don't use the Joneses or the TV sitcom as the "yardstick" or "pattern." We are "not to conform to the pattern of this world."[12] We are just strangers passing through.

Two Cures for Materialism

1. *Sell and give!*[13]
2. *Seek God's kingdom and priorities first!*[14]

Giving our time, money, and belongings liberates us from gripping our "stuff" too tightly. Our security is not in *what* we have but in *who we are* through Jesus Christ. Our heart (the foundation) is being secretly enticed by the enemy. We must be on guard against the enemy's trap!

Then and Now

It is good to look back and see just how far we have come as a society as well as to learn from what previous generations have experienced. History shows that we often go through cycles. I think that it is time that we learned from our more fiscally conservative generations. Note the following rather shocking comparisons.

In 1864, C.H. Mackintoshi taught the following:

> "Owe no man anything" is a precept so plain that the wayfaring man, though a fool, need not err therein. . . .

What right have I, before God and man, to wear a cap or a hat not paid for? What right have I to order a ton of coal, a pound of tea, or a joint of meat, if I have not the money to pay for it? It may be said what are we to do? The answer is plain to an upright mind and a tender conscience, *we are to do without rather than go into debt."*

This seems to be too radical a concept for modern America. I am not quite sure that most of us would know how to live by "doing *without* rather than going into debt." Debt is not a new problem, but the severity has definitely grown. The 1920s were definitely the birth of modern consumer financing. Although the first car buyers paid cash, in 1919, 5 percent of Americans bought a car on credit. In 1925, that percentage increased to 75 percent.[15]

The similarity between the Great Depression and modern America is eerie. The celebration of technology was being embraced then just as it is today. From 1919 to 1929, the number of cars tripled to twenty-three million. By 1922, radio had become a craze. People were debating whether radio should be legal in cars because of the many accidents that were occurring. Sound familiar? How about our cellular phones? The technological impact of the car and the radio parallel the great technological impact of the Internet. However, as we discussed earlier, although we might have progressed in certain areas, we have regressed in others, a prime example being our financial habits and behavior.

Progression or Regression?

THEN	NOW
1950's—12 percent savings rate*	2001—1.6 percent savings rate*[16]
1954—Tax Freedom Day— March 30**	2001—Tax Freedom Day- May 3** [17]
1950—twelve-year mortgage norm	2000's—thirty-year mortgage norm
1960—eighteen-month car note norm	2000's—sixty-month car note norm

1960—1.22 vehicles per household	2000's—1.87 vehicles per household[18]
1960—House is 22% of average budget	2000's—House is 40 percent of average budget
1970—<100,000 annual bankruptcies	2001—>1.4 million annual bankruptcies[19]
1950—Public debt is $257 million	2002—Public debt is $6.0 trillion[20]

* personal savings as a percentage of disposable personal income
** number of full days of salary per year that is allocated to taxes

Our toys are getting bigger and it is taking us longer to pay them off, and ol' Uncle Sam has not helped the situation much. In 1948, the median-income U.S. family paid 2 percent of its income in taxes to the federal government. In the 2000s, that same family pays 24 percent, plus as much as 9 percent in state and local income taxes. The key to keeping more of what you earn is self-discipline and self-denial.

The American Bankruptcy Institute concludes that as consumer debt increases, so do the number of nonbusiness bankruptcy filings. The numbers seem to agree with their assessment.[21]

Figure 7-1
Credit often Leads to Bankruptcy

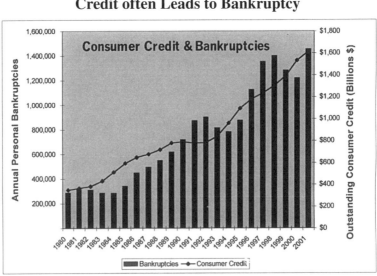

Bankruptcies are on the rampage, hitting an all-time high in 2001 (1,452,030),[22] and consumer credit continues to spin out of control. The consumer credit card dollars depicted in Figure 7-1 do not even include mortgage debt. If you were to include that in the equation, the total consumer debt would be $7.5 trillion in 2001.[23]

The number of bankruptcies is eight times the annual rate of bankruptcies during the Great Depression. The sad thing about bankruptcy is that "the average indebtedness of couples in bankruptcy is only $5000!" [24] Many people would not have to take this path if they could hang in and make some changes. The other sad thing about personal bankruptcy is that only 37 percent of the people who file claim that it is their fault. Most people shift the blame to another person, the economy, the banks, etc.

The first step in becoming financially free is taking responsibility and ownership. I needed to own up to the fact that I had a problem and that I had the responsibility to fix that problem. I had a responsibility to my wife, my future children, myself, and God.

We were acquainted with a couple who refused to take responsibility and knew full well that they needed to make some financial changes. They refused to take me up on my offer of some free counseling. This sounds absurd, but some people just do not want to change. They want the easy way out. This couple continually purchased regularly only name brand clothing and the latest trend shoes for their one-year-old child. They ate out regularly. They bought the latest toys. They had the latest model car. Yet, they decided to declare bankruptcy rather than make a few changes. They did not have an insurmountable debt, but they gave up. Now they are facing the same struggles again because they never dealt with the root of the problem—the foundational issues.

SELAH 7-2

Talk to your parents and grandparents and do some factfinding. Where did you get some of your financial habits? What were you taught? How much did your parents and grandparents save compared to the percentage that you are saving? Did they have car and mortgage notes? How large was their house? How many bedrooms? How quickly did they furnish it? Did they have credit cards or other major debt? Did it affect them? Do you have a higher salary yet seem to be more strapped and more stressed?

We are debt dependent and our debt is becoming "permanent." The results have been more bankruptcies and more and bigger assets that we cannot afford but buy anyway.

In previous generations, the "credit" that was used was temporary and short term. We now are dependent upon "debt," which is permanent and long-term, more of a *state* of owing. Our toys have gotten bigger, but so has our debt. The mind set and bumper sticker that jests, "He who dies with the most toys wins" might be more of a mind set than we would like to admit. It should read, "He who dies with the most toys still dies, and you can't take 'em with ya."

We truly have been blessed. Recent statistics released at the International Builders Show in Atlanta reveal that the average home built in America has grown by more than 50 percent in size since the 1970.[25]

	1975	1980's	1995	2001
Square feet, av. House	1645	1905	2095	2332
Houses with 2½ baths	20%	24%	48%	54%
Median price	$55,000	$75,000	$127,000	$169,000

Yet the average family is smaller. Could it be that we need more space to store more stuff?

SELAH 7-3

Why Do We Have a Sea of Debt?

Answer for yourself personally. Score yourself (High/Medium/Low)

1. I have had little or no teaching in money
   management, debt, and spending.   _____

2. I have lacked self-control in spending.   _____

3. I have let the media/advertising
   influence my spending decisions.   _____

4. I have not had patience in spending.
   (Why wait when you can charge?)   _____

5. I have not been disciplined with my
   budgeting and planning.   _____

6. I have been distant from the Lord
   and His priorities.   _____

7. The government has not set a stellar
   example for me regarding "debt."   _____

8. My focus has been too temporal/
   earthly and not eternal/heavenly.   _____

9. I have tried to keep up with the
   Joneses too much.   _____

10. _____   _____

Our financial institutions, peers, leaders, schools, and even government have taught us that debt is okay. The monster public debt, as we near fiscal year 2003 is now a staggering *$6,005,161,158,767.37.* The following graph depicts the growth of the monster according to the Bureau of the Public Debt.[26] Only in the last fifteen to twenty years has the cumulative public debt grown significantly.

Figure 7-2
The MONSTER

That is six *trillion, five billion, one hundred sixty one million, one hundred fifty eight thousand, seven hundred sixty-seven dollars and thirty-seven cents!*

It is a number so big that it really does not mean anything to us. Here are some down-to-earth terms that we *can* understand.

- This is equivalent to every U.S. citizen's having $23,758 in debt. A family of four would owe nearly $100,000. In 1900 the cost of the federal debt would have been $16 for every U.S. citizen. This is a 1,437 percent increase!

- This is similar to your making $50,000 a year as a salary and paying $10,000 of that toward interest *every year*. We have paid an average of $359 billion[27] in interest a year for the last five years—approximately 20 percent of our annual budget. That is almost $1 billion a day in interest.

- A million dollars is equal to spending $3000 a day for a year. That is beyond my comprehension. It gets silly when a trillion dollars is equal to spending $3000 a day for a *million* years. That is what we owe! Three thousand dollars a day for six million years!

- In a period of eleven years, we accumulated three times the debt accumulation of the preceding 205 years of our history!

Heavyweight Definitions

FEDERAL DEFICIT—When *annual* expenses are greater than income. In some recent years, we have actually spent less than we "brought in" as a country. We have run a surplus rather than a deficit! We have made some progress!

Personal example: If you spent $5000 more than you made in 2002, and put it on a credit card, your *annual deficit* would be $5000.

FEDERAL DEBT—The *cumulative total* of *all* of our *annual deficits*. What we owe as a country. Our *cumulative debt*. This continues to increase and currently stands at six trillion dollars.

Personal example: If you spent $5000 more than you made each year in 2000, 2001, and 2002, your *cumulative debt* would be $15,000 plus interest.

NATIONAL DEBT—This includes *all debt* of federal, state, and local governments', households', and business and financial-sector debt. You will never hear this number talked about, but it gives a good indication of how much *total* debt our society has. According to the Grandfather National Debt Report by MW Hodges,[28] our total U.S. national debt has now soared to *$30 trillion* from $4 trillion in 1960. This is $108,000 per man, woman, and child, or $432,000 for a family of four.

I wanted to prove to myself that some of these "surpluses" over the last few years have not made a dent in our "cumulative national debt." Following are the results of my review of the 431-page *Fiscal Year 2003 Budget of the United States Government:*[29]

Table 7-1

A Dent in the Debt? Nope!

Fiscal Year	Annual Deficit/Surplus	Cumulative/Total Debt
1997	- $22 billion	- $5.4 trillion
1998	+ $69 billion	- $5.5 trillion
1999	+ $125 billion	- $5.6 trillion
2000	+ $236 billion	- $5.7 trillion
2001	+ $127 billion	- $5.8 trillion
2002 (est.)	- $106 billion	- $6.0 trillion
2003 (est.)	- $80 billion	- $6.5 trillion
2004 (est.)	- $14 billion	- $6.9 trillion
2005 (est.)	+ $61 billion	- $7.2 trillion
2006 (est.)	+ $86 billion	- $7.5 trillion
2007 (est.)	+ $104 billion	- $7.8 trillion

The cumulative debt has continued to grow, *even when we had a surplus*! We are not paying off our debt. It is smoke and mirrors, folks. The $6.0 trillion will continue to grow because of the interest charges and because we are not paying anything toward the debt. That $6.0 trillion is currently forecast to be close to $8 trillion in 5 years, yet it rarely gets talked about. That is like saying that you had $20,000 in credit card debt last year and this year you were fiscally responsible enough not to add any new debt to that amount. You just keep ignoring the $20,000 and hope it goes away! But guess what? That $20,000 does not disappear; in fact, it continues to grow because you are not paying anything against it and the interest continues to mount. (See the "throwing-money-to-the-wind" example of personal debt in Chapter 6.) In your personal finances, would you declare yourself a hero and figure out where to spend some of your extra "surplus" you came up with for one or two years? I think not! We are eliminating annual deficits but not the cumulative debt. We are taught that debt is okay. I would direct you to Deuteronomy

28, which clearly talks of signs of blessing being *lending*, not borrowing. It also talks of a cursed country. Is it possible that we are cursed because of our debt?

If you kept your records the way our country keeps its books, you would be sent to jail in the private sector. We have $7 trillion in "off-budget" debt (i.e., Social Security, Medicare, and Airport Trust Funds). The Social Security "surplus" is a lie. We are spending it and not saving it! The five-year budget forecast projects surpluses, but our cumulative debt is forecast to grow by another $2 trillion!

An AP wire service report (March 10, 2000) stated that the U.S. Treasury bought back one billion dollars of the national debt in the government's first such repurchase in seventy years. That is a positive step, but one billion dollars is only 0.00017 percent of the $6.0 trillion debt.

We discussed earlier that we do not even own our own things on which we owe money; rather, the lenders own us. The same thing rings true for the good ol' United States of America. In 1970, foreign countries owned only 4 percent of U.S. debt (treasury securities). According to the U.S. Treasury Department that has now exceeded 42 percent,[30] and that trend is not improving (see Figure 7-3). So we really do not even own our own country!

Figure 7-3
Partially Owned by Others
% of U.S. Debt Owned by Foreign Countries

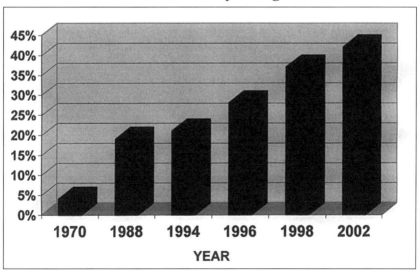

Our early leaders recognized debt as a problem.

"I place public debt as the greatest of dangers. To preserve our independence, we must not let our rulers load us with perpetual debt."
—Thomas Jefferson

We have not done so well. Only nine times has the government balanced its books. We had deficits during the War of 1812, the recession of 1837, the Civil War, the depression of 1890's, and World War 1, but we always paid down the debt. Not today. The Gramm-Rudman Acts of 1985 and 1987 called for the budget to be balanced by 1991. We finally did it in 1998! However, we are still not paying down our *cumulative* Federal Debt.

FALSE ADVERTISING?

The FY2003 Federal Budget summarizes the surpluses and deficits over the years. The surplus for Fiscal 2000 was $236 billion, and the surplus for 2001 was $127 billion. Bill Clinton announced that the national debt had been "reduced by $360B over the last three years." [31] He said that 2000 was "the largest one-year debt reduction in the history of the United States." But was it? The national debt was *higher* than in the previous three years. There was *no* debt reduction! In fact, although surpluses are forecast for the next five years, the $6.0 trillion in debt is expected to grow another $2 trillion. The unsettling vagary of government accounting is a shell game that the average American does not understand—nor cares to. Social Security, for example, is not part of the federal budget. It has its own trust fund. Yet, Congress has spent the money on other things, so it is part of the national debt.

"The Social Security Trust Fund is simply a meaningless record of taxes that have been collected for future needs, spent for current desires, and then recorded and counted as an asset."
—John Harker

We Need a Debt Extinguisher

Alexander Hamilton had some foresight when he called in Federalist Paper #7 for the "extinguishment of all debt." Debt not only causes a burden on our nation but also causes division and unrest in families and marriages and separation from God, and, according to two recent surveys, researchers found that people who reported higher levels of stress about their debts were more likely to have health problems than people with smaller debt loads.[32]

This increase in debt has led to savings rates that are anemic at best and miserable at worst. Look at the trend according to the Bureau of Economic Analysis. We actually had a recent annual period that had a "negative" savings rate (see Figure 7-4).[33]

Figure 7-4
Sinking Savings Rates

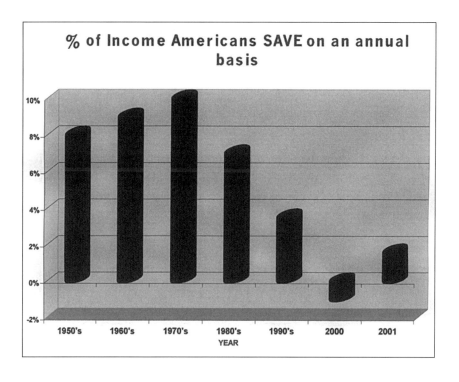

"A personal savings rate stuck for months in negative territory is giving new meaning to the old phrase 'spending like there's no tommorrow.' Consumers are on a spending roll, but this time with a new twist: They're spending completely at the expense of saving. Unlike the wise ant of Proverbs 6, who 'stores its provisions in summer and gathers its food at harvest,' Americans seem to think the harvest season is forever." [34]

According to a recent survey commissioned by the Consumer Federation of America, 53 percent of the respondents said that at least sometimes they live paycheck to paycheck. The problem with living this way is that both saving *and* giving suffer. "A focus on the long term and a willingness to defer gratification are distinctly out of fashion today." [35]

SELAH 7-4

Financial Freedom Thermometer

I can guarantee you that there are more pros than cons to living a debt-free life. I know that ten years ago I would have scored myself negatively in many of the following categories, but not today! Your testimony is coming (if you act)! Score yourself on the following statements using a scale of from 1 to10. Then score yourself on the same statements a year from now.

	Today	Year later
1. I feel unparalleled freedom regarding my finances.	_____	_____
2. I am flexible in my giving and my living.	_____	_____
3. I am fulfilling my life purpose (Life Foundation).	_____	_____

4. I have deep marital and family
   unity and intimacy.   _____   _____

5. I am parenting with purpose.   _____   _____

6. I am confident and not fearful
   of the future.   _____   _____

7. I am content and trusting in God's
   provision and plans.   _____   _____

8. I live a peaceful and stress-free life. _____   _____

9. I live a disciplined and obedient life
   that is pleasing to God.   _____   _____

10. I have a financial freedom testimony! _____   _____

11. I have no credit card debt.   _____   _____

12. I have no vehicle debt.   _____   _____

13. I have *no debt* at all!   _____   _____

If you focus on today's situation, you might want to give up. *Don't!* If you begin making some changes today, you will have the beginnings of a testimony next year!

ACTION POINTS

1. What changes do you believe you need to make to begin affecting your debt?

   _____

   _____

   _____

   _____

   _____

   _____

2. How are you doing on a savings plan? List things for which you need to save.

   _____

   _____

   _____

   _____

   _____

   _____

3. Review Selahs 7-3 and 7-4. Jot down the top five issues in which you need radical change. Pray about those areas.

   _____

   _____

   _____

   _____

   _____

   _____

4. Do you have any materialism traps out of which you need to get? Do you need to deal with any idols?

   _____

   _____

   _____

   _____

   _____

Section 2

Furnishing Your Financial House

"A Giving Plan"

CHAPTER 8

Do You Have a Heart Condition?

B enefits of becoming debt free abound, and I can now say "Amen" to every one of those listed in Selah 7-4. The freedom and flexibility are a welcome change from my financial past. One benefit that has been the most rewarding is the benefit of *giving*.

"Oh, no!" you say. "Here it comes. Time to skip a few chapters."

I ask you not to. You cannot separate giving from financial freedom. You cannot separate the spiritual from the financial. Before we delve into the practical steps of living a financially free lifestyle, the *most important* step is giving. I did not say *tithing*. I did not say giving *money*. I said *giving*. It is not our money that God wants but the surrender of our *will* and our *priorities* in the temporal here and now.

George Barna's website contains a wealth of information. He cited the eye-opening statistic that 33 percent of born-again Christians say that it is impossible for them to get ahead in life because of the financial debt they have incurred.[1] They are referring to the chains about which we talked earlier. This same debt is also a reason that many people say, "I cannot afford to give right now." I know. I speak from experience. Those were my exact words. Just as one is never quite ready for parenting, the expense of a child, or the expense of a first house, one never feels quite ready for giving. We must take the plunge in beginning a life of giving. If you never begin, you will never be the blessing that God desires you to be, and you will never know how blessed you will be because of having given. As a Christian, surrendering our all includes the surrender of our finances. Martin Luther's assessment was sad, but true:

"There are three conversions of the Christian Faith. There is the conversion of the heart, the conversion of the mind, and the conversion of the pocketbook! For many, many Christians, that third conversion, the conversion of the pocketbook, never takes place."

Male-Pattern Deafness

When the topic of giving arises, people have many presuppositions. Presuppositions are "hearing what we want to hear *before* we actually hear." I call it selective deafness. I think that most women would agree that this is a "gift" that has been bestowed upon most men.

Unfortunately, some valid reasons exist for this deafness. I will not consider merely being a man as a valid reason. However, some so-called ministers of the gospel have "peddled the word of God for profit."[2] When some people hear the word *giving*, they might think of a bad TV solicitation experience. They might have had a negative arm-twisting, fund-raising experience. They might have been told that they would go to hell if they did not tithe. If you are like me, you might be overwhelmed by the number of telemarketers and mailings that request your dollars. We need to be sensitive to the baggage that the word *giving* might carry, especially to the unchurched, "dechurched," or "burned churched." Such people must be taught biblical principles of giving and not hear constant, high-pressure solicitations for money. The church must not avoid the subject of giving because of potential baggage; rather, we must be sensitive, yet thorough, in teaching people so that they can drop the baggage.

Spin Doctors

Martin Luther said it best: "The best teacher is the one who does not *bring his* meaning into the scripture, but *gets* his meaning from the scripture." He does not put his spin upon it or pluck a verse to match his belief. Much mischief has resulted regarding interpretation when people have claimed truth in "partitioned" passages while disregarding the rest of God's Word. One must first consider the *context* of any verse (the scriptures before and after the verse) and then "the *entire* scripture" while interpreting or quoting the individual verse. If the teaching does not line up with both the context and the entire Scripture, then a problem exists.

If you doubt that giving is biblical then I ask you to search God's Word. Do not wait for someone else to teach you. In Acts 17:11, the Bereans examined the Scriptures. They intently scrutinized them. They searched them. They had an old-fashioned Bible study. I am afraid that laziness is rampant in the American church. Ooh, tough word! If we can give time to our hobbies and other reading material but fail to crack the Bible other than on Sundays, or if we skip daily devotions, we need a foundation adjustment. I know that I have needed one—we all have at one time or another! Real joy and fulfillment come only when we saturate ourselves in God's Word, not just skimming to find a verse or an answer to a particular question, but really to study it, to study His ways. Unfortunately, laziness in spiritual matters often leads to laziness in financial matters. We need a firm foundation!

I have narrowed the types of listeners to four different kinds that become apparent whenever the conversation turns to giving. I think that you will find some parallels with the parable of the sower in Matthew 13.

1. Those who are totally unopen to talk of giving. (This was me at one point!) Ears seal shut as soon as a word in the giving family (*tithe, offering, gift,* etc.) is mentioned. The person's skin begins to crawl, and their palms get sweaty. Unfortunately, many people have some valid reasons for clamming up and not hearing. Some people have abused teachings regarding motives for giving (bless me, give to get, etc.). Although some of the reasons might be valid, that does not mean that there is no correct teach-

ing on giving. If this leads to an unwillingness to hear the truth, it can quickly turn to pride, a hard heart, or an unsurrendered heart.

2. Those who will hear but will not obey or change their position or just do not understand. This does not excuse the fact that there is truth and that there is also disobedience. We are accountable *after* we are taught correctly or understand the truth.

3. Those who hear and change for a while, then they either become distracted, lose faith, or spout the "I-tried-that-once" line. God is not a flash-in-the-pan, microwave God. He is looking for faithfulness, obedience, and consistency.

4. Those who hear *and* do. Only a few such people exist.

I must admit that at one time I fit squarely in category 1, those who are totally unopen to talk of giving. In fact, foremost among my criteria for church selection when moving to Dallas was whether a pastor talked about giving biblically. I went to more than thirty churches before selecting one. There is nothing wrong with a church's talking about money. Jesus talked about it quite a bit, but most of His teachings were warnings about it's influence.

More than two thousand Scriptures concern finances, but it is *how* one talks about finances that turns most people off. However, talking about *sin* turns people off, too, as does talking about *hell*. And talking about *money* will turn some people off, but that doesn't mean that those things shouldn't be taught!

Note to pastors—if you *are not teaching about money, giving, or financial principles, I can assure you that someone else is teaching your flock—*probably incorrectly. It is similar to teaching our kids about human sexuality. Someone will teach them, and you would probably not approve of their teacher. If you are not comfortable or prepared to teach your people about finances, then get someone else whom you trust to do it. My pastor had me teach on the subject for five to ten minutes per Sunday for eight weeks.

SELAH 8-1

I have seen and heard of a number of reactions when I've taught about giving.

In which of the following categories do you fit? (Check all that apply.) Why?

_____ "The *sweater*"—sweating under conviction; wish the subject would change.

_____ "The *doubter*"—clouded by past experiences; question the speaker's/writer's motive.

_____ "The *searcher*"—sincerely want to do God's will and are open to hearing the truth.

_____ "The *rock*"—already made up my mind about giving; no one will change it.

_____ "The *snail*"—willing to listen but will take no action to change giving patterns.

_____ "The *fast food cook*"—have too many other fish to fry; the message goes in one ear and out the other.

_____ "The *flash in the pan*"—listen openly and even change— but only for a while.

_____ "The *doer*"—listen openly and act upon the areas about which God is speaking to me.

Multiplication, Not Division

Giving does not begin with a tithe! I am not saying this because of my unspectacular testimony of giving (which I will share later) but because giving starts with an attitude of the heart. The book of Jeremiah states, "You will seek me and find me when you seek me with all your heart. I will be found by you."[3] The Lord did not have my finances because He did not have my *whole heart!* David's prayer was "give me an *undivided heart*."[4] Paul speaks of "*Undivided* devotion to the Lord."[5] Ezekiel questioned the Lord about the remnant of Israel's heart condition and God's response was an admonition to remove the idols and have an *undivided* heart![6]

One can be beat over the head with the law to tithe. I have heard different speakers say that I would go to hell if I did not tithe. My anger at hearing this spurred me to action—to seek the truth for myself. I like Ronald Reagan's comment: "Trust, but verify." We must research and verify for ourselves.

Giving is most definitely biblical. It is not found in just a verse or two, across a couple of centuries, or in just an Old Testament-era principle. If you would like a good basis on which to start your study of biblical giving, look at the "Chronology of Giving" in Appendix A.

I will talk about tithing later, but we are not under the Law but under grace.[7] One time, Jesus actually referred to tithing.[8] He did not command it but said, "You *should have* practiced the latter [tithing] without neglecting the former." I know that I fought the Lord over the 10 percent. *I had a heart problem.* The truth is that He owns 100 percent, not just 10 percent. The earth is the Lord's and *all* that is in it!

> *"God can have our money and not have our hearts, but he cannot have our hearts without having our money."*
> **—R. Kent Hughes**

Happy, Happy, Happy

We have such a need for a cultural role reversal, a 180-degree turn in our giving, that it is almost hard to swallow. Second Corinthians 8 and 9 provide a great study of giving. It speaks of not being coerced in our giving (attention: teachers, preachers, and evangelists!).[9] It speaks of a "willingness" to give, a "giving beyond their ability," a giving "liberally." It later speaks of giving "generously," "not as a grudging obligation," and "not out of a necessity." But most importantly, God loves a *cheerful giver* (attention: giver!)[10] The Corinthian church excelled in their giving.

Many churches are excellent in serving and in loving, and they teach both practices. But many churches fail to be excellent in giving. Why? Because the people are not taught to give!

SELAH 8-2

Read 2 Corinthians 8 and 9, and pick out the portions of those chapters that regard giving (see some of them below). Score yourself honestly on the following statement (with 1 being poorest and 10 being near perfect) to see how you are doing.

❖ I give beyond my ability, not just what I can afford to give. _____

❖ I give entirely on my own. I do not need poking/prodding. _____

❖ I view giving as a privilege and not an obligation. _____

❖ I give liberally and not stingily. _____

❖ I give cheerfully and not begrudgingly. _____

❖ I give generously and not selfishly or out of obligation. _____

A church that does these things *excels* in giving! More importantly, an *individual* who does these things excels in giving and has a proper heart condition. It all comes down to one's heart, not law and guilt-laden armtwisting. What is the attitude of the heart? Reading 2 Corinthians 8 and 9 should challenge us to have a proper *heart focus*. The words are foreign to us, yet they jump off the page: *eagerness, enthusiasm, readiness, preparedness, spontaneity, sincerity, cheerfully, generously, entirely on their own, not coerced, willingness, a privilege*. This does not sound like a boring "country club dues" tithe check. If you are a pastor, I say emphasize the heart teaching, and the giving will follow and be properly motivated. I'll have more to say about the tithe later.

The only way to be ready to give is to prepare your heart. Notice the pecking order in 2 Corinthians 8:5. First, they gave themselves to the Lord, and *then* they gave to others. He wants our heart, then we will have *His* heart attitude toward others and giving will not be a chore or a drudgery.

<u>ACTION POINTS</u>

1. What heart condition changes do you need to ask God to help you make? Realize that *you cannot do this on your own.*

   _____

   _____

   _____

   _____

   _____

   _____

2. See Selah 8-1. When giving is taught, why do you react or feel the way you do? Do some soul-searching regarding your reactions. Pray and ask God to reveal or to heal past wounds, or to ask for forgiveness, if necessary.

   _____

   _____

   _____

   _____

   _____

   _____

3. Confess your weaknesses. Pray for the Lord to take out the hard heart and put in a soft heart. Ask Him to enable you to give *yourself* first. If you really don't care and feel numb to the subject of giving, ask Him to soften your heart and give you *His* heart on the matter.

   _____

   _____

   _____

   _____

4. Conduct a study of biblical giving. (See Appendix A.)

CHAPTER 9

That Tough Word—Giving!

When my pastor asked me to teach a series of lessons on biblical giving, I found that I had to spend extra time in prayer to ensure that I was not speaking from my own biases or denominational upbringing. I did not want to tell people what *they* wanted to hear but what *God* wanted them to hear. Thankfully, my pastor has much wisdom and did not want to influence what I taught, so even when I asked him three different times what he wanted me to teach, he would not respond other than "speak what God is showing you. I want God's agenda, and giving from God's perspective."

Wow! That was refreshing. Figuring out God's agenda took an average of eight to ten hours of preparation for five to ten minutes of teaching and *much* prayer to ensure that I taught it with God's heart.

One of my first questions was "Lord, how do I tell people to give? You have taught me, but I was stubborn and hardheaded. How can I pass on what You taught me?"

His response to my innocent but searching question seemed instant. "*You* can't do it; let Me do it. Go to my Word—spend 80–90 percent of the teaching time reading and applying the Word. Let me do the rest."

God's Word is a lamp to our feet and a light to our path.[1] Sometimes we think that His Word is not enough and we need to add a bunch of our own light. The problem is that our added light gets lost in God's massive floodlight. His Word will not return void. It is sharper than any double-edged sword.[2]

> *I think that most people would admit that giving is biblical. So are we walking in obedience?*

Just as many of us want financial freedom without the work and discipline of budgets, reducing expenses, self-control, etc., sometimes we want the blessings from God without the obedience to God. We prefer the dessert without the main course. We like it easy! We often hear only part of the Word of God preached these days. I will take the part that goes down easy, thank you very much. But we must move from milk to solid food.[3] Whatever happened to "I want to know Christ and the power of his resurrection and the fellowship of *sharing in his sufferings*"?[4] It really comes down to the "doing" versus the "hearing." "If you are willing and obedient, you will eat the best from the land."[5]

James 1:22 says, *"Do not merely listen to the word and so deceive yourselves. DO WHAT IT SAYS!"* (I added the exclamation point and capital letters for emphasis.) *Deceive* means "to cheat by false reasoning." We talk ourselves out of it. We cheat ourselves by only hearing. Listening is only the beginning; the prudent man *does* something.[6]

SELAH 9-1

READ: Matthew 7:24–27.

How can you build a firm financial foundation? Build your house upon the rock. Be a *doer!* Wisdom is *hearing and heeding.* I can almost guarantee that if you begin to give and you follow the principles in the third section of this book, you will be *financially* free!

Abraham had an "Isaac testimony" only *after* the test, *after* walking in obedience, *after the action!* God told Abraham, "Leave your country, your people, and your father's household and go. . . ."[7] Did he become a great nation because he merely listened? No, he became a great nation only when he obeyed.

Faith Finds Fulfillment in ACTION!

I guess there is no better time for my giving testimony. Let me preface it with a nonbiblical quotation that I came up with to go along with my testimony:

Progressive obedience is better than disobedience.

As I mentioned, I did not ride my stallion of faith into my budget spreadsheets and begin giving God 10 percent. I could not "afford it," as we discussed earlier. I knew that giving was biblical, so Dana and I agreed that we would start in Month 1 by giving 1 percent (on the gross). On Month 2, we raised it to 2 percent, and so on. We began giving and began disciplined cost cutting at the same time. Forget about saving; that would be step 3 for us.

I am thankful to report that we were giving 10 percent within six months, and God kept honoring our "progressive obedience." We have continued with the "progressive" concept and have been amazed as the percentage keeps growing every year. We have a goal of giving 50 percent of our gross income, and, with God's help, we are more than half way there! Ten years ago, 10 percent seemed impossible! As God provides, however, our faith grows, and the 50 percent does not seem as impossible as we once thought. I can safely say that if it is possible for *me* to obey (stubborn, hard-headed, Rule of Seven), then it is possible for anyone to give!

I never could have done this on my own. I am too selfish. I also have carnal desires and materialistic tendencies. Name someone who does not struggle with obedience. The flesh battles against the Spirit in all of us. But He is pruning the branches, and it is getting easier and easier to give *Him* what is rightfully *His* anyway! To God be the glory!

Obedience means—without challenge, without excuse, without delay.[8]

JUST DO IT!

Multiplication takes two factors: **Faith** *and* **Action.**

Faith + action = results.

A Giving Attack

I can remember standing in front of the congregation one Sunday testifying about what God had done in our finances and our progressive giving and being so excited that I could hardly contain myself. I really had not felt that excited about anything in a while. I felt as though I would burst.

I shared a story about how I was riding home from church after a Monday prayer meeting and the thought popped in my head to give a significant sum of money to some friends of ours who are itinerant evangelists. They had shared with us recently some depressing stories about churches promising to support them and others promising love offerings after their altar times and being lied to time and time again. I was so excited that I could not wait to get home and write the check (after clearing it with my wife, of course). We prayed together about the amount and believed that the Lord was saying the same thing to both of us. Dana has had similar "giving attacks" for buying gifts for people to bless them.

Fun and Worship!

We need to get excited about giving! We need to have some "giving attacks" like we have "spending attacks!" How about some "impulse giving" instead of "impulse spending" once in a while? Paul said that the Corinthian Christians "were ready to give; and your *enthusiasm* has stirred most of them to *action*."[9] (Emphasis added.) If we had more people who were excited about giving and sharing what God has done, we might get some folks stirred up to action. I am not talking about braggadocio, boastfulness, or pride— just enthusiasm and genuine excitement. We have beat the tired,

old, tithe teaching into the ground. It is so much more than Law!
God's Word is not dry! We must testify to what the Lord has done.
That is part of worship. If we do not do it, the very rocks will cry
out! Giving is not only an act of worship but also can be *fun!*

We Need an ACTION ATTACK.

"faith by itself, if it is not accompanied by ACTION is dead."[10]

"Wisdom is proved right by her ACTIONS."[11]

*"Now finish the work, so that your eager willingness to do it may
be matched by your COMPLETION of it."*[12]

Remember, God does not want obedience out of obligation. If
you are in love with someone or have made a covenant commitment
(marriage), you do things for that person because you love him or
her, not out of obligation. Recall dating someone whom you really
loved. You did not buy flowers or become romantic because you
were forced to do so. It was because you desired to do those things.
Does your spouse enjoy receiving a gift or love if it is offered out of
obligation, guilt, or reluctance? I will answer for my wife. No! She
might accept the gift, but she does not desire to have it given that
way. There is no real joy in either the giving or the receiving when
it is done out of obligation or guilt.

If Jesus saved you and rescued you from sin, hell, a life of
depravity, vices or loneliness, then it should be a *joy* for you to
give to Him. Look to the heart, and then obey. The book of Isaiah
mentions that the Lord knew the people's hearts. He made clear
that He had had enough of their meaningless offerings.[13] Giving
should not be a burden. God does not twist arms. He is not into
guilt trips. Man might manipulate, but God does not. He would
rather have us keep our money if we are not willing to give it with
a joyful, cheerful heart.

Pass the Test

I once said, "I cannot afford to give," but when we finally took some risks and started giving, God came to our assistance. We are willing to take risks in our spending. I challenge you to test God to see if He will not take care of you when you step out in faith to give. Although it is an Old Testament truth, God, in Malachi 3:10, tells us, "Test me in this." Nowhere else in the Word does He ask you to test Him. Be a risktaker, not a caretaker or an undertaker. Get beyond the outer court of giving. It is an act of worship. It is an act of obedience. It becomes easier and more joyful to give the more you do it!

Who is in control? Who is governing your life? Who is governing your finances? If Jesus is in control, will He leave you stranded and beat you down because you have been *obedient?* This is where I hear the biggest Christian cop-out: "I will pray about it." Most people who say that do not pray about it. They know the truth, and they have heard the truth, but they have just chosen to disobey that truth.

"Stop delaying and start giving."

When you obey, you will see results. What kind of results? Blessings. We will talk more about them in the next chapter.

SELAH 9-2

Read Deuteronomy 28, especially verses 1–14 to get a taste of the results. Think what we could do as the body of Christ if all Christians gave obediently. I believe that we could take back the ministering function that the government has stepped in to fill as a result of the church's void. We could take care of

➢ the poor,
➢ the single mothers,

➢ the widows,
➢ the elderly,
➢ the sick,
➢ children in need,
➢ those on welfare,
➢ taking the gospel to all nations, and
➢ world hunger.

I believe that if we had a heart for God and were obedient in giving, the results would be staggering!

SELAH 9-3

If you are still struggling with having the faith to give and need strength, read the following four Scriptures:

1. Philippians 4:11–13—Paul could relate. He had much and had little, but he learned to be content.
2. Matthew 26:41—The Spirit is willing, but the flesh is weak.
3. 2 Corinthians 12:10—For when I am weak, then I am strong.
4. Romans 8:26—The Spirit helps us in our weakness.

ACTION POINTS

1. Do some further study of John 14:15, 24; Acts 5:29; Matthew
   25:23; Luke 16:10–11.

   _____

   _____

   _____

   _____

   _____

   _____

   _____

2. Spend a few minutes in prayer, asking for God's specific direction on your "call to give."

   _____

   _____

   _____

   _____

   _____

   _____

3. When God convicts or speaks to you about something, obey! We
   will talk later about the consequences of disobedience. They are
   greater than failed finances (see Leviticus 26, Jeremiah 25,
   Jeremiah 44, and Jeremiah 7).

   _____

   _____

   _____

   _____

   _____

   _____

   _____

   _____

CHAPTER 10

The Results of Giving— Blessing!

E veryone puts on a different shade of glasses when the word *blessing* is used. The biblical meaning of that word has been so twisted because an unbalanced amount of time is often spent on "*financial* blessing." The "give-to-get" mentality has been spewed from too many television screens and pulpits. The Scripture has not been "divided" or "interpreted" correctly; the peddlers have taken verses out of context to fit their theology. Nowhere in the Bible can I find giving with strings attached. Trying to link the financial giving and the financial getting is a dangerous and slippery path to trod.

Looking back on God's favor in *some* cases, we *might* be able to see *financial* blessing as a result from our giving, but that should *not* be our motive. "Giving to get" is like signing a prenuptial agreement with God. Beware of your motive! No strings should be attached to your giving. I even struggle to pray the "prayer of Jabez" because I want to ensure that my heart is pure and that my motives are correct.

Show Me the Money (and the Word)

As we discussed earlier, an unselfish heart does not expect a "hundred-fold" blessing from God. Nor should we request a blessing as a result of our giving. This false teaching is the one that has bothered me the most.

Genesis 26 tells about Isaac's planting crops and reaping a hundredfold, but in no way does it imply that his planting was an attempt to get something back from God. God did bless Him, but for us to believe that our writing a check for $100 will "reap" $10,000 back is twisted.

Other people have tied a number of New Testament Scriptures (e.g., Matthew 13: 8, 23; 19:29; Mark 10:30; Luke 8:8) to this idea, implying that it is a New Testament giving principle. If you read these in their entirety and *in context,* however, they show clearly that the seed is not money; it is *the Word!* The hundred-fold blessing in Matthew 19:29 talks about *leaving all,* not getting! People who leave *all* for the mission field will get *eternal* blessings. God will not be treated as a puppet. "Demanding" that God bless us is not the proper "fear of God" that we should have.

The Meaning of Blessing

Approximately 80 percent of the time that the words *bless,* *blessed,* or *blessing* occur in the Bible, they are used in both the Hebrew and the Greek as an *act toward God*—adoration, thankfulness, or to praise Him. In the other 10–20 percent of cases, they are interpreted as "go forward," "prosper," "happy," "to confer a benefit upon," "count happy," or "fortunate, well-off." These terms do not necessarily refer to money. In fact, God warns us so much about money that it probably does *not* mean money for most of us (e.g., Paul learned to be content, the love of money is the root of all evil, be on your guard against greed, etc.). Putting God in a financial-blessing-only mode is making Him too small.

Does God Bless? *Yes!* Is it always financial? *No!* Is it always in response to giving? No. Can it be? Yes.

Do you want to be blessed, to prosper, to be happy, or to be fortunate or well off? I do, too. But that is not why I give! And neither should it be *your* motive for giving. These things do not occur just as a result of our giving. The Bible is clear about that fact.

How Do We Get Blessed?

We will be blessed if we follow and act upon God's Word.

Is there a formula for God's blessings? Although we cannot put God in a box, He will be faithful to His Word. So much more is required than dropping some money in the offering plate. In my study of God's blessings, I have found nine things that will lead to His blessings.

1. **Obedience**—Genesis 22:18 says, ". . . all nations on earth will be blessed, *because you obeyed me*" (emphasis added). Read Deuteronomy 28:1–14. We are blessed when we obey! First John 3:22 says that we "receive from him anything we ask, because we *obey* his commands and do what pleases him" (emphasis added). James 4:3–4 says, "You do not have because you do not ask. When you ask, you do not receive, because you ask with *wrong motives*, that you may spend what you get on *your pleasures*" (emphasis added). First John 5:14 says that "if we ask anything according to *his will*, he hears us" (emphasis added). It all goes back to our *motives*.

If we obey, He will bless us.
If we ask with correct motives, He will answer us.
If we ask according to His will, He will hear us.

We must take these verses in their *entirety*. The verse that I hear quoted out of context more than any other is "you have not because you ask not." But read the rest of the verse. This is not a "name-it-and-claim-it, blab-it-and-grab-it" theology. The proper ingredients include more than just asking.

Use all of the Ingredients.

√ Ask.
√ Obey.
√ Have pure motives.
√ Ask according to His will.

> *Ask + Obedience + Pure motives + His will = God's hearing*
> *and blessing!*

2. **Be Merciful**—Matthew 5:7 says, "Blessed are the merciful for they will be shown mercy." Show mercy with your money. Give and spend the way the Lord would if He were here.

3. **Help the poor**—Psalm 41:1–3 says, "Blessed is he who has regard for the weak; the Lord delivers him in times of trouble. The Lord will protect him and preserve his life; he will bless him in the land and not surrender him to the desire of his foes. The Lord will sustain him on his sickbed and restore him from his bed of illness." Proverbs 28:27 says, "He who gives to the poor will lack nothing. . . ."

Read Psalm 119:1–2 for the next three points if you need a formula for blessing.

4. **Live a blameless walk.** Holiness will lead to God's blessings.

5. **Keep his statutes.** Obeying His commands and laws will lead to God's blessings.

6. **Seek Him with all your heart.** See Matthew 6:33 for more detail.

7. **Delight yourself in the Lord.** He will give you the desires of your heart (Ps. 37:3–7).

8. **Mix prayer with your giving.** Acts 10:5 gives an example of a man to whom God's angel said, "Your prayers and gifts to the poor came up as a memorial offering before God." Later, in Acts 20:35 is the well-known verse that says, "It is more blessed to give than to receive."

9. **Be His child.** Sometimes God will bless us for no reason at all—just because He is our gracious father and He loves us. I love to buy my kids a small gift occasionally when I go out of town. Do they deserve it? No, not always. In fact, once in a while I will hear about how they treated their mom when I was gone,

and I will want to keep their gift until they have "earned it." but God is not like that. He is full of grace. It is not by "works of righteousness" but by only His grace that He blesses us.

SELAH 10-1
Blessing Readiness

It is difficult really to know one's own heart or motives. The following self-assessment might spur you to do some soulsearching and praying about how well positioned you are to receive God's many blessings. Score yourself (with 1 being poor and 10 being excellent), but do not fall into the trap of "doing" to get His blessing. That is "works" motivation, and we must guard against that dangerous attitude.

_____ Obedience

_____ Showing mercy to others

_____ Helping the poor

_____ Living a holy life

_____ Keeping His commandments

_____ Seeking Him with all of your heart

_____ Delighting in the Lord

_____ Mixing prayer with giving

<u>10</u>___ Just because you are His child!

_____ Giving

Types of Blessings

Think about how God has blessed you. His blessings include *so much more than the financial*! Conducting a study of the word *blessing* proved to me beyond a shadow of a doubt that we have boxed God in with a "financial-blessing-only" mentality. Look at the following ways in which He blessed in the Scriptures.

➤ Children, crops, food, enemies defeated, your work, prosperity, lender (Deut. 28: 1–14)
➤ Mercy, deliverance, protection (Matt. 5:7)
➤ Strength, peace (Ps. 29:11; Isa. 40:29)
➤ Wealth, riches (Gen. 26:12–13; Prov. 10:22)
➤ Spiritual and material blessings (Rom. 15:27—A material seed may reap a spiritual harvest!)
➤ "Noah found *favor* in the eyes of the Lord" (Gen. 6:8)
➤ Favor, make you fruitful and increase your numbers (Lev. 26:9)
➤ Favor with both the Lord and men (1 Sam. 2:26)
➤ He who finds a *wife* finds what is good and receives favor from the Lord (Prov. 18:22)
➤ Salvation (2 Cor. 6:2, Eph. 2:8)
➤ The Lord was with Joseph and gave him success in whatever he did (Gen. 39:23)
➤ Land flowing with milk and honey (Deut. 6:9)
➤ God gave Solomon wisdom and great insight (1 Kings 4:29; 5:12; Prov. 2:6)
➤ Bread and water (Neh. 9:15, 20, 22, 27)
➤ Possessions (Job 42:10). The Lord can give, and the Lord can take away (Job 1:21).
➤ Authority over evil spirits (Mark 6:7)
➤ The Holy Spirit (Acts 11:17; Luke 11:13)
➤ Health, healing, peace, security (Jer. 33:6; Prov. 3:8; 4:22; 14:30)
➤ Grace (1 Peter 5:5)
➤ Refreshing (Prov. 11:24–25)
➤ Friends (Prov. 19:6)
➤ Family (Prov. 18:22)
➤ Heaven, spiritual gifts, job, church, pastor, etc.!

God is not a one-dimensional "blessing" God! He is multifaceted and desires to bless you in many ways.

SELAH 10-2

Take a minute to review the preceding list. List *specific ways* in which God has blessed you. Thank Him and keep the list as a reminder. Add to it regularly as He sends other blessings your way!

Will God Bless Me if I Give?

We have discovered God's many ways to bless us. Now let us look at Scriptures that *do show* a correlation between giving and blessing.

Read 2 Corinthians 9. Paul was addressing the believers at the church of Corinth, and he was specifically talking about financial giving. He discussed the principle of sowing and reaping. "Whoever sows sparingly will also reap sparingly, and whoever sows bountifully will also reap bountifully" (v. 6). I can testify that God began blessing us financially when we began giving. We had a lower/middle income, and we had decided to attempt tithing (progressive obedience) while trying to pay off credit card debt *and* have Dana stay home to start our family. Financial suicide, right? This seemed like quite a mountain, and when I put it on a spreadsheet, it *was* quite a mountain. But God honored His Word, and it seems that the more we gave the more He continued to bless us. He definitely has blessed us in many of the previously mentioned areas, but His blessings were not always financial.

Proverbs 3:9–10 says, "Honor the Lord with your wealth, and with the firstfruits of all your crops; then your barns will be filled to overflowing, and your vats will brim over with new wine." Sounds like blessing to me!

Proverbs 28:27 says, "He who gives to the poor will lack nothing, but he who closes his eyes to them receives many curses."

Luke 6:38-39 says, "Give, and it will be given to you. A good measure, pressed down, shaken together and running over, will be poured into your lap. For with the measure you use, it will be measured to you."

Malachi 3:8-12 says, "Bring the whole tithe into the storehouse, that there may be food in my house. Test me in this . . . and see if I will not throw open the floodgates of heaven and pour out so much *blessing* that you will not have room enough for it."

God does want to bless us. He even desires to bless us financially. But there is no formula. I know that I have often wished that there were a formula. It would be so much easier! "Lord, let me plug the numbers into my spreadsheet so that I can see the results. Lord, if I give you 12 percent this year, how about a bonus and a healthy family? Lord, if I increase my giving to 20 percent, how about Your doubling my income and have my entire family be saved?

Nope. God cannot be bought, manipulated, or figured out. His ways are much higher than my ways, and His thoughts are much higher than mine. Do not box God in!

Blessings in Disguise

Some people have twisted the blessing message to say that you just do not have enough faith and that is why you are not blessed. I heard one so-called teacher of the Word say that suffering and persecution are not for today. If Paul only lived today, he would live a life of abundance and would not need to go through the trials he did. All he would need is great faith.

Hello? Our family had some difficult years, but God blessed us even through those times.

The two most difficult years of my life were shortly after we began "tithing." I had just completed teaching a class at LeTourneau University and presented a devotional on "planning and giving." One of the students (Jack) came up to me and said, "I really enjoyed your devotional on planning relative to your finances. Have you ever thought about teaching it at churches?" Another student made a similar comment the next week.

Hmmm, I thought. *Could this be God?*

Flat on My Back

In a matter of a few weeks, I began having dizzy spells at work and felt as though I was going to black out. This continued for weeks, and I missed a lot of work. The only position in which I could be without blacking out was flat on my back. I missed four months of work while eleven different doctors ran tests, poked and prodded, said "just one more blood sample," and continued referring me to other doctors. During that time, the only thing I could do was read and study. While I was flat on my back, I completed my entire financial seminar, read the Bible through, and studied and researched.

God met me. He blessed me. He had a plan! It was not a financial blessing, but as I walked in the office of Doc No. 12—the scientist, teacher, and man who flies all over the world working with astronauts—lo and behold, the next blessing arrived. He diagnosed me in *two minutes*.

"Bradbury Eggleston Syndrome," he said.

"Okay. You got me. What is that?" I asked.

"It is orthostatic hypotension from your autonomic nervous system failing."

Blank stare. Awkward pause. "That clears it up," I replied. "Come again?"

"Basically, your nerve endings are failing, and when you lie down your blood pressure is a normal 140/70, but when you stand, it drops to 70/30 in two seconds!"

Wow! *That* I could understand. No wonder I was almost blacking out.

To make a long year short, it just "so happened" that the scientists had come up with a drug just six months earlier to combat this very illness! Coincidence? No, I believe it was God's blessing. Here I was—thirty-two years old, flat on my back, and out of work for four months. As far as the experts knew, only about thirty other individuals worldwide had Bradbury Eggleston Syndrome, and most all of them were over sixty. But God saw fit to bless me. He led me to that particular doctor. He had available a medicine with which to treat me. He allowed an agnostic in another state who had the same disease and had never met me to send me e-mail and encourage me through it all. Even the doctor who diagnosed the disease did not fit the religious "blessing model."

During our discussion one day, I asked him whether I could fast. He looked at me incredulously, paused for five seconds, and then said, "Why would you do a dumb thing like that?"

Do not put God in a box. He will use whomever He wants. He will bless you however He sees fit. There *will be* trials and sufferings, but He will be there in the midst of them. Trust Him! Just because things look hopeless for your finances, your family, your church, or even your health, know that through trials and persecutions our faith is tested, as gold is tried by the fire. We make the choice whether to view these times as the best time of fellowship and communion with our heavenly Father or whether to wallow in our misery. Let us choose the Paul and Silas response of worship!

How God has Blessed Me—My Public Thanks!

I have been in five car accidents in which my car has been totaled. I am still alive. I am blessed.

We had four close family members die in a period of twenty-four months. God has given us peace and been with us. We are blessed.

My wife is a Proverbs 31 woman, beautiful, and loves me as I am. I am blessed.

I have three beautiful children who take after my wife! I am blessed.

I have parents that raised me to be a follower of Jesus. They loved me unconditionally, when I least deserved it. I am blessed.

I am a sinner saved by God's grace. God loves me. He is slow to anger and full of grace. I am blessed.

I have a home and daily food whereas many people do not. I am blessed.

I have employment. I am blessed.

I still have Bradbury Eggleston Syndrome. I will always have it unless God chooses to heal me. I have medicine!

I am blessed.

God has allowed me the privilege to teach financial free-dom seminars and teach about biblical giving, and He is allowing me to write this book. I am blessed.

On February 10, 1991, I was saved by God's grace! I am blessed!

We are free to worship God in public and are not martyred or persecuted for the sake of the gospel. In other parts of the world, 200,000 people a year die for their faith in Jesus Christ. We are blessed.

I have a pastor who has spurred me on to works I never would have attempted on my own. He has challenged me to take risks, to be real, and to dream. I am blessed.

We are completely and totally debt free! We are blessed!

If you happen to be going through a season of struggle or a desert experience, that does not mean that God has left you. He will use it to grow you and to teach you to lean on Him. Someday you will call these lean times a blessing!

SELAH 10-3
Blessing List

If you have not already done so, make your personal blessing list.

Why Does God Bless Us?

We said earlier that in some cases we do not receive what we ask for because we would spend it on our own desires and pleasures (James 4). During my studies, I happened on what I believe to be the *main reason* why God blesses us:

   so that you can be generous! (2 Cor. 9:11)

Proverbs 11:24–25 says, "One man gives freely, yet gains even more; another withholds unduly, but comes to poverty. A generous man will prosper; he who refreshes others will himself be refreshed." Wow! That is wisdom.

Do you want to be blessed and be refreshed?

> ## *GIVE!*

ACTION POINTS

1. Think of a time when you gave out of an improper motive (to get or to manipulate, out of guilt, as a "trade/deal" with God, etc.).

   _____

   _____

   _____

2. Make (or update) your blessing list. (See Selah 10-3.)

3. What specifically can you do to be in a better position to receive God's many blessings? (See Selah 10-1.)

   _____

   _____

   _____

   _____

   _____

   _____

   _____

4. How has God blessed you financially?

   _____

   _____

   _____

   _____

   _____

   _____

5. How has God blessed you through some specific trials and sufferings?

   _____

   _____

   _____

   _____

   _____

   _____

CHAPTER 11

That Controversial Question— How Much Should I Give?

I discussed the condition of the heart first before this always-controversial question of "how much" because I really believe that the condition of the heart is of foundational importance. I struggled with the question of "how much" for years, and I never really thought that I received the proper teaching on the subject. I had always heard "tithe," but I never heard *why* other than "because the Bible says we should."

That wasn't good enough. I needed some more specifics. It also did not sit well with me because I had heard more than once that I probably would not make it to heaven if I did not tithe. I knew that this view was hogwash, but I needed to prove it for myself.

When I see all of the affluence and prosperity in our land but the amount of giving is decreasing, I do believe that a problem exists with the heart generally. Matthew 6:21 seems to indicate that the way a believer spends money might be the clearest indication— perhaps like a thermometer—of the spiritual condition of the heart.

"For where your treasure is, there your heart will be also."
—Matthew 6:21

The question of "how much" has deeply divided pastors, Christian leaders, and denominations, and it has been a turnoff to many people who have seen the "church" through only the televised financial appeals. Taking offerings as we do today was apparently not done until the twentieth century. Varied approaches were used over the years, including the following:

➤ Pledges;
➤ laypeople raising the money;
➤ taxation approaches;
➤ public lists that detailed the amounts given, which encouraged social pressure to give;
➤ pew rental and sales;
➤ enforced tithe;
➤ collections; and
➤ public processionals.

Methods used in India included door to door collections and asking for commitments for the next year. Some modern churches still use the public processional to the front, where tithers are asked to stand. Pledges, faith promises, and passing the plate seem to be the most prevalent methods in use today. We use "responsibility baskets" near the exit in our church with low-key, low-pressure teachings about giving.

The Bible does not treat money as an "off-limits" topic, but for the most part the church still prefers the hush-hush, noncontroversial approach and spends minimal time talking about it. Compartmentalization and separation of our faith from our finances or other areas is dangerous. Our faith in Christ should affect *every* area of our life. Survey results from Robert Wuthnow and noted in Behind the Stained Glass Windows by John and Sylvia Ronsvalle[1] showed that 82 percent of those who attend church do not discuss personal finances with friends. Ninety-three percent have not talked with clergy about money matters, and 95 percent had not discussed it with fellow church members! Keeping it hidden is not the solution!

Finances is an important *spiritual* topic. We get advice from the marketers on how to spend our money. They saturate us with thousands of commercials a day—on billboards, grocery store floors,

TV, newspapers, bus seats, and radio. We must combat materialism and teach giving. We must not shrink from talking about it from a godly perspective.

"The materialism of our culture is the dominant issue, and the church has not combated materialism, with its own set of values."
—Wes Willmer

Pastors are forced into crisis fundraising and hiring "stewardship" letter-writing marketers who are known to increase giving. They rightfully struggle because "giving" teachings are not well received by some people because of their "heart condition." Some preachers do not address the topic because it makes them seem to be raising their own salaries and beefing up the petty cash fund to serve their own interests. Some churches are using the plaque, tile, or brick fund-raising approaches. Preaching about giving from the pulpit is about as popular as preaching about sin, judgment, discipline, self-sacrifice, trials, suffering, and hell. It just is not done that much, and when it is done, it is not done correctly.

Shepherds have the difficult role of depending upon the sheep for their income. Some preachers face a real challenge in having to look to the owner of the sheep for their livelihood. Many sheep attempt to control the shepherd, and many other sheep grumble, complain, or even leave a church if the preacher talks about money or giving. Many people will leave whenever sin is discussed or if they are corrected or disciplined biblically in love. I do not want this to sound too harsh or make this matter too trivial, but Galations 1:10 gives good guidance: "Am I now trying to win the approval of men, or of God?"

If giving is taught correctly and in love, I believe that people will appreciate the "discipline" and "teaching" and will not leave. They might not like it early on, but they will grow to appreciate the truths that have been shared with them, and they will thank the teacher or pastor later (not now, *maybe* later). If a pastor is not comfortable providing this teaching, then he should find someone else to teach it.

SELAH 11-1

Take a few minutes to pray for your pastor(s). Send a card
or call to tell them how much you appreciate them.

If giving numbers are an indication of the condition of the heart,
the fervor of church members seems to be cooling. "In a 1968
survey of twenty-nine mainline evangelical denominations, the
average Christian gave 6 percent of his or her income. This was a
peak in giving. In 1995 the same group gave 4 percent of their
income."[2] In the late 1990s, Americans were more than 400 percent
richer after taxes and inflation than they had been in the Great
Depression, yet Protestants were giving only 2.6% of their incomes
to churches in 1997.[3]

According to Barna Research Group, four of ten adults gave
nothing to churches in 2000, a rise of 15 percent among those refus-
ing to support churches. However, among born-again adults, there
was a 44 percent rise in those who gave nothing last year! Barna
reports that tithing is rare: 32 percent of born-again believers claim
to tithe, but by the pollster's calculations, the actual figure is only
12 percent.[4]

If giving is declining during a period of blessing, what will
happen if we have a severe economic downturn? We need to practice dependence upon God *now* so that we can *really* trust him in
times of need.

**More affluence. Less giving. We are not "excelling in
our giving."**

The most troubling fact is that no major difference exists
between believers and nonbelievers in charitable giving. The average giving for Christians in the 1990s was 2.5 percent, and for
nonbelievers it was 1.7 percent. It is easy to convince ourselves that
we will *give* more when we *have* more, but that does not seem to be
happening. We really are not *giving* any more although we seem to
be *getting* more.

An even more troubling trend is that those who have been blessed *more* seem to be giving *less*. We are not being obedient to the biblical call, "From everyone who has been given much, much will be demanded."[5] Americans in the lowest income range donate three times more of their income (by percentage) than do middle-income Americans and are twice as generous as wealthier U. S. households. Interestingly, the more money one makes, the less likely he or she is to tithe (see Figure 11-1).

Figure 11-1
The greater the affluence, the less given

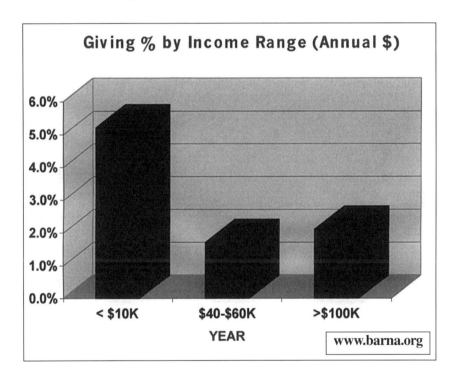

How we can trust God with our salvation but not trust Him with our money is surprising and difficult to understand. It seems that the more one has, the less he trusts in the Lord. We learn to become self-reliant with our wealth. That is why the Bible warns us so often about putting our trust in riches and wealth. To do so is idolatry.

*"We trust not in idols; so every idolater will allege,
but if either you or they in God's honor do anything contrary to
God's word, you show yourself to put your trust in somewhat else
besides God, and so are you idolaters."*
—John Knox, 1554

Voluntary or Tithe? Privilege or Obligation?

Most synagogues set dues and bills for members. That is *one way* to increase giving. It might teach responsibility, but it is not "heart" or "voluntary" giving. That method would make giving more of an obligation than a privilege. More is taught in the Bible about heart (voluntary) giving than about the tithe, especially in the New Testament. I have always wondered why the percentage 10 percent is taught so much? I believe that it is because of the heart problem. It is because of the information shown in the preceding figures. Because people are not willing to give voluntarily, cheerfully, and generously, we must resort to legalism.

Does the Lord want us to give out of fear or guilt? No! He wants us to give to Him because we love Him. We should give because of what He has done for us. I hope that God is dealing with you about your giving. If He does deal with you, it will not be to make you feel guilty or to condemn you. He does not want to focus on a percentage or a law. He desires to be worshipped, and giving is an unselfish act of worship that comes from our heart.

My biggest struggle as a Christian was the battle over the 10 percent. I did not want to hear it—and I definitely was not giving it!

The Old Testament contains thirty-four references to tithing, and the New Testament contains three such references. As a New Testament Christian, I do not believe that we are commanded to tithe. The New Testament *encourages* it, but it doesn't issue a "thou shalt." We are not under Law but under grace.[6] "Therefore, when Christ came into the world, he said: 'Sacrifice and offering you did not desire, but a body you prepared for me; with burnt offerings and sin offerings you were not pleased.' "[7]

Abraham and Jacob practiced both voluntary giving and required tithing. The Old Testament Law included different types of giving, some of which included taxation. Some tithes were as high as 25 percent or even 33 1/3 percent. Do we throw out the Old Testament? No, it, too, is inspired by God. Do we follow every Old Testament custom? No. Do we offer blood sacrifices? Thankfully, no. But we can offer firstfruits, thank offerings, and tithes. These are some ways to bless and thank the Lord for all that He has done for us! We should take the Bible in its entirety! We should not ignore either the Old Testament or the New Testament. Some people say that tithing was only "the Law," but Abraham's tithing to Melchizedek actually *preceded* Mosaic Law.[8]

Another great standard by which we could live would be 2 Chronicles 31: 4–10. In this passage we learn that a need was presented, and the people responded by giving immediately and generously. Those are two fairly difficult words—*immediately* and *generously!*

SELAH 11-2

Read Matthew 23:23 and Luke 11:42.

These verses say, "Don't neglect either." They neither condemn or command tithing! The danger in making the "tithe" law, totally black and white, is that it is too much legality (obligation) and not enough heart (New Testament—cheerful, a privilege, voluntary, not coerced). Some people can write that 10 percent check, have their conscience eased, and their commitment or obligation is done, but they are not blessed the way we discussed earlier. The tithe is not meant to be some country club dues or fee that we pay with no joy or purity of heart.

I believe that the biggest problem with teaching the rigid tithe is that many people could do so much more, but they stop once they reach "the 10 percent plateau" because "their dues are paid." The 10 percent has been drilled into us for so long that people think that they have reached the peak of the mountain when they hit the magical 10 percent. It is actually limiting God by pinning Him down to a particular percentage. People are missing additional blessing by stopping at 10 percent.

Hebrews 7:1–10 talks about Abraham's giving Melchizedek a tenth of everything. It doesn't talk about *punishment* for not tithing. Rather, it teaches *missed blessing!* Read Malachi 3 again, which says that God will pour out His *blessing*. I believe it, and I have a testimony that God proved His Word true.

I believe that 10 percent is a good benchmark. It is a good guideline or starting point, but it is not the upper limit or a do-or-die number. If you are looking for a benchmark, none is lower. Many types of offering in the Old Testament, however, were *greater*. If you are a die-hard New Testament giver, then take a peek at Zacchaeus, who gave 50 percent. But Zacchaeus stood up and said to the Lord, "Look, Lord! Here and now I give half of my possessions to the poor, and if I have cheated anybody out of anything, I will pay back four times the amount."[9] Why not use Zacchaeus as the model? Fifty percent? Salvation affected his financial attitude!! There was evidence! There was action!

Or how about the widow's offering of two lepta (mites)? She gave her *all* (100 percent)! "I tell you the truth, this poor widow has put more into the treasury than all the others. They all gave out of their wealth; but she, out of her poverty [lack], put in everything— all she had to live on."[10] The two lepta were the smallest bronze Jewish coins in circulation in Palestine. They were worth just a fraction of a penny. She could have kept one and nobody would have cared or known. But she wanted to give her all, her best, to God. It was not the *amount*, but the *heart attitude* that mattered. It was the amount of sacrifice. Proportionally, she gave the most. Her two lepta were more than your $50,000!

So we have a few models—10 percent, 25 percent, 33 1/3 percent, 50 percent, 100 percent. Take your pick. Multiple choice.

> *"First of all, I think 10 percent is too small. I fight the concept that God owns 10 percent and I own 90 percent.*
> **God owns it all."**
> **—Ron Blue**

Ron Blue actually gives 50 percent. His clients give an average of 15 percent. Our personal goal is 50 percent, but I will not be constrained or bound by a percentage. I think that 10 percent is a good target and a starting point, but it should not be used to beat people over the head, nor should it be an end all. If we use it that way, we might miss additional blessings, but, more importantly, we might miss an opportunity to help others in need if we are not sensitive to God's leading.

Our giving is about so much *more than money*. We cannot possibly repay our debt to the Lord in dollars and cents. I love Matt Redman's worship song "I Will Offer up My Life":

> *I will offer up my life in spirit and truth*
> *Pouring out the oil of love as my worship to You*
> *In surrender I must give my every part*
> *Lord, receive the sacrifice of a broken heart*
>
> *Jesus, what can I give, what can I bring*
> *To so faithful a friend, to so loving a King?*
> *Savior, what can be said, what can be sung*
> *As a praise of Your name for the things You have done?*
> *O my words could not tell, not even in part*
> *Of the debt of love that is owed by this thankful heart.*
>
> *You deserve my every breath for You've paid the great cost*
> *Giving up Your life to death, even death on a cross*
> *You took all my shame away, there defeated my sin*
> *Opened up the gates of heaven and have beckoned me in*[11]

How Much? Other guidance?

The disciples each gave according to his ability. They each gave. No one was exempt.[12] They made the decision; then they acted.

The New Testament is clear about the words *generously and liberally*. "Out of the most severe trial, their overflowing joy and their extreme poverty welled up in *rich generosity*. For I testify that they gave *as much as they were able*, and even *beyond their ability. Entirely on their own. . . .*"[13] (emphasis added) That took faith, not logic!

The original meaning of *rich generosity* was "liberality; bountifully, sincerely, not self-seeking, singleminded."

Paul talked more about giving than any other New Testament

writer, and he never used the word *tithe*. "Now about the collection for God's people. Do what I told the Galatian churches to do. On the first day of every week, each one of you should *set aside a sum of money* in keeping with his income, saving it up, so that when I come no collections will have to be made."[14] This passage clearly implies a systematic, weekly collection. They gave a "portion" or a "percentage" of their income.

Sowing!

Although we do not give to get, the Bible is clear that a blessing (not just financial) will result from our giving (see chapter 11). If you give a little, you will be entrusted with little. If you give a little, you will be blessed a little.

SELAH 11-3

Read 2 Corinthians 9:6–12.

This passage says that "whoever sows generously will also reap generously." Luke says, "Give, and it will be given to you. A good measure, pressed down, shaken together and running over, will be poured into your lap. For with the measure you use, it will be measured to you."[15] How much do you want to be blessed? If you had told me ten years ago that we would be giving as much as we are today and that I would desire to give even *more*, I would have laughed you out of my house. God will bless and provide for His people but not so that we can squander it on our own desires. God will meet all of your *needs* according to His glorious riches.[16] We are very blessed in this country to be able to claim a tax deduction for our giving. But we must be careful when we're analyzing motives that our level of giving is not driven by the tax code but rather by our heart condition and our love for Jesus.

Stop Giving!

Can you imagine ever hearing such a phrase from a pulpit or television screen in America some day? That is my desire. We have precedence for it. Consider Exodus 36:3–7: "The people continued to bring freewill offerings morning after morning." Then the workers said to Moses, "The people are bringing *more than enough* for doing the work the Lord commanded to be done." Then Moses gave an order to restrain the people from bringing more "because what they already had was *more than enough* to do all the work." Notice that these were *freewill* offerings. If we gave as God desired us to give, no one would have to *ask* for money! Does it start with the preacher, or the church, or the pope? No, it starts with you and me.

Leftovers!

Another great testimony of giving is found in 2 Chronicles 31:1–10. Hezekiah assigned the leaders to offer burnt offerings and fellowship offerings. "[T]he Israelites *generously gave* the firstfruits of grain, wine, oil and honey and all that the fields produced." Then the chief priest reported, "Since the people began to bring their contributions to the temple of the Lord, we have had enough to eat and plenty to spare, because the *Lord has blessed* his people, and this great amount is *left over*" (emphasis added).

Wow! They had *more* than enough!

It is all about the heart. "The Lord said to Moses, 'Tell the Israelites to bring me an offering. You are to receive the offering for me from each man whose *heart prompts him to give.*'"[17]

God desires *all* of our hearts. He is not concerned so much about the number or the percentage. When my heart was finally in the right place and I began to give joyfully, cheerfully, and liberally, then the 10 percent became smaller in the rear view mirror.

"What is needed is not simply an increased giving, an enlarged estimate of the "Lord's share," but a **radically different conception, of our relations to our possessions."**
—Josiah Strong, 1885.

ACTION POINTS

1. Have you struggled with giving? _____ What are the main reasons for your struggle? _____

    _____
    _____

    Are the reasons valid to you? To God?_____

2. Have you increased your giving as your affluence has increased? _____

3. Have you been bound at all by the "tithe" teaching? Why or why not? _____

    _____
    _____

4. Research, pray, and develop a position on how much you should be giving. Talk to your spouse about this and reach an *agreement*—then act on it! Unity on this issue is important, and God does not want a disagreement over giving to drive a wedge between you and your spouse.

    _____
    _____
    _____

5. Are you average? Review the giving graphs in this chapter. Why has giving by Christians decreased over the years whereas prosperity has increased? Is it a heart issue? Was the Corinthian church average? What is the difference between "average" and "excellent" in your giving life/plan?

    _____
    _____
    _____

CHAPTER 12

Who Gets My Money?
Going Once, Going Twice. . . .

Just as the marketers are crying for our money, so are many ministries, outreaches, and churches that are in need of money. This chapter looks at who should get your hard-earned money. First and foremost, we ought to go to the Bible to get God's advice on the subject. Second, we ought to pray for specific guidance. God may direct you specifically to help a widow in your church, a missionary on the field, or a laid-off coworker for a season. God wants to give us specific direction. Will we seek His advice? So, to whom should we give?

The Storehouse

The Bible contains eight references to a "storehouse/storage facility."[1] The most often quoted passage is "Bring the whole tithe into my storehouse, that there may be food in my house."[2] A storehouse was a special room or rooms in the temple for keeping tithed grain.[3] It was a depository, cellar, or secret chamber. Most of our churches do not have grain storage, nor can you consider the local grocery store a holy house, so, where is the modern storehouse? I believe that 1 Corinthians 9:11–14 gives us the best clue: "If we have sown spiritual seed among you, is it too much if we reap a material harvest from you?"

Give where you are fed.

Let me clarify. If you are having spiritual seed sown into your life at your church, that is where you need to give. Obviously, we need to be certain that our motive for attending church is not just to "get fed." We ought to be just as concerned about "feeding" others. Hopefully, we are beyond the bottle-feeding stage of our Christianity. There is a time for bottle feeding, but there is also a time when our purpose for being part of a body is to participate. I do not have a useless part of my body; every part functions for a specific purpose. Yes, we all need to get fed, but we also need to do some feeding.

However, if no food is in your storehouse (church), maybe it is time to move along. If it offers only junk food, maybe it is time to move on. If your church is full of tradition and religion but void of life or purpose, or if God is nowhere to be found in it, maybe it is time to feed somewhere else. If the Word is not being preached and you are getting only self-help, milk-toast, *Reader's Digest*-type anecdotes, or items from a preacher's quotation book, then I question whether you are getting fed. If God's power is nowhere to be found in your church, then maybe it is time for you to move on.

Am I Getting Fed?

Do not get in the mode of looking for a perfect church or ministry, you will look for a long time and never find it. In fact, if you find the perfect church, do not go there because you will ruin it. We must, however, be sensitive to the Holy Spirit and pray regarding where we are involved and to whom we give.

SELAH 12-1
Feeding Scorecard

Although it is somewhat dangerous to score or rate your church or a ministry, I think that praying about and meditating on whether your investments in giving line up with God's Word and are having an eternal impact is healthful. Following are some questions to help you determine whether a ministry or church is involved in biblical "feeding." If feeding is occurring, then you ought to be giving to that ministry. (Evaluate your church and one to three other ministries by giving grades of A–F on each of the following questions.)

Evaluation question	Your church	Ministry #1	Ministry #2	Ministry #3
Are you personally learning/ challenged?	_____	_____	_____	_____
Is your family learning/ challenged?	_____	_____	_____	_____
Are your children learning/ challenged?	_____	_____	_____	_____
Are you being touched?	_____	_____	_____	_____
Are you being blessed (not financially)?	_____	_____	_____	_____
Have you been moved spiritually?	_____	_____	_____	_____
Is the ministry alive/ passionate for Jesus?	_____	_____	_____	_____
Are traditions/rites valued above Jesus?	_____	_____	_____	_____
Is your relationship with Jesus growing?	_____	_____	_____	_____

Evaluation question	Your church	Ministry #1	Ministry #2	Ministry #3
Is the focus mostly on "internal" (members)?	_____	_____	_____	_____
Are only the members being fed?	_____	_____	_____	_____
Are you feeding the lost "spiritually"?	_____	_____	_____	_____
Is there a focus on evangelism/outreach?	_____	_____	_____	_____
Is your life better because of this ministry?	_____	_____	_____	_____
Is Jesus, not man, lifted up?	_____	_____	_____	_____
Is the Word of God used and taught?	_____	_____	_____	_____
Is the mission biblical?	_____	_____	_____	_____
Is the focus on eternal things?	_____	_____	_____	_____
Are the teachings on giving biblical?	_____	_____	_____	_____
Is there accountability for the finances?	_____	_____	_____	_____
Are the leaders servants?	_____	_____	_____	_____
Do the leaders have a heart for God?	_____	_____	_____	_____
Are there continual "crisis" appeals?	_____	_____	_____	_____
Is there a "give-to-get" focus?	_____	_____	_____	_____
Do you see fruit of the ministry?	_____	_____	_____	_____
Are heart/head knowledge balanced?	_____	_____	_____	_____

Evaluation question	Your church	Ministry #1	Ministry #2	Ministry #3
Is wise financial stewardship practiced?	_____	_____	_____	_____
Are disciples being made?	_____	_____	_____	_____
Is there genuine fellowship?	_____	_____	_____	_____
Is Jesus and the Cross taught?	_____	_____	_____	_____
Is sin preached about?	_____	_____	_____	_____
Is grace/love taught? Does the worship draw you to God?	_____	_____	_____	_____

The preceding questions should also be asked of ministries to which you give. You should be familiar with the ministry, its finances, its mission, and its zeal for souls. Pray and evaluate the ministries before giving to them. Do not be driven to give by an emotional plea or because of an impressive speaking or singing performance. When in doubt, use the seventy-two-hour rule: if God is still dealing with your heart seventy-two hours after the appeal, then maybe it is God and not merely an emotional plea that moves you. Many people are manipulated out of their money because they do not wait. On the other hand, God may in fact deal strongly with you to give immediately. Let the Lord help you with your giving decisions. Giving $1000 that you do not have to someone you do not know because of a promise of a hundred-fold return or a release from your debt situation is presumption and is testing God foolishly!

Remember that getting fed does not mean that you like the pastor's suit, think he preached well, or agree with everything that the pastor said. Being fed doesn't mean that no one offended you on a particular Sunday, the seat cushion was comfortable, the building suited you, the temperature was correct, the music was the right volume, the right instruments were played, or your "felt needs" were met. Feeding is not self-seeking. It is not getting your own way. A church or ministry that "feeds" focuses on: (1) Jesus, (2) love, and (3) the Bible.

The fact that 16 percent of church members gave *nothing* to their church last year[4] means one of two things: either that person (1) is not getting fed *at all* (which is hard to believe, but, if it is true, then get out, find a Bible-teaching, nonlukewarm church, and give there), or (2) is a stingy freeloader. If you are attending a "feeding" church and give somewhere else, I liken that to pulling up to the Chevron station, filling up with gas, and then going across the street to pay for that gas at Exxon! If your "storehouse" is feeding you and others, then give to it!

The Workers/Ministers

In addition to giving where we are fed (the storehouse), we are to support God's leaders through our giving. The priests and Levites were supported through the offerings of the people. Aaron the priest received support in exchange for his work.[5] The ministry was a source of income for the priests. It was their compensation. We need to pay our pastors! First Corinthians 16 and 2 Corinthians 8 and 9 also address this issue.

The Poor and the Widows

The Bible addresses giving to the poor more than other group. An angel said to Cornelius, "Your prayers and gifts *to the poor* have come up as a memorial offering before God"[6] (emphasis added).

"But when [not *if*] you *give to the needy*, don't let your left hand know what your right hand is doing"[7] (emphasis added).

"He who *gives to the poor* will lack nothing, but he who closes his eyes to them receives many curses"[8] (emphasis added).

Jesus, talking to the rich young ruler, said, "[G]o, sell your possessions and *give to the poor,* and you will have treasure in heaven"[9] (emphasis added).

Paul said, "[C]ontinue to remember *the poor,* the very thing I was eager to do."[10]

Proverbs says, "He who is kind to *the poor* lends to the Lord. . . ."[11]

Jesus said, "[W]hen you give a banquet, invite the *poor,* the crippled, the lame, the blind, and you will be blessed."[12]

If we give just to the wealthy or to those who are not in financial need, we are not giving in proper balance. One of the most overlooked, undertaught passages in the New Testament is this: "Our desire is not that others might be relieved while you are hard pressed, but that there might be *equality*. At the present time your plenty will supply what they need, so that in turn their plenty will supply what you need. Then there will be equality, as it is written: 'He who gathered much did not have too much, and he who gathered little did not have too little.' " [13]

America does not have equality with other nations regarding our prosperity.

One year, I felt really impressed to focus a significant amount of my giving on the poor. This practice was followed during Old Testament days: "At the end of every three years, bring all the tithes of that year's produce and store it in your towns, so that the Levites . . . and the aliens, the fatherless and the widows who live in your towns may come and eat and be satisfied, and so that the Lord your God may bless you in all the work of your hands."[14]

One of my biggest blessings occurred on a business trip. While I was eating at a fast food restaurant, I noticed that one of the workers was dressed shabbily. She also seemed to be quite depressed and sad. On my way out, I handed her $5 and told her that Jesus loved her. A joy came over her, and she began crying. It was a moment that replays over and over in my mind, and I will never forget it. Never underestimate the impact of your giving and the mention of Jesus! It does not take much, but we need to be sensitive to whom God wants us to give.

Your Enemy

This point could possibly give you the most satisfaction. It might be difficult, but you also might be in line to see some great results.

"If your enemy is hungry, give him food to eat; if he is thirsty, give him water to drink. In doing this [meet his need], you will heap burning coals on his head and the Lord will reward you."[15]

One of my coworkers daily gained significant joy out of ridiculing, persecuting, and chastising me both privately and publicly. He nearly fainted one year when I gave him a Christmas basket that my wife had prepared. It was the last thing he expected. You could feel the heat of the coals! We began getting Christmas cards from him and his wife after that!

The Weak

Paul's last words to the Ephesian elders were, "You yourselves know that these hands of mine have supplied my own needs and the needs of my companions. In everything I did, I showed you that by this kind of hard work *we must help the weak*, remembering the words the Lord Jesus himself said: 'It is more blessed to give than to receive' "[16] (emphasis added). Find a low-visibility ministry that touches the weak; that cannot afford TV, radio, or advertising; and bless them with your time or a gift. Seek out single parents, low-income families, or widows at church or work, and help them.

Children

"And if anyone gives even a cup of cold water to one of these little ones because he is my disciple, I tell you the truth, he will certainly not lose his reward."[17] Give of your time, tools, talents, and finances to your church's children or youth ministries. Find a ministry that touches children in need.

Missionaries

During Paul's third missionary journey (Romans 15:23–28), the churches at Macedonia and Achaiah supported him. The Church of Antioch supported Barnabus and Paul (Acts 11:29). Paul's missionary journey included raising money for the needy (1 Corinthians 16:1–3). As indicated in Philippians 4:15, not all churches support missionaries. If your church does not, I encourage you to begin doing so. It will bless both the missionaries and you greatly.

Anyone and Everyone

They practiced this principle in Acts: "Selling their possessions and goods, they gave to anyone as he had need."[18] It was not socialism or communism but voluntary giving and sharing (community). The parable of the sheep and the goats in Matthew 25:34–36 gives a great "laundry list" of those to whom we should give. Watch and listen for opportunities in your church or on the job. Seek out single parents, widows, or others in need. Find the needs referenced in the parable, including the following:

> ➢ the hungry,
> ➢ the thirsty,
> ➢ strangers,
> ➢ those needing clothes,
> ➢ the sick,
> ➢ prisoners, and
> ➢ "the least of my brethren."

God is the champion of the poor and needy. *Jesus cared about the oppressed, the downtrodden, the Samaritans, the leper, and the widow.* He reserved His harshest words for the Pharisees (Luke 10:14—"they loved money") and those who clung to material possessions: the rich young ruler, the moneychangers in the temple, the rich man who built bigger barns, and the rich man with Lazarus at his gate. They all received harsh words and actions from Jesus. "But woe to you who are rich, for you have already received your comfort. Woe to you who are well fed now, for you will go hungry."[19] "God knows your hearts. What is highly valued among men is detestable in God's sight."[20]

The Bible assists us by guiding our giving. The bottom line is that we should *be sensitive to whom God wants you to give!*

ACTION POINTS

1. How can you help your church "feed" better? Pray, then act!

   _____
   _____
   _____
   _____
   _____
   _____
   _____
   _____
   _____
   _____

2. Review the chapter, and consider some new avenues by which you can give to the following groups of people:

	WHO	*WHAT*
Workers/ministers	_____	_____
The Poor/widows	_____	_____
Enemies	_____	_____
The weak	_____	_____
Children	_____	_____
Missionaries	_____	_____
Other	_____	_____

CHAPTER 13

A Land of Rich Young Rulers?

Wealth can entangle us all. It is an American reality that we must face constantly. Is it possible that a direct correlation exists between income and spirituality? We must, of course, guard against pigeonholing people or judging them based on their incomes, but the Bible warns us more about riches and money than about any other area.

One of George Barna's recent surveys showed that income seems to be inversely related to identifying oneself as an "evangelical Christian." Only 26 percent of those who earn more than $60,000 a year call themselves evangelical. Forty-five percent of those earning less than $60,000 a year identify themselves as evangelical Christians.[1]

One area of difficulty for some Christians is the balance or tug-of-war between "eternal investing" and "temporal investing." A fine line exists between hoarding and investing. To *hoard* means to "lay up," to "store up," to "keep." Many individuals and families chuckle (or grimace) at the thought of actually having some money available to invest. Some people are just struggling to make it from payday to payday. But part of the journey toward financial freedom is the balance of giving and saving or giving and investing.

Is It Biblical to Save and Invest?

Solomon commended the ant for its initiative in saving and storing: "Go to the ant, you sluggard; consider its ways and be wise! . . . it stores its provisions in summer and gathers its food at harvest." [2] The Bible says that "a foolish man devours all he has." [3] The parable of the talents says, "[Y]ou should have put my money on deposit with the bankers, so that when I returned I would have received it back with interest." [4] It also is biblical to leave an inheritance for our children: "A good man leaves an inheritance for his children's children." [5]

If we are "working for the Lord, not for men," and if it is the Lord Christ whom we are serving, then we need to be mindful not to focus excessively on building our own kingdoms with the income with which He has blessed us. *He* is in fact our "employer/boss"; and the earth is the *Lord's,* and everything in it. . . . We are just "house sitting." He is giving us our *eternal* inheritance. Our final payday is coming! Hallelujah!

So When Does Investing Become Hoarding?

It's too bad that we don't have a black-and-white checklist that tells us when we have crossed the line between investing and hoarding. This issue is a matter of prayer and reflection. It is a heart issue just like the others about which we have talked throughout the book. Following are some warning signs that you might have crossed over that fine line between investing and hoarding:

1. you thirst for more, and your thirst for more never seems to be quenched;
2. you watch the stock market or your investments more than you read the Word or pray;
3. you spend more time considering your temporal investments than you do planning and strategizing your giving; or
4. you worry or are afraid. (Read Matthew 6:24–27: "[T]he birds . . . do not . . . store away in barns, and yet your heavenly Father feeds them."

*"I have made many millions, but they have brought me
no happiness."*
—John D. Rockefeller

Even the blessing of receiving an inheritance can be fodder for lust and covetousness. One godly man told me how he had fallen into the trap of coveting his own inheritance soon to come. This is easy to do. We must guard against it! Even the things that we at one time acquired in purity or with which God has blessed us, can become idols.

It is so easy for us to hoard. We have so much financial protection in our society. If we are not careful, we can push away our dependence upon God and not truly live one day at a time, without worry about tomorrow. We have insurance. We have 401k's. We have retirement accounts. We have pensions. We have Social Security. We have IRAs. We have college funds. We have savings accounts. We have unemployment benefits. We have Medicare. We have government aid and assistance. We have financial aid and grants. If we are not careful, we can come to think that our security and solace are ourselves and our bank accounts.

SELAH 13-1

Read the following two Scripture passages: Job 31:24–28 and Luke 12:13–21.

If we put our faith in things, money, or bank accounts, we have said of them, "You are my security." It is also easy to get caught in the trap of rejoicing over our wealth. If we do either of these things, we have sinned and been unfaithful to God. To consider these acts sin is difficult because they are not overt and such is the norm even among many Christians. But the Bible calls such attitudes *sin*. We are walking a tightrope of idolatry and comfort similar to the rich man mentioned in Luke. His intention was to lay up good things so he could take life easy. Cushy Christianity is not biblical. God called him a fool! We must beware! We must be on our guard against all kinds of greed.

No matter how much we get, it never seems to be enough! We "need" more for every want, desire, and contingency. Fear awaits us at every turn. College tuition, retirement, energy crisis, stock market crash, inflation, recession, depression, layoffs, war, a call to the ministry or the mission field—FEAR, FEAR! But God has not given us a spirit of fear!

For What Are You Thirsty?

This is a good soul-searching question that I ask myself as a measure of my spiritual temperature and to keep myself honest in my struggle for simplicity.

For what are you thirsty? It is a question worth asking twice (seven times for me!). Am I thirsty for more entertainment? More toys? More money? More promotions? More hobbies? More temporal things? More TV? Or am I consumed with a passion and a thirst for more of Jesus? More prayer? More time in the Word? More time at church? More serving? More witnessing?

What a tug of war! In the battle for eternal focus and eternal investing, we must be on guard against both the enemy and our own flesh. The following Scripture is worthy of a thorough reading and meditation.

> One man *gives freely*, yet gains even more; another *withholds* unduly, but comes to poverty. *A generous man will prosper*; he who refreshes others will himself be refreshed. *People curse the man who hoards* grain, but blessing crowns him who is willing to sell. *Whoever trusts in his riches will fall*, but the righteous will thrive like a green leaf. (Prov. 11:24–26, emphasis added)

Based on this passage alone, I would choose giving over hoarding. I would rather err on the side of giving too much instead of hoarding or investing too much. No, I will not leave my children broke. I will leave them a spiritual inheritance and hopefully a financial inheritance. But I will focus on storing eternal treasures with my giving! Our neighbor or coworker is not the yardstick for our "investing" and "giving" decisions. Just because *they* "need" $1 million to retire does not mean that *I* need it! Just because *they* have the latest car or fashionable clothing does not mean that *I* need it! Just because *they* are consumed with stocks and market analyses and quarterly financial statements does not mean that *I* need to be!

Warning!

We ought to note that we are *all* rich here in America (see Figure 13-1). James issues a warning to rich people. He talks of hoarding wealth in the last days. He talks of financial injustices, but I think that the most incriminating verse could possibly describe America as a land of rich young rulers: "You have lived on earth in luxury and self-indulgence. You have fattened yourselves in the day of slaughter." [6]

We can use our wealth either on ourselves or to advance the gospel and to help those in need. It is a choice that each of us makes *daily*. A "soft life," a "life of luxury," is an option for many American Christians and a challenge for even the most saintly and superspiritual. Will we hoard? Will we spend on ourselves? Or will we give? How will we invest our resources?

Figure 13-1
Putting things in perspective [7]

Country	Population	People/ km²	Gross Domestic Product	Gross National Prod./person	Literacy	Infant mortality	TVs
United States	267,115,000	29	$6,952,020,000,000	$ 26,980	99%	0.7%	99%
India	929,005,000	312	$324,082,000,000	$ 340	52%	7.2%	5.1%
Bangladesh	118,229,000	909	$29,110,000,000	$ 240	38%	7.8%	0.6%
Ethiopia	56,404,000	56	$5,287,000,000	$ 100	36%	10.7%	0.4%
Mozambique	17,260,000	22	$1,469,000,000	$ 80	40%	11.0%	0.4%

If you ever doubted that you were wealthy, Figure 13-1 should help clarify just how blessed we are! The U.S. median income is

311 times greater than that of Mozambique! According to the U.S. Census Bureau, the American median household income is now $42,148.[8] Of the 6.1 billion people in the world today, 4.8 billion (80 percent) live in the Third World.[9]

- ❖ 3 billion live on less than *$700/year*, [10]
- ❖ 1.3 billion live on less than *$350/year*,[11]
- ❖ Nearly 3 billion lack basic sanitation,[12]
- ❖ 1.6 billion have no access to clean water,[13]
- ❖ 1.2 billion do not have adequate housing,[14]
- ❖ 1 billion do not have access to modern health services,[15]
- ❖ In less developed regions 20% of children do not attend school through age 5, [16] and
- ❖ 1–2 billion individuals have *never* heard the gospel.

In fact, according to Joshua Project, 494 people groups have no known church planting efforts.[17]

This is not a guilt trip. It is the facts. It is the mirror that we Americans do not want to hold up. It is so easy to change the channel or tune out this information. We need to face the music once in a while. We are making great progress in spreading the gospel, but we still lack in proper priorities and *equality*. If only we could grasp these truths, we could help change our world!

We are blessed with so much that we can share with others. God honors your desire to give and your acts of giving. I think that the most appropriate scripture that obligates the American church to care for our brothers and sisters laboring in other countries is as follows:

> Our desire is not that others might be relieved while you are hard pressed, but that there might be *equality*. At the present time your *plenty* will supply what they *need*, so that in turn their plenty will supply what you need. Then there will be *equality*, as it is written: "*He who gathered much did not have too much, and he who gathered little did not have too little.*" (2 Corinthians 8:13–15, emphasis added)

How are we doing on equality? Only 23 percent of the world's population live on more than $700/year. (See Fig. 13-2.) We Americans are in that blessed 23 percent, and most of us live on fifty to one hundred times that much! Yet Americans spend more on dog food annually than on foreign missions.

Figure 13-2
Not the Average Joes

Average Annual Income (World Population)

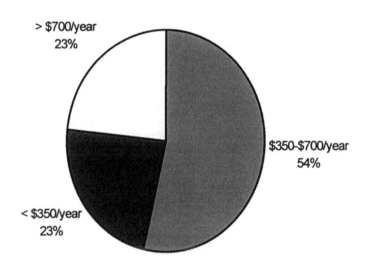

- We spend an average of $1251/person yearly on entertainment. [18]
- We spend an average of $1091/person yearly on clothing.[19]
- We spend an average of $1517/person yearly on eating out/food away from home.[20]
- We spend an average of $186/person yearly on tobacco and smoking supplies.[21]
- We spend an average of $292/person yearly on alcoholic beverages, and $156/person yearly on non-alcoholic beverages.[22]
- We spend an average of $5243/person yearly on transportation (vehicle, gas, and insurance). [23]
- We charge an average of $1150/household on credit cards during

the Christmas holiday season. [24]
- Estimates show we spend $60 to $250 billion a year on Gambling. Twice the entire GDP of Bangladesh. [25]
- We spend $27 billion a year on pet food and services. [26]
- We spend $20 billion a year on cosmetics and fragrances. [27]
- We spend $8 billion a year on box office movies. [28]
- We spend $24 billion a year through jewelry stores sales. [29]
- We spend $13 billion a year on chocolate in all its forms. [30]
- We spend $36 billion a year through vending machine sales. [31]

Yet,

√ We give only $2.9 billion a year to Overseas Missions. [32]

√ 1579 people groups (more than one billion souls) have yet to hear the gospel. [33]

√ The Bible is not available in whole or in part in 4267 of the world's 6500 languages. [34]

√ More than 25% of the children die before age 5 in: Afghanistan, Angola, Niger, and Sierra Leone. [35]

√ More than 15% of the children never reach the age of 1 in: Afghanistan, Angola, Liberia, Niger, and Sierra Leone. [36]

√ The Philippines spends 52 percent of its income on food. (We spend 10 percent.) [37]

√ U.S. citizens consume six times as much grain per person as do people in lesser developed countries. [38]

√ In developing countries, 40 to 60 million people die from hunger and hunger related diseases each year. [39]

√ The dollar value of the food North Americans throw in the garbage each year equals about one-fifth of the total annual income of all the Christians in Africa. [40]

√ One source estimates that $70-80 billion would impact the worst of world poverty, and $2.5 billion could end most of the 11 million annual deaths of children under age five. [41]

√ If church giving increased from an average of 2.5% per person to 10% per person, we could give an additional $78.4 billion a year to overseas Missions. [42]

According to the Executive Office of National Drug Control Policy,[43] Americans spent $66 billion on illegal drugs, "establishing that Americans spend more annually on illegal drugs than they contribute to all charities, education, and religion *combined*."[44]

Do I cite all of these statistics to make you feel guilty? No! I do so only to provide perspective. When 85 percent of the world's population lives in the Third World, and the Bible is for everyone, *the Scriptures about hoarding do not apply to very many countries or people.* Are we doing our personal part?

Should we feel guilty? No. Should we be convicted and make a change in our lifestyles and in our giving and missions support? I will leave that decision up to you and God. I am accountable for *me,* and the answer for *me* is *yes* on all counts.

Ten years ago, we made a goal of giving 50 percent of our income—ten percent to the local church and 40 percent to missions/outreaches. I have been stretched by the likes of R.G. LeTourneau, who gave 90 percent of his income, and others who have shared their giving testimonies with me. I believe that it can be done! It seemed impossible for us, but God works through us when we make the proper spiritual and practical adjustments to our life and our finances.

If the world's population were one hundred people,

- fifty-seven would be Asians,
- fourteen would be North or South Americans,
- sixty-six would be non-Christian,
- seventy would be nonwhite,
- eighty would live in substandard housing,
- seventy would be unable to read,
- fifty would suffer from malnutrition,
- seventy-five would have never made a phone call,
- one would have a college education,
- six would own half of the world's wealth, and
- all six would live in the *United States of America.*
  —*Unknown Source*

The book that most changed my life and my perspective on missions is *Revolution in World Missions—Final Thrust to Reach the 10/40 Window* by K.P. Yohanon. I give the book away at my seminars, and I will give a *free copy* to anyone who purchases a copy of *Ease the Squeeze* (see order form on back page). If you would like to order a copy directly from Gospel for Asia you can contact them at 1-800-WIN-ASIA, www.gfa.org, or drop them a line at:

Gospel for Asia
1800 Golden Trail Court
Carrollton, TX 75010

Our family goal is to support Gospel for Asia in building one or two churches a year and to add a new missionary to our support each year. It costs only $3000–5000 a year to build a church for one hundred to two hundred worshipers. They do not require much. It costs only $90–120/month to support an indigenous missionary through Gospel for Asia.

Worthwhile ministries worthy of support exist right here in our own backyard. Since the 1960s, the government has recognized an official poverty line. According to the U.S. Census Bureau, more than thirty-one million Americans live below the poverty line, currently set at $18,267 annually for a family of four with two children.[45]

If you are looking for other worthwhile ministries to which you might give, a few that I might suggest include the following:

- Gospel for Asia—reaching the unreached people groups:1-800-WIN-ASIA; www.gfa.org
- Dallas Metro Ministries—reaching the inner city of Dallas: 214-744-0848; www.metrodfw.org
- Metro Ministries International—reaching the inner city of New York: 718-453-3352; www.metroministries.com
- Feed the Children—feeding the children of the world: 800-627-4556; www.christianity.com/feedthechildren
- Compassion International—feeding and educating children of the world: 800-336-7676; www.compassion.com
- Voice of the Martyrs—supporting the persecuted church around the world: 918-337-8015; www.persecution.com

Chinese Christian leader Samuel Lamb, a prisoner for twenty years, stated, "Our churches in China are undergoing persecution; your churches in the West are undergoing delusion." Are some of our teachings so fashioned that we can maintain our selfish, comfortable lives? Eighty percent of Christians do not live in the pampered West, yet we are the most gospel-rich nation on the face of the earth. We have more ordained pastors, more Bible colleges, more full-time Christian workers, more Christian radio and TV, and more Christian publishing houses *than the rest of the world combined.* Is prosperity really a test from God? Will it be a drug or a tool?

We are blessed beyond, and must continually be mindful of our purpose here on earth. I have been challenged by the words of a Greg Long song titled "The Sacrifice:"

Who am I to choose to walk in green pastures?
As if that's what I deserve.
I try and try to live my life for what really matters.
Anymore, I am not so sure.
I get so caught up in the good things you have given me.
I pray I don't forget to see the sacrifice—
the cross of Christ ...[46]

Multiplication!

I love the optimistic perspective of my friend and neighbor, Matt Schonoff: "When we give our 10 percent to a church, the impact is not 10 percent but actually 11.1 percent! If you make $50,000 a year and give $5,000 to your local church, that church quite possibly gives $500 to another ministry or mission. In turn, that mission may give $50 away, and so on. Multiply your money!

Just imagine if we could follow the principal in 2 Corinthians 8:13–15. We could change our world!

SELAH 13-2

Ask the Lord how you should be involved in furthering the gospel around the world. Act now; do not delay. Time is short, and the laborers are few. The fields are awaiting. You can influence your world. What can you do?

Are You Called?

Many Christians are called to the mission field but cannot go because they are chained by debt. If that is you, then the urgency for resetting your life plan and financial plan should take on greater importance for follow through. Begin today!

It breaks my heart as I talk to believers who know that they have a call that they are not fulfilling. God still has not given up on you! He will restore the years that seem to be wasted. Begin anew today! The tools in Section 3 of this book will help get you started.

Three Cures for Hoarding

The Scriptures offer at least three cures for hoarding.

1. "Freely you have received, freely *give*." [47]
2. "[D]o not be hardhearted or *tightfisted* toward your poor brother. Rather be *openhanded. . . Give generously* to him and do so *without a grudging heart;* then because of this the Lord your *God will bless you* in all your work and in everything you put your hand to." [48]
3. The man with two tunics should *share* with him who has none, and the one who has food should do the same. [49]

These three cures actually boil down to one cure—*give*. Frances J. Roberts says it better than I can:

God Spoke

Blessings are released when the soul of a man is content with nothing of earthly value.
The spirit is prepared for worldly success only after it has learned to care nothing for it.
I fill the hand that lies open in worship.
The hand that grasps shall be forever empty.

Learn to leave to my love and wisdom all your destiny.
Nothing ought concern you but the health of your soul and the outflow of your life.

Man looks upon the income.
I watch for the outflow.
You will free your soul as you refuse to seek anything and desire
only to give.
Then shall I bless you with increase and only then will it not
impoverish your spirit. [50]

The balance between hoarding and investing/saving is difficult. God will guide you in your endeavors. We must shift our thinking radically from an emphasis on how much we should give to *how much we should keep.*

ACTION POINTS

1. Do you need to reconsider the balance of your temporal investments and your eternal investments (giving)?

   _____

   _____

   _____

   _____

   _____

   _____

   _____

2. Have you considered or prayed about the dilemma of hoarding versus giving?

   _____

   _____

   _____

3. Pray about your current and future involvement in World Missions. What can you do today?

   _____

   _____

   _____

4. Consider ordering a copy of *Revolution in World Missions—Final Thrust to Reach the 10/40 Window* by K.P. Yohanon.

CHAPTER 14

Keeping it All in Perspective— Temporal vs. Eternal

I believe that one of the most difficult challenges for the twenty-first-century American Christian is keeping an eternal perspective in our *living* and in our *giving*. The so-called "normal" American Christian is hardly characterized as a pilgrim, a sojourner who is just passing through. We have blended quite well with a secular, humanistic society. We must pinch ourselves to keep it all in perspective.

Only one life, will soon be past; only what's done for Christ will last.

SELAH 14-1

The Thermometer Test

It is time for a quick, introspective look at what we are doing with our time and how it all looks in the light of eternity.

189

Read James 4:13–15—We are a mist. Neither our time nor our life is our own.
Read Ecclesiastes 2:1–11—Consider Solomon's thesis on his life.

How can I apply these Scriptures personally to my life?

_____

_____

_____

Obviously, both James and Solomon were referring to more than money. However, how we "invest" our money—temporally or eternally—matters to God and will eventually matter to us. Jesus stated in His Sermon on the Mount, "Do not store up for yourselves treasures on earth, where moth and rust destroy, and where thieves break in and steal. But store up for yourselves treasures in heaven, where moth and rust do not destroy, and where thieves do not break in and steal. For where your treasure is, there your _heart_ will be also."[1]

The Giving Gauge

In Jesus' interaction with both the rich young ruler and the widow who gave her two mites, He teaches that what we do with our money and possessions is a direct reflection of our hearts. I believe that someone can get a pretty accurate reading of my priorities in this life by viewing my checkbook register or credit/debit card statements. They provide a pretty good "eternal giving gauge."

Pinches

I recall how my grandmother pinched me during church services to help me refocus or keep me from nodding off. Ecclesiastes is filled with "pinches" of reality and wisdom regarding our lives. I think that Ecclesiastes ought to be mandatory "pinch" reading for Christians once a year. "Whoever loves money never has money enough; whoever loves wealth is never satisfied with his income. This too is _meaningless_. I have seen a grievous evil under the sun: wealth hoarded to the harm of its owner, or wealth lost through some misfortune, so that when he has a son there is nothing left for him. Naked a man comes from his mother's womb, and as he comes, so he departs." Solomon says that hoarding wealth is a "grievous evil" and "harmful" to its owner.[2]

How can *we* really take hold of the life that is truly life if Solomon and James took so long to figure it out? I think that Paul has the answer: "Command those who are rich [that is all of us here in America—if you doubt it, read Chapter 13!] in this present world not to be arrogant nor to put their hope in wealth, which is so uncertain, but to *put their hope in God*, who richly provides us with everything for our enjoyment. Command them to do good, to be rich in *good deeds*, and to be *generous* and *willing to share*. In this way they will lay up treasure for themselves as a firm foundation for the coming age, so that they may *take hold of the life that is truly life*." Here is what we should and should not do:

DO	DON'T
—put our hope in God	—put our hope in wealth or self
—get our enjoyment from Him	—get our enjoyment from stuff
—do good deeds	—hoard or be selfish
—be generous and willing to share	

Result: *Take hold of the life that is truly life! Sounds like a guaranteed return!*

To help keep an eternal perspective, I believe that setting goals is a critical exercise to maintain proper focus spiritually, financially, and personally. (If you need a refresher, see Chapter 2!)

It really comes down to our choices. Sometimes we despise black-and-white issues or certain Scriptures because they force us to deal with both ourselves and God. The parable of the rich fool says that we can have either an eternal perspective or a temporal perspective: "*store up things for yourself* or *be rich toward God*."[3]

Not too many "guaranteed investments" or "sure stocks" exist in our temporal walk here on planet Earth. The Bible, however, is clear about a guaranteed bank, where the insurance cap does not stop at $100,000 like that of the FDIC. "Provide purses for yourselves that will not wear out, a treasure in heaven that will not be exhausted, where no thief comes near and no moth destroys. For where you treasure is, there your heart will be also."[4]

> *"We should give what we cannot keep to gain what we cannot lose."*

Our *glances* should be toward our stuff, our money, and our investments. Our *gazes* should be more on eternal things. "Cast but a *glance* at riches, and they are gone, for they will surely sprout wings and fly off to the sky like an eagle."[5]

An interesting thing about God is that He will entrust some of us with worldly wealth. Unfortunately, many members of the body of Christ have not been trustworthy in handling God's money. However, we are not accountable for how *others* have handled God's money, and they are not accountable for us. We all must take responsibility for handling our own personal, temporary wealth with which He has entrusted us. If we are faithful, then He will put us in charge of more.[6] "So if you have not been trustworthy in handling worldly wealth, who will trust you with true riches?"[7]

Oh, to be found faithful. I want the Lord's cry to be, "Well done, good and faithful servant!"

Two men who were later put in charge of much started off being faithful with only a little. Consider their examples.

> *R.G. LeTourneau*, a Christian businessman and teacher, started a moving equipment company and now has a fruitful Christian university in Longview, Texas. He was known for living on 10 percent of his income and giving away 90 percent! His legacy lives on through his university and a foundation to support Christian work.

> *Robert Laidlaw*, a New Zealand billionaire, determined to tithe at the age of eighteen. He continually and incrementally increased his giving until he was giving 50 percent by the time he was twenty-five!

Wow! These exemplars challenge me! Many people think that they will get an eternal perspective when they "hit it big," when the kids move out, or when the next promotion comes. No! We get an eternal perspective when we live selflessly *now* and store up for ourselves eternal treasures.

The only way to do that is to have our hearts and minds set on things above rather than on earthly things. We must live in accordance with the Spirit and have our minds set on what the Spirit desires. Our minds must be controlled by the Spirit to please God. Our citizenship is in heaven, so we must live as such![8]

SELAH 14-2

Pray the following (or a similar) prayer from your heart:

"Lord, I confess that I have not lived with an eternal perspective. I am sorry. Please forgive me. Thank you for your patience with me. You have blessed me so much. I truly want to begin again and live selflessly and with a godly, eternal perspective, but I need your help. Please show me what to do and how to do it. I need your wisdom, and I know that nothing is too difficult for you. I love you, Father. Amen."

ACTION POINTS

1. Go back to Section 1 of the book and review the Action Points on goals and some of the priorities sections. Reevaluate your goals and priorities in light of eternity (spiritually, financially, family, etc.). What changes will you commit to making now?

   _____

   _____
   _____
   _____
   _____
   _____
   _____
   _____
   _____

2. Are you managing your time and money effectively in the light of eternity (Selah 14-1)?_____

3. Take a journey through Ecclesiastes and get a wealthy man's perspective on this thing called life.

4. What are your giving goals?

   _____

   _____
   _____
   _____
   _____
   _____
   _____
   _____

CHAPTER 15

The Spiritual vs. the Practical

The tendency when teaching about or listening to a lesson on the subject of giving is to focus too much on either the spiritual aspects of giving or the practical side of giving. The truth of the matter is that we need a balance. Jesus lived an extremely spiritual life, but He also ate, slept, and showed emotions. He had a spiritual side and a practical side. He was real! Giving includes a *spiritual* side and a *practical* side. Thus, giving should be both *spontaneous* and *planned.*

We must be careful to plan and consider the cost, but we must also be flexible with our plans and be willing to have God *override* them. We must also involve Him *while* we are making the plans, *not after* we have made them.

Recently, our family has encountered a number of "unplanned" giving situations. Some friends of ours are itinerant evangelists, and a number of churches had promised to give them love offerings, but they never followed through. Another church took up a sizable offering for them, but they never received it.

While I was driving home from a prayer meeting, I had an extremely strong burden of intercession and a heavy heart for them. It occurred to me immediately that we needed to bless them with a sizable check. Two numbers popped into my mind. I have heard people say that the smaller amount is the devil speaking and the larger amount is God speaking. In this case, I concurred. I was so excited that I could not wait to get home and tell my wife. If you have never had a "giving anointing"—or a "giving attack," as I call it—there is nothing quite like it. I have had a "buying attack," and I usually end up with buyer's remorse. But a "giving attack" is much more satisfying, especially when you know that God is in it!

Another giving attack came when my wife wanted to bless a single mother in our church with a care basket of food, clothes, coupons, etc. Both situations were different and both were very God inspired (i.e., spiritual).

Spontaneous giving attacks are great, but most of the time we need to plan our giving or it will not happen. As a new Christian, I used to dump whatever cash I had in my wallet into the offering on Sunday. If I spent less on my Saturday evening outings, then God fared OK. If I splurged, then He received the pocket change. I have heard the "write the first check/first fruits" approach, and I believe it is a very good one if you are new to giving and need the discipline. It should be the first check written, non-negotiable, and a part of your budget (to be covered in a later chapter). If we obey what we know is correct, and practice cheerful, generous giving, and most importantly not live beyond my means, we will not be putting God to the test and He will act for us!

That Nasty Demon of Debt?!

Recently, I received a letter from a ministry asking for money so that I could be "delivered" from the *spirit of debt*. I do believe that God can and does work the supernatural; however, if we do some honest soul searching, I believe that most of the time our financial situations resulted from some practical occurrences or events rather than a demon of debt. Each of us has journeyed through different financial quicksand in our lives—a lack of self-control, materialism, a lust for things (1 John 2:15–17), a spousal issue, a bad relationship, or a bad business deal.

Sometimes, however, the blame game is the easy way out. It is easier to blame the situation or blame Satan for our situation. It is also easier to request a financial "deliverance" than to dig our way out slowly. The "write-a-check—free-me-God" approach is definitely easier on the flesh! It definitely avoids some of the "tough words" and "disciplines" about which we talked earlier. We need the mixture of practical disciplines and the supernatural, awesome help of an Almighty God. He will do it! But do not try to manipulate Him by writing a check or letting someone else hear from God for you.

It is not my intention to ridicule the ministry that sent me the "demon-of-debt" letter, but that financial plea had no scriptural basis, and it reeked of manipulation. I doubt that this was a ministry that would pass the "feeding scorecard" that we discussed earlier. We must be wary of such solicitations. Verify. Investigate. Wait. Pray and fast if you feel strongly. I do believe that Satan comes to steal, kill, and destroy, and he *will* attack your finances. I believe that he has succeeded, spiritually, in our land in this area—the idolatry, the greed, the lust for things, and the manipulation—are all spiritual things. But his power can be broken through practical changes, obedience, and much prayer as well as by God's supernatural intervention.

Practical Planning

Our church is embarking on a building program, and a good example of practical planning is our praying *today* and planning for what I will give six months from now. If I make my decision the day of the commitment, my giving will be lazy and full of my doubt, fear, and the check probably will be too small! Many times, if we are honest, we do not pray about how much we should give because we are afraid of the answer! I know in this case that I believe that God wants me to give sacrificially. I have not done that more than two or three times in my life. It is somewhat frightening! I had better involve God, my spouse, and my family in the decision. I must pray and give the matter more than a day's thought!

You need to pray and plan *now* about your future giving. If you do not pray, then the only voice you will hear on the matter is your own. If your voice has the same influence that mine had on me, then you will definitely want God's influence!

When I began my "tithing" journey, I had a plan. I would start at 1 percent and then increase to 2 percent, 3 percent, etc., as my debt load decreased. I did not wish it into existence, and I did not pray that I would have more income. I just planned it in my budget and wrote that check first.

We can plan our finances and our spending, but if we do that *before* we have a life plan and a giving plan, then our priorities will not show up correctly on our spreadsheets.

P-P-P (Proper Priorities in Planning)

1. A Life Plan
2. A Giving Plan
3. A Financial Plan

Planning is good, and better than that—planning is biblical!

Biblical Planning

"Go to the ant, you sluggard; consider its ways . . . it stores its provisions. . . ."[1]

"Ants . . . store up their food in the summer. . . ."[2]

"[A] foolish man devours all he has."[3]

"Now about the collection for God's people: Do what I told the Galatian churches to do. On the first day of *every week*, each one of you should *set aside* a sum of money in keeping with his income, *saving it up*" (emphasis added). [4]

SELAH 15-1

I think that my favorite "planning" scripture regarding finances is found in Luke 14:28–30. Take a minute to read that passage and apply it to your financial situation. Do you need to be planning anything financially? Are you planning properly for your giving?

1. How well do you plan your giving?_____ (Grade yourself A, B, C, D, F)

2. How well do you respond to spontaneous giving opportunities? _____ (Grade yourself)

Benefits!

The benefits of planning include not only the obvious benefits such as a balanced budget or increased giving ability but also the following "hidden" benefits:

√ increased self-control,
√ more discipline,
√ reduced risk of hoarding your money,
√ opportunities for teaching your children, and
√ priorities that are consistent with actions.

A definite balance between the spiritual and the practical aspects of giving is required.

Yuck! The Two "S" Words!

Deuteronomy 15 talks much about the proper heart condition of giving. "Give generously and do so without a grudging heart," "be openhanded," "supply him liberally," "Give to him as the Lord has blessed you." The following words and phrases are *not* self-seeking adjectives:

➢ generously,
➢ without a grudging heart,
➢ liberally, and
➢ as the Lord has blessed you.

Second Corinthians 8:3 says, "[T]hey gave as much as they were able, and even *beyond their ability*."[5] *Beyond their ability* seems to imply sacrifice. I used to drop a twenty- or fifty-dollar check in the offering whenever I felt like it. That was not sacrificial giving. We really do not understand the two S's: *self-denial* and *sacrificial giving.* What are they?

The example that I gave earlier of the time when we gave our friends the equivalent of two months' worth of giving (no, we did not skip our church tithe those months!) was not really sacrificial giving, but it was more than our ordinary offering. When I say *sacrificial*, however, I mean something different. If it sounds a little scary, it just might be!

What is sacrificial giving? It is giving that

- is beyond what *you* believe *you* can do (faith comes into play),
- affects your lifestyle,
- makes you sweat,
- forces you to trust,
- requires a commitment on your part,
- requires some changes on your part,
- requires hearing from God,
- requires (most likely) giving up something,
- gets nothing in return and has no expectations,
- makes you dependent upon God,
- frees you from the slavery of self-seeking materialism, and
- forces you to trust in God's provision rather than your own ability to provide (see Exodus 16 for the example of the manna).

Just as a baseball player lays down a sacrifice bunt, which does nothing for the batter himself, a sacrificial gift, on the surface, does nothing for the giver. But it definitely benefits the "team"—the body of Christ, God's kingdom—and, in this case, actually blesses the giver beyond measure. And a sacrificial gift will test us.

The ultimate sacrificial gift was a mixture of the spiritual and the practical about which we have been talking. Consider the case of Abraham and Isaac. This was not Abraham's first test. After all, he had left his country and family.[6] He had to wait on the Lord for his "stars."

SELAH 15-2

You might want to grab your Bible and a cup of coffee for this one. Open your Bible to Genesis 22. I would suggest reading Genesis 22:1–19 first to get the whole story, and then this application will make more sense. This is not an application that you would find in a typical Bible commentary, but hopefully it will be applicable to your finances and your giving.

God tested and proved Abraham (v. 1). This whole encounter was a *mixture* of the *spiritual* and the *practical*. God desires both in our lives.

Verse 2 is spiritual—the call to sacrifice Isaac: God initiated this call by speaking to Abraham. Abraham now had a choice. My guess is that a spiritual battle might have ensued at this point.

Verse 3 is practical—Abraham prepared: he gathered two servants, cut wood, and then set out. He prepared and planned for the act of sacrifice. Abraham's response: he neither fought nor questioned. He did not double check with his advisers or a committee. God had spoke. Abraham simply obeyed. This action was not simple, but it was practical.

Verse 5 is spiritual—Abraham worshipped: he initiated and moved toward God. This was a spiritual act that he most likely needed. After God speaks, we need to initiate. It is not a one-way relationship.

Verse 6 is practical—Abraham planned and prepared some more for the sacrifice: he took the wood and placed it on Isaac. He carried the fire and the knife. He took practical steps.

Verses 7–8 are spiritual—Abraham exercised his faith: he spoke to Isaac about His faith that God would provide the lamb. God was working in him and preparing him.

Verses 9-10 are practical—Abraham built the altar and arranged the wood: he bound Isaac and reached for his knife. These were practical steps, most likely the most difficult practical steps of all.

Verses 11–12 are spiritual—The angel of the Lord spoke, rescuing Isaac!

Verse 13 is spiritual—The Lord provided!

Abraham obeyed, and God provided! They worked together both spiritually and practically. Another great story of obedience followed by provision is found in 1 Kings 17. God sent the ravens to feed Elijah.

Step Out

We will have moments of sacrificial giving (money, time, or other). When they occur, they most likely will require a mixture of the spiritual and the practical. *The Lord will provide the strength, the faith, and the finances!* These opportunities will also require communication with God and others.

One of my personal "Isaacs" was laying down a personal dream that I had so that I could focus better on my family. It was big to no one but me—and God. He knew my heart, and He has blessed me in so many ways for that one sacrifice that I could fill a book just on the blessings of being obedient!

You will probably be able to count your sacrificial giving acts on one hand for your entire life. They will be challenging, but you will grow so much and be blessed beyond belief.

We had to step out in faith when we began tithing. We could not afford to give, but we mixed faith and action—the spiritual and the practical—and made it a priority. We stepped out in faith when we had kids and could not afford it. God provided the strength, the faith, and the finances. God will do the same as you move forward in your calls to give sacrificially.

"God is looking for leaders through whom He can do the impossible. What a pity that we plan only the things we can do ourselves."
—A.W. Tozer

Plan in Pencil

Plan, but do not live and die by your plans! Write them in pencil; write them in the sand. God might have other ideas.

Recently, I had to change some of my financial spreadsheet plans. God was challenging me to give more. We must plan and prepare. We need a budget or a spreadsheet or a goal, but do them in pencil—God might change your plans. I had to move some of my investments to more liquid/available money to have it available for some giving that He wants me to do. I do not throw my plans out; I just learn that His plans are better, and I need to be flexible.

A Unique Plan

You are unique in God's eyes. Thus, your spiritual and practical mix will differ from mine. Your faith tests and sacrificial giving calls will be different than mine. That is why it is critical that you stay in tune with the Lord. Ask, seek, and knock! He will not speak to each of us in the same way or at the same time. He knows that He needs to start early with me to plan for a sacrificial gift. But He knows that He can trust me with His money because I have been faithful with the little things—the coupon clipping, the giving, the laying down of my Isaacs, etc. God will not set up a budget for me, but He will give me wisdom, direction, strength, and spiritual guidance to mix with my practical actions.

Our lives are a mixture of the practical and the spiritual. That is why God should be included in every area of our lives. He should not be left out of any of them.

<u>ACTION POINTS</u>

1. How can you plan your giving better?

_____

_____

_____

_____

_____

2. How do you support your spouse's giving patterns? Planned? Spontaneous? How can you do better?

_____

_____

_____

_____

_____

3. Have you ever had to give "sacrificially"? Are you willing to give sacrificially if God asks you to do so in the future?

_____

_____

_____

_____

_____

4. What plans do you have written in ink or etched in stone with which you do not want God to mess? How can you change them to pencil? Ask God to help you now.

_____

_____

_____

_____

_____

A Few Final Ponderings

SELAH "Ponder 1"

When God is included in every area of our lives, we *will* give. Why then is giving so difficult at times? Check all of the following reasons that apply to you.

_____ I was not taught.
_____ I have not been asked to give.
_____ I was not taught about giving from a biblical perspective.
_____ I struggle with selfishness.
_____ Many people and groups are clamoring for my dollars (marketers, bill collectors, credit card institutions, our children, etc.).
_____ I struggle with my life priorities.
_____ I struggle with my "motives" or "heart condition."
_____ I do not plan or budget my giving very well.
_____ I do not think I can "afford it."

Facing the mirror and asking why we struggle to give is half of the battle. Many people do not want even to understand the "why." The second half of the battle is the obedience factor. If you have dealt with the "why," then God will help you with the "how."

SELAH "Ponder 2"

Take a few minutes to reflect, ponder, and pray about the next steps in your "giving plan."

Read the following Scriptures to help you understand your responsibility of "stewardship": Deuteronomy 8:1–13; 1 Chronicles 29:11–17 (David's prayer); Psalm 24:1; Luke 16:1-13.

More than the Dough

So far, we have limited the word giving to mean only money. Yes, our ability to produce wealth and our money all belongs to the Lord, but so does our

- time,
- talents ,
- life (Prov. 23:26),
- families (1 Sam. 1:11), and
- desires.

SELAH "Ponder 3"

Onto what else have you been hanging that you can give
to the Lord?

We must be balanced in our giving, our saving, and our spending. Balance is one of the most difficult things to achieve in our Christian pilgrimage, especially in America.

Final Ponderings on Giving (I promise!)

1. Give cheerfully!

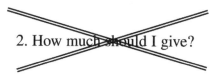

2. How much should I give?

How much should I keep?

3. When in doubt, *give,* don't hoard (Luke 12:16–21).

4. Increase my giving before increasing my lifestyle.

5. Give where you are fed (spiritually).

6. Give to those who are "feeding" others.

7. Law = 10 percent; Grace = 0 percent

Law = 10 percent; Grace = 100 percent

8. Give to the poor.

Section 3

The Brick & Mortar

"A Financial Plan"

CHAPTER 16

The Path to Financial Freedom

During my years of research, months of writing, and many nights of reading, I have asked myself one question more than any other: "What exactly is *financial freedom*"? I have read many different definitions of it in both secular and Christian books. Most all of the definitions and solutions are focused on a "black-and-white" financial answer. We like to package our answers into sound bytes that make everything seem simple. But life is not simple, nor is pursuing financial freedom an easy, simple task.

My hope is that through this book you have come to realize that financial freedom begins with a foundation that is much firmer than just your current financial situation. The solution begins with a firm foundation—Jesus Christ—and is built on Christian lifestyle principles and priorities that affect every area of your life. Financial freedom is not "more stuff." In fact, it is not just "getting out of debt." I believe that one can be out of debt and still not be living in financial liberty and freedom, especially if he or she is ignoring the other foundational issues.

As I struggled to define *financial freedom*, I began to draw. (For those of you who know my artistic abilities, you will be thankful that I was "drawing" at the computer.) I envisioned a pictorial representation of financial freedom as shown in Figure 16-1.

Figure 16-1

A Financial House in Order

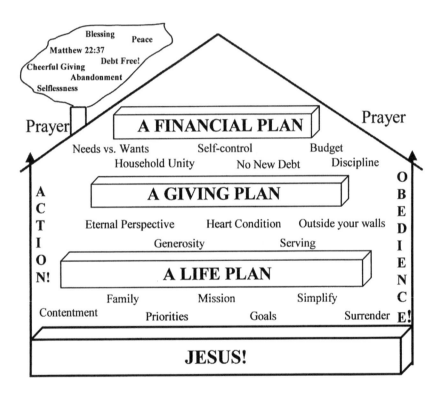

SELAH 16-1

Circle the areas in the "Financial House" (Fig. 16-1) with which you are struggling. Star the areas on which you are making some progress. Take a few minutes to reflect on and pray about these areas; ask the Lord for wisdom in moving forward. Do not be discouraged if you circled many or even most of the areas. God will assist you in your journey!

Our society has been saturated with what Wall Street and the American dreammakers have told us is financial freedom. We really should step back, look into the mirror (God's Word), and look beyond the "stuff." One of the most rewarding and fulfilling moments of our life was when we could say that we owed no man anything. We are completely and totally debt free! *That* is real freedom! We feel free. We no longer feel handcuffed. We are free to give. We are free to pursue God's dreams. But there is more to it than just owing no man anything, as the "Financial Foundation" house Figure 16-1 shows.

You are free *financially* when you

1. are completely and totally debt free (owing no man);
2. can truly feel *content* with what you have;
3. truly know that *everything*—100 percent—is God's, and you live like it;
4. give cheerfully, generously, completely, and immediately;
5. have conquered the tithe "law," are not bound by 10 percent, and give freely above that amount;
6. obey when God speaks and give sacrificially (beyond what you can foresee);
7. can properly balance temporal and eternal investments;
8. and your family are united;
9. know where your money goes (see Fig. 16-2);

10. have a plan;
11. are free from excesses;
12. live selflessly;
13. serve others *above* yourself and bear fruit for Jesus (i.e., you have an external focus); and
14. conquer the tough words: *discipline, obedience*, and *self-control.*

Do some of these goals seem unachievable? Join the club! Although we have not yet achieved all of these goals, with God's help and our own self-discipline, we have accomplished most of them. Some of these goals will require a continuous, daily challenge and struggle and will not be achieved once for all. However, we are living proof that you can and will achieve them in life—if you practice two simple (not really) things: *action* and *obedience.*

ACTION and OBEDIENCE

When you put a life plan, a giving plan, and a financial plan into place, I can assure you that you will experience incredible relief from worry and fear about your bills and debts. You will have a clear conscience before both God and others. You will have freedom from the bondage of debts, freedom from envy and covetousness, freedom from greed, and a peace that passes all understanding!

Wow! It is worth all of the effort!

- Freedom is having no credit card debt, owning your cars completely, and owning your home debt free!
- Freedom is being able to give freely and generously when God speaks!
- Freedom is being able to go to the mission field or into ministry when you are called!

After my seminars, I have talked to individuals who were in tears because they knew that they were called to "go," but knew that they could not go because of Visa and MasterCard debts and the resulting lack of freedom. If that is you, begin today. Obey today!

It has been said that the road to financial freedom is 80 percent behavior and 20 percent knowledge. Finding super investments, magical formulas, or get-rich-quick schemes is not the answer. Effective planning, setting goals, acting on those goals, giving, and discipline *are* the keys. Information first, then action! The next few chapters will give you some practical tools to assist you in planning and acting on the information that is pertinent to the financial freedom journey that is ahead of you and your family. Buckle your seat belt—here we go!

Most people want the easy way out. They want to believe that it is strictly an income problem rather than a spending problem. Most folks do not believe that they can cut any more of their "fat." For example, I was viewing the evening news, and the reporter was describing a couple who were being forced by some neighbors to remove mounds of trash and wood from the side of their house. When interviewed, the husband said that he could not afford to pay for the removal of the heaps of trash. I noticed in the background was a satellite dish, a late-model car, and some other items of value in their yard. He had money for those things; why not money to get rid of the rubbish?

We basically afford what we *want* to afford, and we spend what we *want* to spend. Obviously, some exceptions exist of which I do not want to make light, but my point is that *everyone* has *some* areas where they can cut.

Unfortunately, most of us have not looked long enough in the mirror, or we will skip the trip to the doctor, or bypass the scale in the bathroom because we do not want to deal with reality. It *might* be an income problem, but it also might be an expense problem. I contend that it is easier on "the flesh" to make more money than it is to cut expenses or change habits. Step on the financial scale. It is time to look at both the income *and* the spending.

The Most Important Couple of Financial Pages in the Book

I have talked to many people who claim that they have no way of coming up with extra money to pay off their debts. Their hands are tied. They are already cutting corners to save money, etc. In 95 percent of the cases, I respectfully disagree. Everyone has some fat to trim, some financial calories to burn—they just do not know it or really have not done the homework to validate that truth.

Prove Me Wrong!

I have challenged people to prove me wrong. I have asked every individual and couple whom I have counseled that if they hear nothing else, if they do nothing else, they *must* do the Daily Spend Sheet for at least sixty days, preferably for ninety days. I have never once been proven wrong. I practice tough love by not conducting the second counseling session unless the individual or couple has completed this exercise. It shows the degree of seriousness of their intent. Completing the Daily Spend Sheet is the closest you will come to the "magic pill" that will take care of all your financial problems. It will shed light on many problem areas and stimulate many ideas that you otherwise would not have found. It will be a major step as you begin your journey on the road to financial freedom!

One young couple whom I counseled told me that they had no "fat" to cut, and the husband said that he needed to get another job immediately. I asked them to wait for sixty days. After completing the Daily Spend Sheet, they realized they were spending *double* what they had projected on eating out and groceries and were spending in excess of $300/month on a hobby, cable, and cell phones. They were shocked. I then presented to them some alternatives to the second job that could cover their shortfall, allow them to have more time with the family, and avoid a second weekend job.

"O money, money, money, I'm not necessarily one of those who thinks thee holy, but I often stop to wonder how thou canst go out so fast when thou comest in so slowly."
—Ogden Nash

When Dana and I kicked off our personal financial journey, we continued using the Daily Spend Sheet for nearly a year because of the radical results it achieved, and we have reinitiated it when we felt our finances slipping out of control again.

A Wake-up Call!

After doing this simple exercise, I realized that I was frittering away *$1500 a year* at work on coffee, periodic lunches, and vending machine purchases. That daily pocket change added up to $1500 a year! Wow! It was a real wake-up call.

It is not always easy to begin a new daily habit. Collecting receipts and writing down all of my purchases and fast-food trips at the end of the day was tough initially, but it became simpler after a couple of weeks of discipline. They say it takes three weeks to create a new habit, and another three weeks to make it for a lifetime. If you make one financial change out of this book other than giving, it should be to complete this simple spreadsheet. I can almost guarantee that it will have a positive impact on your financial situation when the alarm clock goes off after sixty to ninety days.

"First you make a habit, then a habit makes you!"

Figure 16-2
The Daily Spend Sheet

Completing the Daily Spend Sheet for your family for two to three months is really the only way to see how much you are truly spending. We *think* that we know what we're spending, but we really do not. The tool simply documents every nickel that you spend and totals the dollars by day and by category. Many other more sophisticated tools and software exist that you might use to track your expenses, but I suggest this simple, manual method that maximizes your participation. You can enlarge this sheet, create your own, or access the full-size version at www.financialfoundationbuilders.com. Following is an example.

Figure 16-2
The Daily Spend Sheet

	1	2	3	4	5	6	7	8	9	10	11	12	13	14	15	16	17	18	19	20	21	22	23	24	25	26	27	28	29	30	Tot.
Income Categories																															
Salary 1																															
Salary 2																															
Interest/Dividends																															
Other Income																															
TOTAL INCOME																															
Income Tax																															
Total Net Income																															
Expense Categories																															
Payroll Deductions																															
Tithe/Offerings																															
Mortgage/Rent																															
Home- Maintenance																															
Home- Furniture																															
Home- Lawn/Land																															
Electricity/Gas																															
Water																															
Telephone																															
Internet/Computer																															
Groceries																															
Food- Eating Out																															
Food- Vending/Misc																															
Miscellaneous																															
Recreation/Entertain.																															
Health/Beauty																															
Medical/Dental																															
Childcare/Babysit																															
Children's Recreation																															
Allowances																															
Clubs/Organizations																															
Books/Magazines																															
Newspapers																															
Cable																															
Dry Cleaning/Laundry																															
Auto Insurance																															
House Insurance																															
Health/Life Insurance																															
Investments																															
Savings																															
401K																															
Gifts																															
Misc.- Husband																															
Misc.- Wife																															
Misc.- Children																															
Automobile Payment																															
Auto Maintenance																															
Auto Tags/Inspects																															
Gasoline/Oil																															
Vacation																															
Clothing																															
Education/Tuition																															
Credit Card #1																															
Credit Card #2																															
Credit Card #3																															
TOTAL EXPENSE																															

What is the Purpose of the Daily Spend Sheet?

⇒ To pinpoint *exactly* where your money is going.
⇒ To establish accountability for your expenditures.
⇒ To instill discipline in your financial record keeping.
⇒ To set you on your way toward financial freedom!

The output from this worksheet will have you on the road to financial freedom within a few months. The first two to three months will show you whether you are serious about breaking the chains of debt and choosing a different financial path. These first few months are also the most difficult because they require you to get out of your comfort zone and become *disciplined*.

The main purpose of this worksheet is to document where *all* of your money is going. Most people *think* that they know—until they use this document for sixty to ninety days.

> *"Be sure you know the condition of your flocks, give careful attention to your herds; for riches do not endure forever."*
> **—Proverbs 27: 23-24**

Document *all* of your expenditures *every day*. To ensure that you do not miss anything, you might want to carry a business card in your wallet to document your expenditures or a piece of paper in your purse, or record your expenses in a daily planner. You might want to identify a record keeper who will coordinate the daily summarizing of expenditures. It is important to hold family members accountable. *Keep every receipt* in case you miss a day.

You will not know what you need to change until you have a true and accurate picture of exactly where your money is going *today*. So *do not change your spending patterns* for *sixty to ninety days*. Document everything! Keep all of your receipts and explanations for all expenditures so that you can analyze your spending patterns. Have a central location (a basket or a folder) in which to keep your summary and receipts. We kept our Daily Spend Sheet on our refrigerator to remind us to update it every day.

At the end of each month, total your expenditures for each category. As you move through the record keeping, you might find that you need to add additional line items. Later, when you develop your budget, you might decide that you want to combine, add, or delete some of the categories that you are using for your Daily Spend Sheet. At the beginning, the more detail you have the better.

ACTION POINTS

1. Review Figure 16-1. Do you agree with the way that the financial house is constructed? Are you excelling in any of the three areas—a life plan, a giving plan, or a financial plan? What will you do to move from average to excellent? Has your house been upside down regarding priorities?

   _____

   _____

   _____

   _____

   _____

   _____

   _____

2. Will you commit to completing the Daily Spend Sheet for the next sixty to ninety days? How committed are you to attaining your financial freedom? On what date will you begin the Daily Spend Sheet?_____ Where will you post it?_____ Who will hold you accountable to ensure that you are keeping up?_____

3. You might start a Foundation Folder (a three-ring binder) in which to store your documents and spreadsheets. Hopefully, you will soon begin to accumulate some valuable information that you will use for months and years to come (e.g., your Life foundation, family goals, Daily Spend Sheet, and many more to come).

CHAPTER 17

Digging Out of Debt

M any people who begin the debt-payoff journey never totally solve the problem because they have not made a commitment to *no new debt!* Too many individuals file bankruptcy or get a home equity loan to pay off debt, only to dig a new hole even deeper than the first one. Rather than just saying that you will do better, it is time to get radical and say, absolutely, positively *no more credit card usage—period!* Switching to a debit card, just writing checks, or focusing on cash as much as possible will help force you into the "digging-out" discipline.

> *"The way to stop financial joy-riding is to arrest the chauffeur, not the automobile."*
> **—Woodrow Wilson**

Digging Yourself Out

If you have significant credit card debt, begin by calling and/or writing letters (see Fig. 17-1 for an example of such a letter) to customer service managers (get their names) at the credit card companies, requesting that they freeze or reduce your interest rate. Send a list of all of your current debts and your current monthly cash-flow shortfall. Ask for late fees to be eliminated. Tell them some of your sad financial story and that you are committed to paying off the debt. Inform them that once you alleviate some of your current financial debt, you will be able to make the proper payment. Send them a list of your other debts, income, and expenses that show a negative monthly cash flow. Many of the companies will work with you. Keep moving up the chain of management until you are successful. Agree to pay the reduced amount faithfully—and then do it!

Figure 17-1
Sample Creditor Letter

January 1, 2003
Moneypit Bank Credit Card Division
P.O. Box 123
Grand Rapids, MI 49503
Attention: Mr. Schwoopie

Reference: Account # 1002

Dear Credit Department Manager,

Regarding the above referenced account, we have sought financial counsel to assist us in making restitution for the amounts due. Our advisor mentioned a number of alternatives. Filing bankruptcy is an obvious solution based upon the Attachment A figures. Before we reach that decision, however, he advised that we send a letter detailing our monthly cash flow (see Attachment A). As you can see, our overall monthly shortfall for debt and the basics of life is a minimum of $_____ per month. Our overall liabilities include > $_____ for consumer debt, more than $_____ of which is credit card debt As you can see, it is impossible for us to make the minimum payments referenced, especially in light of the fact of the following circumstances: [recent layoff, recent divorce, recent health problem, repossession, etc.]

As an alternative to bankruptcy or third party intervention, we would like to attempt to make biblical restitution with our creditors, but we need your assistance. Would you please consider taking the following actions?

1. freezing all finance interest charges on the subject account and moving forward;
2. crediting our account retroactive for all of current year and previous year finance/interest charges to reduce the total balance owed;
3. freezing and reversing all past late fees retroactive to reduce the total balance owed; and
4. working with us to agree on a payment plan of $____ a month for a twelve-month period while we get back on our feet, work out a budget, and seek to increase our income. At that point, we can reevaluate based on our payment consistency.

Our desire is to pay your company back in a timely manner, but we would kindly appreciate your assistance relative to these items. We will attempt to pay back more than the $_____ per month, but we would appreciate your accommodations in working with us. Without your assistance, we will be faced with the alternative of not making the payments that we desire to make.

Thank you for your consideration of and response to this request. Feel free to call me with any questions.

Sincerely,

Name
Phone

If you have multiple, high-interest credit cards, you might consider consolidating them to one low-rate card. Do this only if you are committed to *no new debt!* Read the fine print on "no-payment-for-twelve-months" or low-rate credit cards. Fine print can often lead to big headaches. After a period of time, some "low" up-front interest rates often escalate astronomically and might be retroactive if you do not pay on time. Interest may also begin at the date of the purchase. See www.cardweb.com or www.bankrate.com for low-rate card alternatives and detailed offers.

> *"He that goes a borrowing goes a sorrowing."*
> **—Benjamin Franklin**

If you have struggled with credit card debt for more than a couple of years, I would recommend destroying all but one card (for emergency use only) and make a vow (verbal or written) not to use credit cards again until you have regained control. We destroyed all but one card and did not use it for approximately two years. Now we use credit cards for only emergencies (or frequent flier miles) and pay them off at the end of each month.

Read My Lips—No New Debt!

I have known some people who became radical in their new debt-free journey. They froze their credit cards! Then if they had a "spending bug" hit them, it would be very difficult to use the card. Others have cooked them at 350 degrees until they melted and then framed them as a reminder of their commitment. We just cut our credit cards in half and moved on.

If you desire to make your commitment to no new debt visible, I suggest that you create a "We Commit to No New Debt" certificate! Sign it and post it visibly as a reminder of your commitment. Maybe ask a friend, relative, or pastor to sign it with you to help hold you accountable.

The Debt Hit List

In parallel with completing the Daily Spend Sheet, you should take a "photograph" of how much debt you currently have. This exercise will help you determine how you want the picture to look in three months, six months, one year, three years, etc. The Debt Hit List is a simple tool that documents *all* of your current outstanding debts.

> *"A purse is doubly empty when it is full of borrowed money."*

What is the Purpose of the Debt Hit List?

⇒ To begin accountability to a specific plan for becoming debt free.

⇒ To set specific goals for specific debts.

⇒ To establish a timeframe/long-term plan to be totally and completely financially *free!*

⇒ To encourage you to end the addiction of debt.

Begin by listing each of your current debts and the total balance owed, including the following:

• credit cards,
• automobile debt,
• department store debt/lines of credit,
• student loans,
• consolidation loans,
• mortgage, and
• other consumer loans.

Also identify the current minimum payments for each debt so that you can identify your minimum monthly outlays and establish your monthly budget based on your debt payments.

Next, prioritize the payoff of your debts. Always prioritize to eliminate the *smallest* debt *first!* This will allow you both to see immediate progress and to apply the previous monthly allocation to the next highest debt as soon as it is paid off. I always recommend paying off the cards with the small balances first so that you can gain some momentum.

Set a target date for each payoff, which will help you identify major milestones: credit card payoffs, automobile payoffs, and finally the mortgage! Identify a reward for major milestones in your journey to debt freedom. You will see a snow-ball effect (the *freedom multiplier*) as you apply the amounts that you were previously paying towards numerous debts to the quickly pared-down list of debts.

You will be surprised at the momentum with which your debt payoff proceeds as you continue to add monthly dollar increases to your "freedom multiplier." Additional funds will be added to your "freedom multiplier" after sixty to ninety days of tracking daily expenditures and after establishing a budget. When you further change your spending patterns, your "freedom multiplier" will grow progressively! Soon, the days of juggling bills will be over!

I recommend requesting amortization schedules for your automobile and mortgage notes. These detailed summaries will show you how much of each of your payment is going toward principal and how much is being allocated to interest. It will also help you to set some longer-term goals for achieving total financial freedom!

As you set long-term goals (six months, one year, three years, etc.), do not get locked into these goals. Sometimes you will beat your goal, but at other times your goals will beat you. I advise that you conduct a review every three months so that you can make appropriate revisions. It is important to set both short- and long-term goals. We actually set seven-year goals with this spreadsheet because that was our target date for getting completely out of debt. It took us seven and a half years!

Figure 17-2
DEBT HIT LIST

DEBT	Total Owed	Min. Pmt.	Payoff Priority	Payoff Target	Reward	Jan. bal.	Feb. bal.	March bal.	3-mo *Goal*	Apr bal.	May bal.	Jun bal.	6-mo. *Goal*	1-yr. *Goal*	3-yr *Goal*
Visa	100	20	1	15-Jan	Lunch	0	0	0	0				0	0	0
MasterCard	300	25	2	15-Feb	Dinner	250	50	0	0				0	0	0
Sears	500	30	3	1-Apr	Dinner	475	445	200	150				0	0	0
Foleys	500	30	4	1-Jun	$50	475	450	420	450				0	0	0
Target	750	45	5	1-Sep	$50	725	690	655	650				300	0	0
Best Buy	900	50	6	1 yr	Hotel	875	835	790	750				500	0	0
Carpet World	1000	75	7	18 mo.	Bed & Brk	950	900	840	800				600	300	0
Automobile	5000	300	8	2 yrs	$100	4800	4575	4350	4400				4000	3000	0
Truck	7000	350	9	3 yrs	Vacation	6800	6570	6300	6500				6100	5750	0
Mortgage	75000	900	10	7 years	Cruise	74950	74885	74800	74900				74700	74000	72000
Total Debt	91050	1825				90300	89400	88355	88600				86200	83050	72000

This exercise will not only help you set goals for you finances but also show you how much you are currently paying out monthly toward debt. I would highly recommend keeping this goal chart visible to the entire family and updating it faithfully every month. With your budget, it is your main scorecard to show results and progress from your financial actions.

SELAH 17-1

Complete your own Debt Hit List. You can use the blank worksheet in the Appendix or create one yourself. You might not be able to solidify your goal columns until you have ninety days' worth of daily expenditures tracked and a budget established.

When you better understand your expenditures (Daily Spend Sheet), know what you owe (Debt Hit List), and have set goals for paying off the debts (Debt Hit List goals), you are ready for the next critical tools: the Big-Ticket List, the Cash-Only Control List, the Save-to-Spend List, and finally *the budget!* NOTE: I would recommend revisiting your debt pay-off target dates and amounts after you conclude the next chapter.

Act Now!

Procrastination is a "failure to act," or a "putting off of what should be done today." Are you procrastinating anything? Don't procrastinate; do it *now!*

ACTION POINTS

1. What is financial freedom to you? Ask your spouse or family members.

   _____

   _____

   _____

   _____

   _____

   _____

   _____

2. Have you set goals for paying off your debts? _____
   When do you believe that you can be completely and totally debt free? _____ How much are you paying in total interest every year? _____

3. Review the goals that you set in Chapter 2. Do they need some updating based on your "real debt situation"? Do they need some updating based on changes to your giving goals?

   _____

   _____

   _____

   _____

   _____

   _____

4. Are you committed to NO NEW DEBT?

   _____

   _____

   _____

CHAPTER 18

Determining Your Destiny

In 1994, the Public Agenda Foundation conducted a study on retirement needs and planning.[1] The survey found four financial personality profiles that influence how we spend our money. Each of us must come to grips with how one's personality affects the way we spend our money. Go get the mirror; it is time to take a peek.

1. **Impulsive spenders**—have trouble denying themselves, worry little about the future, live for today.
2. **Strugglers**—fearful, overwhelmed, think that things are out of their control.
3. **Deniers**—refuse to worry, blindly optimistic, waiting on a rescue, avoid reality of debt.
4. **Planners**—know exactly what their goals are, have clear anticipation of the future, know where they spend their money, use debt cautiously if it all.

Each of the profiles contains some key words that can have a major impact on your destiny.

Key Words

Deny self—We discussed self-control, patience, and saying no in earlier chapters.

Future—The future will be here before you know it. You must plan and prepare!

Today—We must live for not only today but also tomorrow.

Fear—We cannot be controlled by fear; rather, we must take control of fear and give it to God.

Control—You must take *more* control over your finances—or *others* will!

Worry—Worrying about tomorrow is not biblical; planning for it is!

Optimistic— Optimistic and blindly optimistic are not the same. Be realistically optimistic.

Rescue—Someone else will not rescue you. You must take the lead.

Reality—Being a realist and dealing with the issues is the most important first step.

Goals—The worksheets in this and other chapters will help you target your goals.

Where—As was discussed in Chapter 16, you must know *where* your money is going!

SELAH 18-1

Take a few minutes to jot down which of the four personality profiles best describes you? What about your spouse, other family members, and your parents? Do you see in them some of the same traits that you "learned" during your upbringing? Are you passing on those traits to the next generation? What are you doing to change some of the "negative" traits?

_____

_____

_____

With which of the preceding key words do you struggle most? Take a minute to pray, asking the Lord to help you in these areas. _____

_____

_____

SELAH 18-2
Honesty Check

Call it a hassle check or an accountability check. You might recall the quotation from Herbert Spencer in the introduction of the book: "The great aim of education is not knowledge, but action." Question: Have you *acted* yet regarding to starting the Daily Spend Sheet? Will you use it for at least sixty days? If you answered no, why not?

_____ a. I am already financially free.

_____ b. I am reading this book as a favor—the author is my friend/family.

_____ c. I do not need to cut my expenses—I have already cut them to the bone.

_____ d. It takes too much discipline, too much work—I do not have time.

_____ e. I need to focus on more income, not less expenses.

_____ f. I am lazy and a procrastinator—I will get to it next month (maybe).

Most people never begin the journey. They feel better about studying, reading and attending seminars, but they never take the big step—*changing, improving.* I usually hear that letter (c)—"I have already cut them to the bone"—is the most common reason people will not record every nickel that they spend for sixty days. If that is your answer, I say that you are wrong. We can *all* cut expenses somewhere. It might not be the entire answer, but you will really never know until you try it! I have never had anyone confess to option (f), but, to be honest, that was *my* reason for delaying.

Get the mirror out. I challenge you to try the Daily Spend Sheet for sixty to ninety days, and see if you discover any surprises. Reread Chapter 16 if you need a jumpstart!

One of the major areas of planning that people avoid is preparing for their *major expenditures*. They usually avoid this area for a couple of reasons. First, if they analyzed it too much, they would realize that they really could not afford many "big-ticket" items. Many people are just struggling to pay their current bills, and they want to avoid the reality of the necessity of cutting back on some expenses. Second, most people do not plan more than a week ahead in their finances anyway.

Reasons for planning major expenditures abound, but the most important one is to do a reality check and see if you can afford the items you want to buy or if you might need to re-prioritize your needs/desires.

Why the Big-Ticket List?

⇒ To avoid surprises that will cause you to slip into the credit trap.
⇒ To prioritize your major expenditures.
⇒ To look toward the future so that you can save in advance.
⇒ To help you spend less than you make!

The entire family should generate this list annually. It should include all potential "big-ticket items" that you expect to purchase during the next twelve to eighteen months. (See the example in Figure 18-1.) After you have completed the list, you should target an expenditure *month* and an estimated *cost*. After your budget is complete and you have an idea of your cash flow situation, this list will give you an idea of what you can afford and cannot afford. This list will also help you differentiate between your *wants* and *needs!* After the Big-Ticket List is complete, everyone involved should agree on a priority order and an estimated timeframe for the purchases. You will almost always find that your desires exceed what you can afford. This is where self-control and prioritizing come into play.

Figure 18-1

BIG TICKET LIST

Priority	Item	Month	Cost
2	Lawn mower	April	$ 300
8	DVD player	February	$ 200
12	Entertainment center	April	$ 1,000
7	Join health club	January	$ 300
3	Paint house	May	$ 1,000
1	25th anniversary present	June	$ 300
4	Weekend trip to San Antonio	June	$ 500
5	Tires	July	$ 300
9	Car for daughter	September	$ 2,000
10	Carpet	October	$ 2,000
11	Landscape backyard	August	$ 500
6	Computer	February	$ 2,000
13	Caribbean cruise	November	$ 3,500

Expenditure totals   **$13,900**

Monthly savings required   **(18 months)**   **$772**

SELAH 18-3

Complete your own Big-Ticket List for the next eighteen months. Use the blank example in Appendix C or the one at www.financialfoundationbuilders.com. After you've made the list, estimate an amount and the month when you plan to spend the money. Total the amounts and divide by eighteen to come up with the monthly savings required, just as Figure 18-1 depicts. You will use this information later.

Usually after completing this list, people experience a little bout of depression after looking at the monthly amount required to cover the "big buys." That is an indication that you might need to adjust your spending patterns. Figure 18-1 shows some seemingly "normal" things for a middle-class American family. The first problem is that the "normal" middle-class American family does not *need* much of what it has or does. Second, the "normal" family is waist deep in debt.

We should not be the "norm." Is a Caribbean cruise evil? No. If it comes before obedient giving to others, or if you are not able to pay cash, however, then maybe that goal should be changed to a weekend family camping trip or postponed until the thirtieth anniversary party. Is the entertainment center wrong? Maybe or maybe not. Maybe the timing is wrong. Maybe you can find one for three hundred dollars? Nothing is wrong with making major purchases; the key is in the timing of them.

You should update the Big-Ticket List at least every three months because priorities do change and new desires always come to mind. This list should be a living, breathing, ever-changing document. The key is flexibility! Include the items on this list in your annual budget and in both your Save-to-Spend List (which we will discuss shortly) so that you can save money appropriately on a monthly basis to purchase these items outright rather than use credit. You might want to include these items as separate budget line items if they are major.

Think Before You Buy!

Always ask the following questions before making a major purchase:

1. Is it on our Big-Ticket List?
2. Should I discuss it with the rest of the family? (Set a minimum dollar amount that *requires* family approval before purchase. We use $50.)
3. Can we afford it?
4. Do we need it *now?*
5. Can it wait until next year? How long can we delay the purchase?
6. Can we buy it used?

7. Is it on sale?
8. Have I priced it multiple times so that I know what a *great* price is?
9. Have I waited sixty days once I get the desire to buy a Big-Ticket item?
10. Is it a *want* or a *need?*
11. Have I prayed about it?
12. Will this purchase affect my giving priorities and commitments?
13. What will I need to give up or sacrifice as a result of making this purchase?

One pastor (or maybe it was his wife) asked me to devise a clever way for him to remember some of these questions while he was shopping. One simple way to capture a few of the key questions is the "debt test." Ask the following four questions before you binge!

THE D.E.B.T. TEST

D = Is it a Desire or a need?

E = Is it of Eternal value?

B = Is it Budgeted?

T = Is the Timing right?

When I purchase something that is outside of my normal budget, I often go through a thought process that asks some additional questions, including the following.

- What will I get in return for this purchase?
- Will I really get my money's worth, or is it an impulse purchase?
- What kind of eternal impact will it have?
- How does it line up with the goals that I set earlier?

"That for which I long becomes that to which I belong."
—Richard A. Swenson

SELAH 18-4

Using the D.E.B.T. test, take a break and go back to your personal "Big-Ticket" List. How many of those items can you identify as a "D"? An "E"? A "B"? A "T"? This exercise might help you reshuffle the priorities on the list.

Cash Control!

Independent financial advisor Dave Ramsey references a recent Dun and Bradstreet study that showed that you *spend as much as 64 percent more when using credit cards versus spending cash.* "You do not emotionally register the pain that you do when you lay down cash. When you use cash it hurts and you tend to spend less. Cash is visual and emotional and a great behavioral management tool."[2] That is reason enough to manage a portion of your expenses with cash. The Cash Control list will definitely help you with items that you or your spouse think need near-term attention based on the results of your sixty to ninety days of using your Daily Spend Sheet. These items usually will be categories in which you spend more than you think you do. They are areas for which you might use ATM cash: hobby areas, impulse purchases, or time-saving purchases (fast food, coffee, lunches, etc.).

After Dana and I completed our Daily Spend Sheet for six months, I realized that I needed an "allowance" for certain areas. When the "allowance" is gone—it is gone!

This is not necessary for every expense area, but it is necessary for some areas. My vending machine weakness could have paid off three credit cards in a short period of time! We discovered that we needed to make some immediate changes.

"If you can't pay as you go, you are going too fast!"

Why the Cash-Only Control List?

⇒ To aid you in monitoring specific budget line items.
⇒ To help you develop new spending habits and to break you of your old habits.
⇒ To make your money more difficult to part with. (Cash is harder to spend than credit!)
⇒ To focus you on specific areas that can quickly affect your debt pay-off plan.

Cash control does not need to be a permanent part of your freedom plan, but you should use it until you get a firm grip on your spending and budget. A one-year focus on cash and no new debt might be realistic. Accountability is extremely important to ensure success in this area. We all have weaknesses; leaning on someone else's strengths can help us identify and deal with our "blind spots." A little friendly debate and compromise within the family will most certainly need to occur on the specific items that might require a "cash focus," especially when you are establishing the actual dollar amounts! Be gentle! To avoid too much conflict, you might want to start conservatively and then get more aggressive as you pursue debt reduction!

You should develop the Cash-Only Control List (see Fig. 18-2) after you have monitored your Daily Spend Sheet activity for a couple of months and you know exactly where your money is going. This is necessary so that your initial cash decisions will be realistic and not overly challenging. Setting expectations that are too high could cause you to give up out of frustration. Include this list as part of your overall budget, which we will cover in Chapter 19.

Typically, the types of items that should be included in the Cash-Only Control List are those that fit into one or more of the following categories:

◊ areas for which you currently spend cash,
◊ areas where you see an opportunity to reduce your expenditures but need to train yourself to live by a budget, and
◊ another family member thinks that your expenditures might be excessive in this area. (Be nice!)

You will want to develop the Cash-Only Control List as a family, but typical items to be included are the following:

- recreation/entertainment,
- dining out,
- vending machine purchases/coffee,
- groceries,
- books/magazines/music,
- hobbies,
- clothing,
- health/beauty,
- allowances, and
- miscellaneous. (Beware of lumping too much into this category!)

After you have identified the areas that need a cash focus, agree on some preliminary amounts for each category and create a storage location for your cash accounts. Storage ideas include envelopes, cookie jars, Pringles cans, and soup cans. Label each account separately and include a detailed expenditure list nearby to monitor your spending for each item. You might want to assign family members to each account to increase accountability.

Figure 18-2
Cash-Only Control List

Cash-Only Accounts	JAN 1–15	JAN 16–31	FEB 1–15	FEB16–28	MAR 1–15	MAR16–31
Groceries—Bought	200	200				
Food—Eating out	25	25				
Food—Vending/misc.	20	20				
Recreation	25	25				
Entertainment	20	20				
Health/beauty	15	15				
Allowances	25	25				
Clothing	50	50				
Books/magazines	10	10				
Misc.—Husband	20	20				
Misc.—Wife	20	20				
Misc.—Kids	10	10				
Hobby	10	10				
TOTAL CASH ACCT's	450	450				

Figure 18-2 identifies thirteen "envelopes" that need to be created with funds of $450 every two weeks. Once paychecks are received, the cash should be allocated to each envelope or storage location *immediately!* The more accounts that you manage by cash, the better control you will have over your spending. It would be best to start with too many envelopes rather than too few. You can always cut back later.

The beauty (or frustration) of this system is that when your monthly allocation of cash is gone, *it is gone!* This exercise will help wean you from credit and can actually be fun if you have a competitive nature. Flexibility is key. If your envelope or jar is empty in one account and you want to dip into another, that is perfectly okay. However, if this is a consistent occurrence, you might want to adjust your budget, which will occur frequently early on. You might want to make notes and keep accurate balances on whichever envelope from which you borrow.

You should include the items on the Cash-Only List in your annual budget, which will need to be modified as you better understand your expenditures. We will discuss the dreaded "B" word in more detail later.

Dana and I used about ten "cash" envelopes and simply wrote the name of each "Cash Account" on the respective envelopes. Payday occurred every two weeks, so we put the same amount in the envelopes every two weeks and began to establish discipline in the areas with which we were struggling. Do not go overboard and pay for your mortgage or car note with cash! It is unwise to keep thousands of dollars of cash in your mattress or envelopes! Address only the pertinent areas over which you need extra control as we discussed earlier.

Opinions may differ within the family about which accounts should be handled with cash. You might consider using a quick spreadsheet to come to some sort of agreement on the categories, how important each is to your future financial freedom, the priority (high, medium, low) of each category, and the amounts to be considered for each category (see Fig. 18-3). The purpose of the priority is to help understand better how strongly your spouse feels about the necessity of making a spending change in a particular category.

We did not decide upon our cash-only items until we had used the Daily Spend Sheet for sixty to ninety days. You need to see actual expenses before you take a wild guess and have a meaningless family feud!

Figure 18-3
Cash Control List Decision Spreadsheet

Spending category	Husband	$/mo	Wife	$/mo	Agreement
Clothing	High	$30	Low	$100	$50/mo
Recreation—Golf/ baseball	Low	$100	High	$30	$50/mo
Eating out	Med.	$50	Med.	$50	$50/mo

SELAH 18-5

Take a first cut at your Cash-Only Control List (similar to Figure 18-2). You might use Figure 18-3 to get your spouse's input! A blank form is available in Appendix C, or you could use one available at www.financialfounda-tionbuilders.com. After completing your Daily Spend Sheet (Figure 16-2) for a couple of months, you will know which items over which you need tighter control. Create envelopes for these items, take the monthly (or biweekly) amount, and distribute it into the labeled envelope, and get started! You have now taken some major steps toward financial freedom!

Save-to-Spend List

Another area of struggle for some people is nonregular expenses that seemingly pop up at the worst possible time. Money for such expenses usually is not available because most people typically do not save regularly for such expenses. A local newspaper conducted a survey after Christmas and asked how many people had actually saved money for their Christmas gifts in advance and paid cash for them. The response was only 27 percent.[3] We know that these "nonregular" expenses are coming. Many of them occur on the same day and time each year; yet, we do not plan accordingly. We do not limit our spending when we are fully aware that we cannot pay cash for them. Some typical examples of such expenses include the following:

- insurance,
- home improvement,
- furniture,
- Christmas gifts,
- other gifts,
- automobile maintenance and tags,
- vacation,
- pet,
- medical, and
- some of the "Big-Ticket" items listed in Figure 18-1.

Generate your "save-to-spend list" for those expenses that occur nonregularly throughout the year. This list actually will be part of your budget and should be adjusted accordingly as you become more familiar with your spending patterns and cash flow. (Some examples of items that could be included in this type of savings are included in the sample budget to be discussed later.)

Why the Save-to-Spend List?

⇒ To save money for expenses that you know will occur through-out the year.
⇒ To plan for those minisurprises.
⇒ To help you avoid borrowing from others (and paying interest) and to begin borrowing from yourself.
⇒ To encourage you to live within your means.

Many of these items might not show up on your Daily Spend Sheet for the first sixty to ninety days because of the timing of the billing or expenditure. Some of them might require an estimate until you get a handle on your actual expenses.

Figure 18-4

Save-to-Spend Balance Spreadsheet

Save to Spend Balances	JAN 1–15	JAN 16–31	FEB 1–15	FEB16–28	MAR 1–15	MAR16–31
Home—Maintenance	15	30				
Home—Improvements	15	30				
Home—Furniture	20	40				
Home—Lawn	15	30				
Computer software	10	20				
Medical/dental	30	60				
Clubs/organizations	5	10				
Auto insurance	50	100				
Gifts account	40	80				
Auto—Maintenance	30	60				
Auto—Tags/inspects	10	20				
Vacation account	100	200				
Pet account	10	20				
TOTAL SAVE TO SPEND	350	700				

This example identifies thirteen nonregular spending accounts that need a plan for which to save money. The estimated total amounts are $350 every two weeks. Note: This list is different from a "Save-to-Invest" account in that you will access these accounts weekly. You need the flexibility to borrow from different accounts as needed, especially early on in your financial planning. The reality of your financial situation might be such that you cannot afford all of the items on this list. You might need to reduce these items or delay some of your "Big-Ticket" items until your debt is paid off or reduced significantly. Radical changes might be necessary in some cases.

Even if you cannot currently afford to save for these items now, you will be able to do so within a few months as you reduce your debt. This goal can be achieved through changes made in your spending patterns and by implementing the savings ideas that will be addressed in future chapters.

SELAH 18-6

Take a first cut at a Save-to-Spend Account List like the one in Figure 18-4. Go back to your Big-Ticket List (Figure 18-1) and your Daily Spend Sheet (Figure 16-2) to help generate your list.

Save-to-Spend Account Activity Sheet

You should keep a separate "Account Activity" sheet for each "Save-to-Spend" item to monitor activity and increase your discipline to save for specific items. For example, if your $1200 insurance premium is due on June 30, you should be saving $100 per month toward this account. If you have estimated that you will spend $1000 on gifts per year, you will need to save approximately $80 per month toward this account.

Figure 18-5 details an example of deposits and expenses for two months for a home maintenance account. Note the February 18 activity for which insufficient funds had been saved, thereby necessitating a "loan" from the vacation account that must be paid back later. (A blank form for this purpose is provided in Appendix C or is available on the Internet at www.financialfoundationbuilders.com).

Figure 18-5

Save-to-Spend Account Activity Sheet

ACCOUNT: Home Maintenance   Amount/check: $15

DATE	TRANSACTION DESCRIPTION	DEPOSIT	WITHDRAW	BALANCE
15-Jan	Home Maintenance—Deposit	$ 15.00		$ 15.00
31-Jan	Home Maintenance—Deposit	$ 15.00		$ 30.00
4-Feb	Withdrawal—Paint for kid's room		$ 23.00	$ 7.00
15-Feb	Home maintenance—Deposit	$ 15.00		$ 22.00
18-Feb	Withdrawal—Fertilizer, saw blade		$ 29.00	$ (7.00)
18-Feb	Borrow from vacation account	$ 7.00		-
28-Feb	Home maintenance—Deposit	$ 15.00		$ 15.00
28-Feb	Payback vacation account		$ 7.00	$ 8.00

SELAH 18-7
Save to Spend

Create a separate account sheet for each Save-to-Spend item (see Figure 18-5).

The simplest way to budget these items is to estimate your annual expenditures and then divide by twelve and save that amount in a separate account. Instead of borrowing from the creditors when you have a nonregular expense, borrow from yourself. Do not get discouraged if you have to modify your Save-to-Spend account list frequently or if you have to borrow from one account. Just continue to keep good records and pay back your borrowings. You will *always* have unplanned expenses. This activity just helps you learn to plan for them.

"Make all you can, save all you can, give all you can."
—John Wesley

The best way to separate these funds and accounts is initially to set up a separate money market or checking account so that you will not be tempted to dip into this account regularly. Larry Burkett's *Money Matters* software has a great envelope system if you prefer that to the manual spreadsheets. One major caution is that by not having a separate account for your "Save-to-Spend" items you might be setting yourself up to be tempted, especially if you lack discipline as I did. I recommend opening a separate checking account as soon as you have enough extra monthly money to begin saving for your "Save-to-Spend" items.

All three of these lists (Big Ticket, Cash Control, and Save to Spend), coupled with your Daily Spend Sheet data, will be combined to form your budget! You are 90 percent complete with the dreaded task of developing your budget, which will help you *determine your destiny!* Other than living on your budget, the hard part is nearly done. Keep reading to finalize your plan, which is the subject of the next chapter.

ACTION POINTS

1. Because this was SELAH STOP paradise, we have already discussed most of the actions in this chapter. If it seems too overwhelming, spread it out and do only one task at a time.

   _____ Complete the Big-Ticket List.
   _____ Complete the Cash-Control List.
   _____ Complete the Save-to-Spend List and the
   account sheets.

2. Start your "cash" journey by creating the cash envelopes for the items that you have identified as needing an immediate change and more self-control. In conjunction with this task, *pray for self-control!*

CHAPTER 19

The Dreaded "B" Word— Budget!

This is one of the most frightening words in the English language. Someone has estimated that only 3 percent of Americans actually have a budget. Most people have attempted a budget at one time or another in their lives, but then they drop it altogether after they failed at that single attempt. If a budget is unrealistic and cannot be achieved, it is nothing more than a piece of paper. However, if the tool is used correctly it can be a rudder for your family finances. That does not mean that you will face no wind or waves. It does not mean that you will not sometimes get off course. It does not even guarantee that an unforeseen storm will not capsize the ship. It does, however, provide direction and guidance and, as we discussed in Section 1 of the book, it is your financial plan on paper.

The budget is the one document that addresses your life plan (your priorities), your giving plan (your tithes, offerings, and missions giving), and your financial plan. It ties them all together. It should also encompass your long-term goals. For example, if your plan is to get out of debt in five years, then the budget should include a line for each debt with a pay-off plan for each. If your goal is to give 15 percent of your income within five years, the budget should include a line that addresses to whom you want to give and how much. If you have a goal of helping to pay for your child's education in three years, then the budget should include a line for that, etc.

Why?

People have asked many times, "Why do I need a budget?" I believe that a few significant reasons exist for a budget, including the following:

- to know where your money is going.
- to set specific goals and promote accountability for achieving them.
- to have a roadmap (a plan) linked directly to your goals.
- to offer a realistic assessment of where you are today and what changes you need to make. (It will hold you accountable for what changes you are planning.)
- to stimulate communication with your spouse and family on priorities. (This can be painful but is necessary.)

Ease the Squeeze

I believe that just *having a plan* would be a great way to ease the squeeze of stress on an individual's or a family's finances. Having a clear set of financial and personal goals does wonders. Many people spend more time planning their vacation or their technology toy purchase than they do their financial future. If you just do not have the energy or skill to create one, then get some help. If you cannot find someone locally, I offer "e-coaching" for those desiring more one-on-one attention.

Payback?!

Some of the benefits of a budget are obvious, as we've discussed (having a plan, knowing where your money is going, etc.), but other benefits are more practical, including the following:

- to plan for unforeseen expenses.
- to help plan and save for raising children. (Estimated costs for raising a child over a lifetime range from $200,000–300,000.)
- to plan and save for economic uncertainty.
- to pay cash for major expenditures (vacations, gifts, autos, home improvement, big-ticket items, etc.).
- to prepare for retirement, career changes, or a job layoff.
- to plan and save for emergency medical needs.
- to reduce debt quickly and purposefully (financial freedom!).
- to position yourself to be able to give generously, cheerfully, and flexibly.
- to build family unity.
- to plan and save for the children's education.

You can actually *begin* a draft budget after you have tracked your expenditures for at least sixty to ninety days on the Daily Spend Sheet (see Figure 16-2). Your entire family should formulate the budget and agree to abide by it to the best of their abilities (no need to sign in blood). If the budget becomes too rigid, you might have a disgruntled family member quit the plan. Start your budget conservatively and adjust some of your obvious spending patterns as necessary. If you are too aggressive, you might get frustrated and give up altogether. Unity is the key to establishing this budget.

Your budget will be the most important document by which the family will live (other than the Bible) and will be critical for both short- and long-term planning. It also should be flexible enough to change quarterly, if necessary, based on your progress and increased understanding of your spending patterns. Above all, *your budget must be realistic!*

You should set both short- and long-term goals. When do you want to be debt free? Keep referring to the debt goals that you set in Figure 17-1. What will you do with upcoming raises? What big-ticket items are a priority? Are your Save-to-Spend and Big-Ticket Lists tied into your budget? As you become more familiar with your spending and accounts, you might want to streamline and/or combine your budget items. You do not want to make this a full-time effort.

Budget Characteristics

Your budget should be:

- realistic,
- attainable,
- challenging (less challenging early on and more challenging down the road), and
- specific (especially in the first year).

The following budget is a sample generated from the "Daily Spend Sheet," the "Debt Hit List," the "Big-Ticket List," the "Save-to-Spend List," and the "Cash-only Control List." Note that some categories have been combined so that the document is not three pages long. I would suggest more detail in the beginning and then combining some accounts down the road after you are more comfortable with understanding your spending. In fact, our very first list of budget categories was almost identical to the Daily Spend Sheet in Figure 16-2. However, because I was paid every two weeks, we changed the daily columns to an "every-two-weeks" plan.

Figure 19-1
Sample Budget

INCOME CATEGORIES	FEB 1-15	FEB16-28	MAR 1-15	MAR16-31	APR1-15	APR16-30	MAY1-15	MAY16-31
Salary 1	1750	1750	1750	1750	1750	1750	1850	1850
Salary 2	750	750	750	750	750	750	750	750
Interest	10	10	10	10	10	10	10	10
Other income	250	250	250	250	250	250	250	250
INCOME BEFORE TAXES	2760	2760	2760	2760	2760	2760	2860	2860
Income tax	675	675	675	675	675	675	695	695
INCOME AFTER TAXES	2085	2085	2085	2085	2085	2085	2165	2165

S=Save to Spend, C=Cash

EXPENSE CATEGORIES	FEB 1-15	FEB16-28	MAR 1-15	MAR16-31	APR1-15	APR16-30	MAY1-15	MAY16-31
Payroll deductions	140	140	90	90	90	90	90	90
Tithe/offerings	300	300	300	300	300	300	310	310
Auto insurance (S)	50	50	50	50	50	50	50	50
Mortgage/rent	900	0	900	0	900	0	900	0
Home—Maintenance/Misc (S)	65	65	50	50	50	50	50	50
Utilities/phone/Internet	0	300	0	280	0	280	0	280
Groceries—Bought (C)	200	200	180	180	180	180	180	180
Food—Eat out/vending (C)	55	55	30	20	30	20	30	20
Recreation/entertain (C)	45	45	25	25	25	25	25	25
Health/beauty (C)	10	10	10	10	10	10	10	10
Childcare/babysitting (C)	60	60	60	50	60	50	60	50
Investments	25	25	0	0	0	0	0	0
Children's recreation (C)	10	10	5	5	5	5	5	5
Books/clubs/newspaper (C)	10	10	5	5	5	5	5	5
Cable	0	25	0	0	0	0	0	0
Gifts (S)	40	40	30	30	30	30	30	30
Misc.—Husband (C)	10	10	5	5	5	5	5	5
Misc.—Wife (C)	10	10	5	5	5	5	5	5
Misc.—Children (C)	10	10	5	0	5	0	5	0
Automobile payment	0	500	0	500	0	500	0	500
Auto maintenance (S)	30	30	30	30	30	30	30	30
Auto tags/inspects (S)	10	10	10	10	10	10	10	10
Vacation (S)	100	100	50	50	50	50	50	50
Clothing—Husband (C)	20	20	15	15	15	15	15	15
Clothing—Wife (C)	25	25	20	20	20	20	20	20
Clothing—Children (C)	15	15	10	10	10	10	10	10
Education/tuition	50	50	50	50	50	50	50	50
Pet expense (S)	10	10	10	10	10	10	10	10
Medical/dental (S)	30	30	30	30	30	30	30	30
Credit card #1	0	15	0	80	0	0	0	0
Credit card #2	0	20	0	260	0	0	0	0
Credit card #3	0	25	0	25	0	365	0	495
TOTAL EXPENSE	2230	2215	1975	2180	1975	2280	1985	2385
INCOME LESS EXPENSE	-145	-130	110	-110	110	-110	180	-180

DEBT BALANCES								
Credit card #1	90	90	80	80	0	0	0	0
Credit card #2	285	285	270	270	0	0	0	0
Credit card #3	980	980	960	960	940	590	590	100
Automobile	4800	4800	4600	4600	4400	4400	4200	3950
Mortgage*	74975	74975	74950	74950	74925	74925	74900	74900
TOTAL DEBT	81130	81130	80860	80860	80300	79860	79635	78850

*Note how little of your mortgage payment actually goes to the principal. Order your amortization schedule if you have not already done so.

Figure 19-1A
Save-to-Spend and Cash-Only Accounts

Pull out the Cash (C) and Save to Spend (S) items, and open a separate account for your Save-to-Spend items if you can. If not, begin to attack your debt so that you can do so later. Also, hopefully you have initiated a cash envelope management system for the Cash-Only Accounts, as we discussed in Chapter 18.

SAVE-TO-SPEND ACCOUNT	FEB 1-15	FEB16-28	MAR 1-15	MAR16-31	APR1-15	APR16-30	MAY1-15	MAY16-31
Home—Maintenance (S)	15	15	15	15	15	15	15	15
Home—Improvements (S)	15	15	15	15	15	15	15	15
Home—Furniture (S)	20	20	20	20	20	20	20	20
Home—Lawn (S)	15	15	15	15	15	15	15	15
Home—Other (S)	0	0	0	0	0	0	0	0
Medical/dental (S)	30	30	30	30	30	30	30	30
Other payroll deductions (S)	0	0	0	0	0	0	0	0
Auto insurance (S)	50	50	50	50	50	50	50	50
Gifts account (S)	40	40	30	30	30	30	30	30
Auto—Maintenance (S)	30	30	30	30	30	30	30	30
Auto—Tags/inspects (S)	10	10	10	10	10	10	10	10
Vacation account (S)	100	100	100	100	100	100	100	100
Pet account (S)	10	10	10	10	10	10	10	10
TOTAL SAVE TO SPEND	335	335	325	325	325	325	325	325

CASH-ONLY ACCOUNTS	FEB 1-15	FEB16-28	MAR 1-15	MAR16-31	APR1-15	APR16-30	MAY1-15	MAY16-31
Groceries—Bought (C)	200	200	180	180	180	180	180	180
Food—Eating out (C)	25	25	15	15	15	15	15	15
Food—Vending/misc (C)	20	20	5	5	5	5	5	5
Food—Ordering in (C)	10	10	10	0	10	0	10	0
Recreation (C)	25	25	15	15	15	15	15	15
Entertainment (C)	20	20	10	10	10	10	10	10
Health/beauty (C)	10	10	10	10	10	10	10	10
Childcare/babysitting (C)	60	60	60	50	60	50	60	50
Children's recreation (C)	10	10	5	5	5	5	5	5
Books/clubs/newspaper (C)	10	10	5	5	5	5	5	5
Misc.—Husband (C)	10	10	5	5	5	5	5	5
Misc.—Wife (C)	10	10	5	5	5	5	5	5
Misc.—Children (C)	10	10	5	0	5	0	5	0
Clothing—Husband (C)	20	20	15	15	15	15	15	15
Clothing—Wife (C)	25	25	20	20	20	20	20	20
Clothing—Children (C)	15	15	10	10	10	10	10	10
TOTAL CASH TO W/D	480	480	375	355	375	355	375	355

The Figure 19-1 budget example is a fairly typical example whereby the family sets a budget and then realizes a month later that a few changes must be made because they cannot continue to spend more than they make. This family is spending $275/month more than it makes (–145 for the first two weeks in February and –130 for the second two weeks of the month). Thus, on March 1 you will see some budget changes noted by a box and bold-faced type. Note that many of the changes are in the "cash-only control" accounts. This family reduced its "planned" cash expenditures from $960/month ($480 every two weeks) to $730/month ($375 and $355 every two weeks, respectively). This is a budget reduction of $230 that was immediately put toward Credit Cards 1 and 2 to pay them off by April. They would then apply what they were paying on Card 1 and Card 2 toward the Card 3 debt in April and May. It becomes a snow-ball effect simply by reducing a few dollars here and there on specific accounts that you can affect.

This example budget in Figure 19-1 is extremely aggressive, but it is purposefully planned to be aggressive for three months until all credit card debt is paid off. Then some budget categories are reinstated.

After this family completed a first cut budget (Figure 19-1, February), they realized that they needed to cut some items to make income equal expenses. They took the following actions:

- reduced $100/month from their 401k (payroll deductions) until the credit card debt was paid off,
- reduced $30/month from home projects (put some projects on hold),
- reduced $20/month from the Cell phone/Internet account by cutting back on phone usage,
- reduced $40/month from Groceries by clipping coupons and shopping sales,
- reduced $60/month from Eating out and Vending expenditures by packing their own lunches,
- reduced $40/month from Recreation and entertainment by staying home more and having family nights,
- reduced $10/month from Babysitting by staying home more and taking the kids with them more,
- reduced $50/month from the College savings accounts until their

debts are paid off (Investments),
- reduced $10/month from Children's recreation until the credit cards are paid off,
- reduced $10/month by canceling magazine subscriptions and book club membership,
- reduced $25/month by canceling cable until the automobiles are paid off,
- reduced $20/month by making a few gifts and simplifying,
- reduced $35/month from the Misc. expenses/other account,
- reduced $100/month from Vacations (postponed long vacation),
- reduced $30/month from clothing accounts,
- paid off Credit Card 1 immediately,
- paid off Credit Card 2 in three months, and
- reduced Credit Card 3 to $100 owed in four months.

Wow! Major changes! But this family was serious about making quick and substantial changes. Your actions obviously will vary depending upon your life, giving, and financial priorities. A few bucks here and there do not seem like much individually, but in this example when they are added up, they total > $500/month in savings. This example, however, is not your yardstick; yours might be higher or lower.

It is also extremely important to plan your pay raises. Many people get annual raises, and the money seemingly disappears into the checking account with too much month left at the end of the money. The family in our example is planning for an expected raise on May 1. The net increase of $160/month is planned for increases to Tithes/offerings and increases toward the credit card and automobile debt.

Before making quick assumptions on your budget changes (see the earlier March 1 changes), I highly recommend sitting down and preparing a quick worksheet (See SELAH 19-2) to ensure family unity regarding the budget changes. Your spouse's priorities might be different than yours. Your children's priorities will be different than yours, and what a great training opportunity to involve them in this process.

I also highly recommend that you not make immediately *major* changes to the budget that would cause you to have unrealistic expectations, or set goals that are too lofty. Our example might be somewhat extreme for your situation. However, if you can cut just $100/month in expenses, you can quickly pay down your debt. Continue using the Daily Spend Sheet covered in Chapter 16 for a couple more months, and then get more aggressive with reductions in the Cash Control and Save-to-Spend items in future months. The expenses that you most likely can control in the near term are those on which you typically spend cash or are expenses that you can affect immediately by exercising self-discipline. This is especially true if this is your first budget.

SELAH 19-1
Your First Budget

Before attacking or cutting your expenses to the bone, it is time to establish *your first Budget*. In the preceding example, note that the boxed and bold-faced items assume some "cuts" in spending. Do not cut your planned budget items until you add up your total income and expenses and see by how much you are overspending. Then you can reduce those amounts. You also might want to modify your "Cash Control" and "Save-to-Spend" Lists if you cannot afford these items.

Get all of your spreadsheets, bills, and other financial documents together, including the following:

- Daily Spend Sheet,
- Debt Hit List,
- Big-Ticket List,
- Save-to-Spend List,
- Cash Control List,
- blank Budget Sheet (see Appendix C),
- checkbook register (to help estimate some of the items),
- credit/debit card statements,
- old utility and other bills,

- pencil and an eraser, and
- calculator.

List every possible item that could go into your budget, and estimate a budget amount for each line (monthly or biweekly). Start with the Daily Spend Sheet. Total the numbers in the rows for the entire period that you have been tracking your expenses. Then divide by the number of days that you have been tracking the expenses. Multiply that answer by thirty to determine a monthly average. Use your old credit card and bank statements, check register, Big-Ticket Lists, etc., to ensure that you are not missing any items because your Daily Spend Sheet will not capture all of your expenses. Estimate an amount for each item, and total everything. Subtract the total estimated expenses from the total estimated income.

Do this in *pencil!* You will have to change some of the amounts because you probably will not be able to afford all of them. You can decide what you want to cut *after* you total the numbers. From this point, you can use an Excel spreadsheet; the blank form in Appendix C; or Money Matters, Quicken, or other money-management software.

At the beginning, this will seem like a lot of data, but you would rather have too much detail than not enough. You can combine some of the smaller items or "like" accounts if you prefer. Your initial budget will not be perfect. Your initial budget will take more time than future updates. The up-front time and planning, however, *will be* worth it! Plan on looking at your actual expenditures monthly for about six months using Figure 19-2 (the Scorecard), and adjust the numbers as you move ahead. Remember, be flexible!

Other Potential Changes to Attack Your Debt

One individual reduced his 401k payroll deductions temporarily until his high-interest debt was paid off. Such a decision is difficult and should be factored into your overall financial planning counsel and long-term planning. We personally decided that we would not invest any money until we had taken care of all credit card debt. It was difficult because a 50 percent match was offered on our 401k, but we needed the extra monthly money to get some momentum on paying down our debt and beginning our Save-to-Spend account. We initially did not have enough money to open our Save-to-Spend account. In the preceding example, it would be difficult to begin $650/month ($325 per pay period) in a "savings account" if you were currently saving nothing. But as we slowly progressed with our debt payoff, we were able gradually to build that "Save-to-Spend" reserve.

You will learn that you have to juggle many financial decisions over the next few years. Save, pay off debt, give, etc. Each situation is different, and if you are in doubt, pray first, and then get wise counsel. One possible ranking of priorities might be as follows:

1. giving,
2. credit card debt payoff,
3. Save-to-Spend account,
4. 401k funding (if matched),
5. consider increasing your giving,
6. automobile payoff,
7. increase your giving,
8. mortgage payoff,
9. increase your giving, and
10. investments.

SELAH 19-2
Budget Change Worksheet

After taking a first cut at the budget, you will most likely need to take some immediate steps to cut expenses. Take thirty minutes to sit with your spouse and family and plan out the changes to the first set of numbers. You might want to dust off your Daily Spend Sheet and ensure that the changes that you are proposing are realistic. Also, get out your Debt Hit List (Figure 17-1) pay-off schedule to ensure that your priorities are aligned. Come up with as many budget savings ideas as you can and then identify the level of desire for making the change (low, medium, and high). Then agree on a dollar amount as a goal.

Budget change idea	Husband	Wife	Family	$ Change/ consensus
Increase tithe	MEDIUM	HIGH	MED/HIGH	+50
Eat out once a week	MEDIUM	MEDIUM	MEDIUM	–25
Reduce 401k temporarily	MEDIUM	HIGH	MEDIUM	–100
Cancel 1 cell phone	HIGH	HIGH	HIGH	–25
Cancel cable	LOW	MEDIUM	MEDIUM	–30
Rent movies once a week	MEDIUM	MEDIUM	MEDIUM	–30
Postpone vacation six months	MEDIUM	MEDIUM	MEDIUM	–100
Etc.				
Etc.				

Total changes	**–260/month**
Increase credit card payoff	**+260/month**

You will have made immediate progress toward debt payoff or increased savings by instituting some budget changes and plans for your next raise if you follow through with your ideas and *do not procrastinate*. Did I mention *do not procrastinate?*

Do it *now!* Start the envelope system with your cash *now!* Begin your giving changes *now!* Cancel those items *now!* Open a Save-to-Spend account *now!* The longer the delay, the easier to slip back into old patterns!

ACTION POINTS

1. Do you need to act on anything on the following "DO IT NOW" checklist?

   Start cash envelopes   _____

   Commit to no new debt   _____

   Complete the Daily Spend Sheet   _____

   Change giving habits   _____

   Specific budget/spending changes   _____

   Complete Save-to-Spend List   _____

   Complete a Big-Ticket List   _____

   Complete Cash-Control List   _____

2. After one month of attempting to live on your budget, complete the Budget versus Actual "Scorecard" (Figure 19-2) to see what modifications (if any) you need to make. I would suggest doing this for at least three months and possibly as long as six months to get a good and realistic sense of what your budget should be.

Figure 19-2

The Scorecard

INCOME CATEGORIES	February BUDGET	February ACTUAL	February + / -
Salary 1	3500	3500	0
Salary 2	1500	1500	0
Interest	20	15	-5
Other income	500	400	-100
INCOME BEFORE TAXES	5520	5415	-105
Income tax	1350	1325	-25
INCOME AFTER TAXES	4170	4090	-80

EXPENSE CATEGORIES	BUDGET	ACTUAL	+ / -
Payroll deductions	280	280	0
Tithe/offerings	600	590	10
Auto insurance (S)	100	100	0
Mortgage/rent	900	900	0
Home maint/misc.	130	130	0
Utilities/phone/Internet	300	300	0
Groceries—Bought (C)	400	360	40
Food—Eating out/vend (C)	110	90	20
Recreation/entertainment (C)	90	75	15
Health/beauty (C)	20	25	-5
Childcare/babysitting (C)	120	105	15
Investments	50	50	0
Children's recreation (C)	20	15	5
Books/clubs/newspaper (C)	20	10	10
Cable	25	25	0
Gifts (S)	80	80	0
Misc.—Husband (C)	20	10	10
Misc.—Wife (C)	20	10	10
Misc.—Children (C)	20	10	10
Automobile payment	500	500	0
Auto maintenance (S)	60	60	0
Auto tags/inspects (S)	20	20	0
Vacation (S)	200	200	0
Clothing—Husband (C)	40	30	10
Clothing—Wife (C)	50	40	10
Clothing—Children (C)	30	20	10
Education/tuition	100	100	0
Pet expense (S)	20	20	0
Medical/dental (S)	60	60	0
Credit card #1	15	15	0
Credit card #2	20	20	0
Credit card #3	25	25	0
TOTAL EXPENSE	4445	4275	170
INCOME LESS EXPENSE	-275	-185	+90

DEBT BALANCES	February GOAL	February ACTUAL	February + / -
Credit card #1	100	90	10
Credit card #2	300	285	15
Credit card #3	1000	980	20
Automobile	5000	4800	200
Mortgage	75000	74975	25
TOTAL DEBT	81400	81130	270

C = cash, S = Save to Spend

CHAPTER 20

Freedom in a Flash!

W e have talked much of planning, spreadsheets, and goals. Now it is time for *action!* You thought (or were hoping) that I would not mention that word again right? Wrong!

After completing the many worksheets and tracking your financial health for three months or so, you should have some initial ideas for saving money and what areas need to be cut. Now it is time to challenge yourself further and make your financial impact quick and exponential. You will see a snow-ball effect when you apply a *freedom factor* to your progress. I suggest that you conduct a thirty-minute family meeting to get all of the brain power you can to generate as many ideas as possible. Some ideas will work; other ideas will not. But gather them all.

I would use the brainstorming technique, going around the circle and having each person offer an idea for saving money or making money, and create a "lightning-bolt" list. Do not criticize ideas. If someone is criticized, do not expect either further participation from that person or family unity. No idea is dumb, and it might stimulate someone else's creativity. Keep going until everyone has "passed" and no one has any more ideas.

Once all of your idea power has been exhausted, review the list in Figure 20-1 and consider adding some of those ideas to your list. If you act on some of these ideas immediately, it will create family excitement and add to the impact of your freedom factor.

In case you have slept during the past few chapters, I believe that financial freedom will come most quickly if you do the following:

1. commit to *no new debt*;
2. complete the Daily Spend Sheet for sixty to ninety days;
3. use cash accounts/envelopes ;
4. apply extra money from paid-off credit cards, spending reductions, and raises toward your debt;
5. stick to your budget;
6. maintain your standard of living while applying future increases, raises, and unexpected income to paying off your debt;
7. give to the Lord; and
8. complete a Freedom Factor Lightning-bolt List similar to that shown in Figure 20-1.

Every family and individual has different needs and opportunities. This exercise might also stimulate discussion as to which accounts should be cash-only accounts. You also might have a discussion at some point about going off the deep end and becoming hermits. Have some balance and take small steps, not giant leaps. However, if everyone is ready to take leaps, then take them—the impact will be stunning. We made a six-month commitment to some radical changes and spending "cuts," and guess what—the habits stuck!

Figure 20-1
FREEDOM FACTOR LIGHTNING BOLTS

- Use **coupons**—Groceries, oil changes, store advertisements, dry cleaning, entertainment, eating out, etc.
- Look for double and triple coupon advertisements. Subscribe to the Sunday paper.
- Shop **loss leaders** (an item that is offered at a great price to get you into the store—with the hope that you will then buy items that are *not* on sale.) at multiple grocery stores. Keep a "low-price" list for future purchases. Stock up on sale items.
- Use an entertainment club **discount card**—50 percent off, coupons (entertainment.com, 800-374-4464[1]). This saves us

more than $1000 a year. Fast food, other restaurants, movies, dry cleaning, sporting events, entertainment, museums, videos, hotels, theatre/arts, golf, oil changes, groceries, etc. We use this every week!

- **Eat in**, not out.
- Reduce your recreation/entertainment.
- Pack your own **lunch and take your own coffee.**
- Review your insurance deductibles, possibly increasing them to save money in the short term.
- Use a "sixty-day **waiting period**" on expenditures greater than $100.
- Check garage sales/thrift stores first.
- **Shop around** for major purchases.
- Purchase only items that are on sale.
- Make purchases during the off-season (buy your Christmas gifts throughout the year).
- Make gifts/clothes.
- **Stop bad habits** (e.g., smoking, drinking, gambling, playing the lottery).
- Use the public library rather than buying books.
- Try a furniture clearance center.
- Read *Consumer Reports* magazine.
- Drink water rather than sodas when you eat out.
- Try store brands (some items).
- Avoid purchasing extended warranties.
- **Sell your car rather than trading it in.**
- **Do it yourself!** (e.g., oil changes, carpet cleaning, painting, washing the car, haircuts, lawn care, landscaping, laundry, sewing, making clothes).
- Check the classified ads.
- **<u>Take a missions trip</u>** (your definitions of *wants* and *needs* will change).
- Stay away from the mall if you do not have a specific purpose for going.
- Be wary of mail-order catalog temptations.
- Carry cash only to the mall, leaving your credit cards and checkbook at home.
- Check clearance racks.
- Buy your birthday/wedding cards in bulk or use the computer to

make them.
- Shop after major holidays.
- Delete phone add-ons.
- Do not buy a brand new car.
- Use babysitting co-ops.
- Use a grocery shopping list.
- Buy diapers, formula, health/beauty, and other nongrocery items at discount outlets (e.g., Wal-mart/Target) rather than at a grocery store.
- Change or cancel cable television service.
- Change or cancel cell phone plan if possible.
- **Turn off commercials** and avoid advertisements, which create a want, a desire, and covetousness.
- Write letters or send e-mails rather than making long-distance phone calls.
- Read.
- Try free family entertainment such as parks, museums, picnics, sports, talking, etc.
- Buy checks from a mail-order company rather than the bank.
- **Use the D.E.B.T. test:** Desire? Eternal value? Budgeted? Timing?
- Vacation during the off season.
- **Exercise self-control at Christmas.** Celebrate Jesus, not things. Give more to the poor. Nothing compares with being involved in a Thanksgiving or Christmas project for the needy with your kids. Metro Ministries has opportunities. Your local food and clothing banks have opportunities. Check them out.
- For other ideas, check the "simplify" list in Figure 3-1.

SELAH 20-1

Take thirty minutes to create your own Freedom Factor list. Enlist your family's help. List everyone's ideas. Nothing is out of line. Stimulate some creative thinking. Offer some "commission" allowances to the kids for money that they save. Keep a "recreation" jar for a portion of the money that they save. Score each idea as a high/medium/low priority, and estimate the savings resulting from that idea (compromise!). On a blank sheet of paper, create the following columns:

Freedom Factor Idea	Husband	Wife	Kids	Priority	Monthly $ Savings
Use entertainment card	Med	High	Med	1	$40
Cancel 1 cell phone	Med	Med	Low	2	$30
Etc.					____
TOTALS					$200

After estimating the savings amounts, total the "potential savings." Go back to Figure 20-1 to help spur you on. Then prioritize the list. Your creativity and the impact of your ideas on the total savings will impress you. Some of these small things seem so insignificant, but when they are totaled, they really will assist you in making a major dent in your debt.

Act now! Revisit your budget and debt pay-off plan, and see if you need to make some changes.

Figure 20-2
Our Freedom Factor Savings

Our Freedom Factor list will be different than yours, but the following is a list of *actual savings* from our list after we made some changes for about a year.

Freedom Factor Idea	Monthly Savings
Entertainment club coupon book (half price coupons)[2]	$60
"In-house" or "free" entertainment instead of going out	$20
Take lunches to work	$100
Take coffee to work	$20
No vending snacks	$15
"Eat in" once more a week	$50
Use coupons	$40
Shop loss leaders/stock up on sales	$25
Haircuts at home	$20
Value dry cleaning	$25
Do-it-yourself car wash/lawn fertilizing	$25
Modify insurance deductibles	$20
Delete phone extras	$5

TOTAL MONTHLY FREEDOM FACTOR   *$425*

TOTAL ANNUAL FREEDOM FACTOR SAVINGS $5100

The little things truly add up. Over a period of five years, these "little things" added up to more than *$25,000* in savings—enough to pay off our credit cards and vehicles. Our list is totally different today. Your list will be completely different than ours. But "a little here and a little there" definitely add up. Your savings can be applied to debt, giving, and a save-to-spend account immediately.

Can I Testify Again?

Once your "freedom factor" begins to snowball, you will get excited as you will be able to reduce your debt swiftly. We were paying $450 a month in credit card minimum payments. When we applied our "freedom factor" savings of $425 a month, our debt was reduced quickly. Then the real snow-ball effect occurred after the credit cards were paid off. We now had $875 a month ($450 + $425) extra! We immediately applied that to our vehicle debts which were $385 a month. Once those were paid off, we now had $1260 ($450 + $425 + $385) a month extra! At some point during your progress (if you have not yet been able to do so), you will want to begin a Save-to-Spend account to save for future expenses.

We also committed income tax refunds and raises/bonuses toward our debt. That worked out to be an additional $200/month, which meant that we could now apply nearly $1500 ($450 + $425 + $385 + $200) a month extra toward our mortgage, additional giving, and Save-to-Spend accounts! Obviously, your Freedom Factor might not be what ours is. But anything that you can do will begin your snowball to freedom! You will be able to get out of debt quicker and give more quickly!

Although this will not happen overnight, it will begin by your starting with one credit card on your Debt Hit List and then adding that extra monthly amount to the next card. When you add in the additional savings by making changes in your spending patterns using your own Freedom Factor Lightning-bolt List, your budget will actually become fun. It just takes planning, discipline, and action.

Figure 20-3 shows our Freedom Story. We started paying off the Saturn first just because it was a much higher interest rate. That thirty-year mortgage could possibly be paid off in less than five years!

Figure 20-3
From the Little to the Free! Our Debt Pay-off Story

Pay-off Start	Debt	Creditor	Pay-off Complete	Time to Pay-off
7/91	$5,852	13 credit cards	5/92	10 months
5/92	$15,684	Saturn note	12/93	1 year, 7 months
12/93	$6,826	GMC truck note	6/94	7 months
1992	$15,000	Mobile home	1994	Miracle
6/94	$58,349	House mortgage	2/98	3 years, 8 months
		DEBT FREE!		
2/98	$50,000	New home mortgage	1/01	2 years, 11 months
		DEBT FREE AGAIN!		

6-1/2 years—> $100,000 in chains removed—totally and completely DEBT-FREE. It can be done!

This is a testimony of God's goodness. We were once in slavery (Nehemiah 5:4–5), but now we are free! It is a testimony of discipline and *action.* Yours can be the same! After we became debt free, my job moved me about thirty minutes away, and we moved into a new home. We took the proceeds from our sold house and were able to set a goal of a "three-year note" on the new house instead of a typical "thirty-year note!" God continued to bless us, and we continued disciplined planning and spending and were again totally and completely debt free in less than three years! We do not plan to have future debt.

The stories of God's provision along the way amaze us. Dana has been able to stay home for the last eight years with the children. Shortly after we began "tithing," we had a mobile home debt forgiven as an unexpected blessing! We received a number of unexpected bonuses. We started this whole process on a family income of less than $40,000 with no end of debt in sight or any ability to "afford" either giving or children. God has been faithful!

If God has entrusted you with little, be faithful with that little. He will put you in charge of more. If He has entrusted you with much, be faithful with what He has given you. We all—rich or poor—are accountable for how we spend the money with which God has entrusted us. Show yourself faithful. We had our trials and challenges, but God saw us through them all!

The Power of the Little

Just in case you still doubt that you can make some changes that will radically affect your financial situation, I will cite a few final examples of the power of the little.

Example 1: A smoker quits his habit

Two packs a day:	$2000/year
Savings:	$20,000 over ten years
	$80,000 over forty years
Potential impact:	Could purchase four or five new vehicles with *cash*
	Could build twenty churches in Asia (at $5000 each)
	Could pay off debt quickly

Example 2: You start taking your lunch to work every day

20–25 lunches a month:	$1300/year
Savings:	$13,000 over ten years
	$52,000 over forty years
Potential impact:	Could pay for kid's college education

Could increase giving from 10 percent to 13 percent

Could pay off debt quickly

Example 3: You get a 4 percent raise (after taxes) on your $40,000 salary

4 percent raise on $40,000:	1600/year
Increase:	$16,000 over ten years
	$64,000 over forty years
Potential impact:	Put $133 a month into your Save-to-Spend account
	Sponsor two or three Gospel for Asia missionaries
	Could pay off debt quickly

Most raises are just frittered away without even "feeling" them. Have a plan when you get the raise. Put it into a separate account. *Do something!*

I think that you get the idea of the "power of the little." Just think what could result if you do more than one of these activities! Your "Freedom Factor Multiplier" will grow quickly!

SELAH 20-2

What are some immediate "little things" that you will commit to changing?

_____

_____

_____

_____

LIGHTNING BOLTS EXTRA CREDIT

A few money-saving ideas have had a significant impact on us during our freedom journey and are worth a little more detailed discussion. Some of you might roll your eyes and say that this is taking it too far. Some people might call it "cheap." Some people might even call it "radical." I call it "frugal" or "Dutch" stewardship. I did get a good chuckle out of a recent statement:

> *"There are two types of cheapskates: natural born . . . and . . . conversions."*

What makes life interesting is when you have one of each type of cheapskate in a family. It makes it even more interesting when you have none in the family.

This next section might stretch you a little bit! Be stretched! I hope to make some converts as a result of this book. Why write it if that is not the goal?

Coupon Capers

Coupons. Some of you cringe at the word. Please give me three paragraphs before you gong me. I would have gonged myself ten years ago. I thought that coupons were for grannies and unemployed hermits. When I was conducting research, I actually read some books on full-time coupon queens that drove me batty. I respected them and was intrigued by their stories of the trips to the grocery store where *the store paid them* money and they walked away with groceries. I'm sorry, but Dana and I live in the real world and have three children and little spare time, so you will not see us with full-time coupon days on our hands or any wild success stories like that. However, I do believe that everyone can benefit from using coupons. I just believe that the level of time that you have will help determine how much time you spend on the effort. Obviously, the amount of time that you spend will directly affect how much you save.

Time = Money

Because we had little time but needed to save a lot of money, our strategy was to take about ten to fifteen minutes a week to clip and sort coupons—and maybe an extra thirty minutes in shopping time. This effort saved our family of five an average of *$75–$150/month,* depending upon whether the grocery stores were having triple coupon days. To us, the extra thirty to forty-five minutes a week leads to savings of $1000–$2000 a year. It will help you cover some of the items on your Big-Ticket List or begin your Save-to-Spend account. One individual I know puts the coupon savings into an envelope and pays for the family vacation every year. It is a reward for doing the coupon-cutting dirty work. The more they save, the better vacation they have. Such simple goals will motivate your kids to participate too! Or you might allocate the savings to support a missionary for a year.

Do not clip coupons that you do not normally need. Doing so could cause you actually to spend more money, and it might turn your ten minutes into thirty minutes. We do not desire to hire a full-time coupon manager in our household. We clip from Sunday's paper and nowhere else. Sorry, no coupon clubs or trading for us. You can take it as far as you desire if you have the time and are committed to it, but radical couponing beyond the basics was just not for us.

Clip coupons *now* even if you do not need them for three months. Soap, toilet paper, dishwasher detergent, toothpaste, and paper towels do not rot very quickly. We rarely pay more than fifty cents for a four-pack of toilet paper or more than $1 for a multibar pack of soap, and we get many of the nonperishable goods for free. We buy when we have coupons and stock up on sale items, not when I am in the shower praying over that sliver of Irish Spring. We stock up on coupons and then when some grocery stores offer double or triple coupon days, we make a *big* trip.

Some stores take competitors' coupons as well if you bring in the competitors' advertisements. Our best day was cutting a $230 bill down to $95. Not bad for an extra forty-five minutes of work! (That's almost $200 an hour!) I could not make that at a part-time job! Recently, we made a special trip because they had triple coupons up to 75 cents. Our savings were $105.02. The original bill was $193.79, but we walked out having paid only $88.77—a 55 percent savings! We did not need all of the items at the time, but we will need them in a few months.

It is free money. You might even call it good stewardship! We rarely buy what we do not need. Once in a while, we will buy some special snacks as a reward for our "coupon capers." Use a coupon organizer or you will really get frustrated shuffling through a handful of coupons while walking (and rewalking!) the aisles. Be patient. This will take some getting used to, but it will be rewarding at the register.

"Loss Leaders" and Sale Items

I estimate that shopping the "loss-leader items" saves us at least $30–50/month ($400–$600/year). Loss leaders are items that the grocer advertises to get you into the store with the hope that you will choose them as your grocer for the week. Ensure that you read your sales advertisements every week. Each grocery store will have their "loss leaders" on sale. Typical items include milk, toilet paper, bread, soft drinks, cereal, chips, and meat. We have learned to "cherry pick the deals." We keep the sales advertisements for two to three grocery stores and then purchase only the sale items at two of them and then hit the road. Fifteen minutes in and out. We save easily $15–$20 with our "loss-leader dashes." We will do our regular shopping at the store that has the best sale for that week.

We stock up on certain items when they are on sale. We now purchase cereal, soft drinks, hamburger, steaks, chicken, apple juice, canned vegetables, soup, toilet paper, and paper towels *only* when they are on sale. They always go on sale; it is just a matter of when. When they do, we load up. We have a small freezer in the garage. Today's cereal box count in our pantry is seventeen boxes. They stay good for a year, but the most important thing was that we paid one-third of the normal price. We bought four boxes of Cheerios when they were 99 cents instead of $2.99. We bought the Frosted Flakes ($2.99)—buy one, get one free. We bought four packs of toilet paper at 69 cents instead of $1.39. We bought four 12-packs of Coke for $1.79 each instead of $2.99. Although this is not a large list of items, we still saved nearly $20, just for a few minutes of extra shopping.

Planning and Flexibility

Part of saving money on grocery shopping includes knowing

when to buy things. You must get to know what a "good price" is. This knowledge will develop over a period of a few months just by your shopping the sales, reading sales advertisements, and paying attention to how much you are paying for things. We know that we sometimes can get ground chuck for 99 cents a pound. We will not buy it the minute we run out but rather plan ahead and stock up or wait a couple of weeks for the next sale. We know that T-bone steaks will eventually go on sale for $2.99 or $3.99; the normal price is $5.99 or $6.99. We know that boneless chicken will eventually be advertised at $1.79–$1.99 a pound. So we do not buy these items until they are on sale.

My kids like multiple cereals. They can do without Lucky Charms until it goes on sale. Meanwhile, we have two boxes of Trix and two boxes of Frosted Flakes that they can eat until that time.

Buy what is on sale—and buy extra. If your memory is as bad as mine keep a "good price" list on regular sale items until you have a good idea of what a "good price" really is. Obviously, you do not want to turn your garage or shed into a minisupermarket, but do what makes sense for you. We have learned to practice flexibility, and our kid's are now being trained to be patient and ask, "Is it on sale, Mommy?"

Blessing Bank

If you actually do have enough time to get wild and radical with your coupon endeavors, you might consider what is called a Blessing Bank. Keep a bank of coupons for widows, single mothers, or a family that is struggling financially. Ask them for a list of brands that they would use. I created a spreadsheet with the key categories. When a great double- or triple-coupon offer is available, stock up on the items and then bless those people by donating the products to them.

For more free information send a self-addressed, stamped envelope to the address on the order form at the back of the book, or check the website at www.financialfoundationbuilders.com.

Random Grocery Shopping Lightning Bolts

- Shop on a full stomach.
- Shop using a list.
- Shop with coupons.
- Shop with your loss-leader list.
- Keep a price list on major items so that you can remember what a "good" price is.
- Minimize trips for just a "few items"; they cost you.
- Use frequent shopper/value cards.
- Buy cleaning supplies, laundry, beauty items, diapers, formula, cosmetics and candy at superstores (e.g., Walmart, Target) rather than a regular grocery store.
- Consider store brands on some items, but on other items—forget it! You could not pay me enough to drink store brand orange juice. But I can handle the vanilla wafers, crackers, pop-tarts, and Windex equivalents.
- Look at unit prices. Bigger is not always cheaper, especially if you often have coupons for that item.
- Beware of bulk buying/warehouse stores. Once you get to know the "good prices" and clip coupons, you will find that many of these bulk deals are not deals at all. We stopped using them for our groceries. We could save more with double and triple coupons and stocking up on sale items.
- Stock up on sale items and nonperishable loss leaders.
- Be brand flexible—one month buy Colgate, the next month buy Aquafresh (be coupon and sale dependent).
- Take advantage of buy-one-get-one-free sales. While completing this section, I noticed a "buy-one-get-one-free" sale in the weekly grocery inserts in the newspaper. They also were having double coupons up to 50 cents and triple coupons up to 39 cents. I grabbed about twenty coupons for items that we would eventually need. I bought only what we needed. The result? The original bill was $153.95, but after coupons and "buy-one-get-one-free" items, the real bill was only $86.79—a 44 percent savings! We saved $67 for an extra fifteen minutes of work and a purposefully timed trip to the grocery store!

Grocers' Tricks of the Trade

- The highest-priced items are often at eye level.
- The high-ticket impulse items, which are not on sale, are put in convenient places. Do not fall for them.
- Products are grouped to provoke impulse buying (e.g., hot dog buns and chips).
- Staple items and loss leaders such as bread and milk are placed at the back of the store so that you have to walk past (and possibly end up purchasing) other merchandise that is not on sale.
- Read the fine print on advertisements, sales, coupons—everything. Tiny print often means big headaches.

Other Miscellaneous Savings Ideas

- If you eat at a restaurant, order water for your beverage. Have dessert and coffee at home. Desserts and drinks are among the high-mark-up foods.
- Join the frequent shopper programs.
- Shop around on local, long-distance, and cellular phone rates. Many options from which to choose are available. (See www.trac.org.)
- Always get two or three prices before buying big-ticket items.
- Buy a phone card for long-distance calls or for when you travel. Hotel phone rates are ten to twenty times higher than normal long-distance rates.
- Shop at resale stores. You can get some first-rate clothes and other miscellaneous items at great savings. My wife is unbelievably skilled at doing this wisely.
- Take in a late afternoon matinee and then dinner to cut your movie expense in half.
- Use coupons when you eat out.
- Comparison shop.
- Have a garage sale. Simplify.
- Stay away from the mall.
- Don't take your credit cards or checkbook if you are just "window shopping," or you might come home with the window.

Other Tidbits

Cars/Travel

- Buy two- to three-year-old used vehicles under warranty and save up to 50 percent.
- Compare the sellers asking price with the "bluebook" NADA price list. Your library or bank should carry them.
- Do not be in a rush. A vehicle is a major expenditure. We knew that we wanted a Honda Odyssey, but we knew that we did not want to pay $25,000 for a new one. We read the classified ads for four months and finally a two-year-old Honda Odyssey with 24,000 miles became available. We paid $13,700 for it!
- Get to know a mechanic. Have him check over the car before you buy it. The $50 spent now might save you thousands later.
- Sell the vehicle yourself and save 10 percent or more. Use classified ads, Auto Trader magazines, or the Internet. Do not trade. Be patient.
- Keep vehicles at least five years.

> *"The cheapest car you can ever own is the one you are driving now."*
> **—Ron Blue**

- Carpool.
- Before renting a car, check with your insurance agent to see if you need to purchase the various waiver and insurance adders.
- You can lower your airline ticket prices by purchasing them more than twenty-one days in advance and staying over on a Saturday night. Your flexibility with departure times can save you a lot of money, too.
- Check out the Travel Discount websites in Appendix A.

Insurance

- Get multiple quotes to include a package deal, both homeowners and auto insurance.
- Ask about discounts for defensive driving, airbags, fire hydrants, etc.

- Consider increasing your deductibles until you've taken care of your debt.

Other

- Before making major purchases, go to the library and review *Consumer Reports* and other consumer reviews for quality, prices, and feedback about those products.
- Before buying new furniture, take your time to look at classified ads and garage and estate sales.
- Purchase checks from mail-order companies (e.g., Current, 800-533-3973; Checks in the Mail, 800-733-4443). You will see ads for these companies in Sunday papers. This idea will save you $10–20.
- Cut out the bad habits. If I had limited my college spending habits, I could probably retire today. Review the "power of the little" examples and do the calculations for a bad habit or an addictive hobby that you have.

Eating Out

- Use coupons! For us, it is now a habit.
- Look for Kids-Eat-Free-Night deals. We found three restaurants this month that were offering "Kids-Eat-Free" deals on particular nights. Our family of five ate at each of these restaurants for less than $10. Two of these restaurants had all kids eating free for every adult entree purchased. I took the kids for date night and all four of us ate for less than $7!
- Use the Entertainment Club Dining Card (see www.entertainment.com). This card saves us easily $500–1000 a year and costs a mere $35. We use it for movies, dry cleaning, entertainment, and sports but mostly for eating out.
- We almost always drink water at meals. It hurts me to pay $1.50 for a 25-cent drink. I would rather save the $5 and buy a case of Coke later!

Entertainment/Recreation

- Stay in. Have Family Fun Nights.
- Visit museums.
- Take a trip to the library.
- Take a trip to the park.
- Read.
- Walk.
- Participate in sports and exercise instead of paying to watch it.
- Play a round of Frisbee golf.
- Fly a kite.
- Go sledding (not in Texas!).
- Garden.
- Review the simplicity section in Figure 3-1.

A Book of Her Own!

My wife Dana has taught a "Christmas on a Budget" seminar at our church women's group. She could write a book of her own on all of the savings ideas and creative things that you can do to reduce expenses, create family traditions, and involve the children to make Christmas extra special—and inexpensive. Following are a *few* of the many other things she does to help our family.

- Garage sales—Before making major purchases, she at least checks out local garage sales.
- Donations—Two or three times a year, she goes through our "stuff" and donates it to a local charity. We are able to bless them and are blessed with a tax writeoff as well.
- Christmas on a Budget—Dana could write a book about creativity and savings ideas that make our Christmases so very special. My description would not do her justice.
- Buy things the day after Christmas. You will save 50–75 percent, and you will need them next year anyway (e.g., cards, lights, wrapping paper, stocking stuffers for next year).
- Buy things the day after Thanksgiving—We make this a family event and rise at 4:00 a.m. to do about half (or more) of our shopping with a "Sale Hit List." We have fun and save a ton!
- Dana buys year round and looks for the sales and clearance racks.

I wear a $4.99 polo shirt, and Dana has a pair of $15 Guess jeans. She just came home from a winter clearance special at two department stores where almost everything was 75 percent off. She found some dress shoes for herself—regular price: $65; Dana's price: $15. She found some Esprit boots for Emily—regular price: $40; Dana's price: $9. She found two sweaters for me— regular price: $50; Dana's price: $9. She found a hooded Nike sweatshirt for Jacob for next year—regular price: $35; Dana's price: $2.99.

- Dana makes some very creative gifts. Investing her time and heart by putting her personal touch into making such gifts has blessed many people outside of our family.

ACTION POINTS

1. Are you committed to no new debt?_____

2. Create a Lightning Bolt List of Saving Ideas. Even if you do not need to get out of debt, you can use this to give more or save more!

   _____
   _____
   _____
   _____
   _____
   _____
   _____
   _____

3. Can you begin immediately doing any "little things?"

   _____
   _____
   _____
   _____
   _____
   _____
   _____
   _____

4. Review the "Lightning Bolts Extra Credit" Section. Can you begin to practice any steps now that would affect your monthly "Freedom Factor" savings?

   _____
   _____
   _____
   _____
   _____

CHAPTER 21

The Eighth Wonder of the World

"The greatest invention is compound interest."
—Albert Einstein

I think that we all have good intentions. We want to give. We want to be out of debt. We want to save. When we are handcuffed financially, however, someone else is getting the benefit of our slavery. We are actually paying others a premium for money that was once ours but no longer is. We borrow money because we do not have it; yet, we do not have the patience to wait to pay cash. As was detailed in Chapter 6, the lenders are quite pleased to have you pay them for the longest time possible. They will gladly reduce your minimum payment or gladly give you a five-year car note instead of a three-year note, all for the sake of gaining your hard-earned dollars. Interest can work powerfully *against* you or powerfully *for* you.

"Compound Interest is the eighth wonder of the world."
—Baron Rothschild

There are two kinds of people: those who pay interest and those who collect it. In which category are you? The financial institutions know the power of compound interest. How valuable is your money to you?

I got angry when I started adding up how much interest I was handing over to other people every year. For us, it was nearly $10,000 a year (including our mortgage)! That is $300,000 over thirty years, and we knew from the Chapter 6 tricks of the lenders that our credit cards would *never* be paid off at our current minimum payment schedules! I became increasingly angrier as I realized that I could possibly make $1–2 million over the next thirty years and end up paying $300,000 of that to lenders! The money that you *intend* to save draws no interest. The money that you *owe* is interest that you are paying to others that you could be giving or saving!

Considering that the cost of raising a child (from birth to seventeen) ranges from $121,000 to $241,700,[1] depending upon your income level, I would say that the money you are spending on interest could be put to much better use.

SELAH 21-1
The Interest Exercise

Gather up all of your credit card statements, car notes, your mortgage amortization schedule, and any other debts that you might have. You might have to order your car and mortgage amortization schedules from the lenders. Create a spreadsheet to determine how much interest you are paying monthly and yearly. It might be a wake-up call to spur you to make some quick changes.

Debt description	Monthly principal	Monthly interest
Visa	$27	$23
Department card	$20	$22
Automobile	$250	$125
Truck	$300	$130
Mortgage	$50	$700
Monthly TOTAL	**$647**	**$1,000**
Yearly TOTAL	**$7764**	**$12,000**

Your Mortgage

If your mortgage note is relatively new (i.e., less than five years), you will discover that 90 to 99 percent of each payment goes to interest. According to Larry Burkett, in 1929, 95 percent of all homes were bought for cash and only 5 percent were mortgaged. Today, 95 percent of homes are bought with a mortgage. Before 1945, practically no cars were financed. It was considered unthinkable (even immoral by some people).

We are a long way from that culture today. We have a debt culture in America. I am not suggesting that you wait to pay cash for your house. We did not, and we would just now be moving into one if I had waited to pay cash. I am suggesting, however, that you have a plan to pay off *all* of your debt. No extra money should be put toward your mortgage until all other debt is paid off because of the tax deduction that we are still granted for mortgage interest.

However, delaying paying off your mortgage to get a tax break is foolishness if you are not getting a greater rate of return than your mortgage rate. That dollar of interest that you are paying yields only a 25- to 35-cent tax break, and you are still throwing 65 to 75 cents on the dollar out the window. The average consumer unit (husband/wife) with an annual income of $53,232 spends $1703 per year on mortgage interest.[2] Some people say that paying off your mortgage early is ignorance because you can yield a much higher rate of return on your money. I will agree that this is *possible* and agree with the word *can*. But there are no guarantees. Ask the market investors in Korea, Japan, or even here in the United States about the year 2000. They would have been thrilled then with 7–8 percent.

Do Not Assume

We can hang on to risky and faulty assumptions that could lead us down a dangerous path. Some such assumptions are as follows.

- The market will not crash.
- It is always wise to buy now.
- Borrowed money is paid back with cheaper dollars in the future.
- Use of OPM (Other People's Money) is always the right choice.
- Appreciation, appreciation, appreciation. (Ask real estate owners in the South in the 1980s about this!)
- We will always have tax deductibility for mortgage interest.

Should I Pay Off My Mortgage Early?

"Though it is often trumpeted that home *ownership* is at an all time high (67% of Americans), in reality, less than 2 percent *own* their own homes; the other 65 percent have their own *mortgage*." [3]

The mortgage is the largest purchase and investment that most people ever make—and the one on which the financial institutions make the most money. On average, homeowners pay $3 for every dollar they are loaned over the life of the full thirty-year note. Many people fall into the trap of pursuing a home equity loan. About 13.2 percent of Americans have some form of home equity loans. The problem is that 40 percent of these loans are used to reduce debt, and 29 percent are used for home improvement.[4] This might be a band-aid for a deeper problem, and many borrowers end up in a vicious cycle of getting back into debt because they have not dealt with the root of the problem.

My intention is not to change your mind if you do not desire to pay your mortgage off early. It was our desire to pay off *all* of our debts simply because the Bible has so much to say about the subject, none of it positive and not even close to neutral. That was enough for me.

This is not a book on investments or the risks and tradeoffs of those decisions. We prayed about our mortgage, and *our* desire was to pay off *our* mortgage. All that I ask is that you involve God in your decision. It might not be the correct decision for everyone. We never even thought that it was a possibility for us until we put the tools to use that we have discussed earlier and made some changes in our spending and giving patterns. You might not need to make the decision today, but begin to pray about it.

For those who desire to pay off their mortgage early, you will save thousands of dollars in interest payments.

Example:

$100,000 loan at 7.5 percent over thirty years = $699 payment
(principle and interest)
Total interest over thirty years = $151,000
Total cost of home over thirty years = $251,000

After all of your other debt is paid off, you might consider paying off your home. Having interest work for you is a powerful thing. Look at the exciting impact and power of compound interest when you make extra payments on your mortgage debt:

	Prior # yrs.	New # yrs.	Prior total cost	New total cost
Paying an extra $100/month	30	21	$251,000	$195,000
Paying an extra $200/month	30	15	$251,000	$171,000
Paying an extra $300/month	30	13	$251,000	$157,000

Just a little extra a month put toward the principal on your mortgage yields a powerful reduction in the number of years that you are in debt. We made this an exciting monthly challenge to see how much extra we could put toward the debt and marked our progress directly on the amortization schedule. We could scratch out five or six payment lines after each payment because of the extra monthly amounts. Once you have paid off your credit cards and cars and have made some "Freedom Factor" changes to your budget, you will be able to pay off your mortgage quickly if you so desire!

Mortgage Tidbits

Following are two issues for your consideration related to mortgages:

1. Just because you "qualify" for a certain amount doesn't mean that you should borrow that amount. Lenders use financial ratios that do not include "giving" considerations and do not consider all of the spiritual and life priorities that might affect you downstream. If you are even considering having a spouse stay at home, ensure that you plan your monthly payment around one income. Ensure that you fully understand your budget and your long-term goals for other debt payoff before you get in over your head with a hefty, stressful, monthly mortgage payment.

2. You pay a monthly amount called Mortgage Insurance Premium that in many states does not get reduced or cancelled automatically. You can possibly cancel this amount once you have greater

than 20 percent equity in your home and have lived there for a few years, assuming that you have a decent payment record. Contact your lender for details.

Investment Priorities

Let me say clearly that I am not a certified anything—unless you count a certified "believer" worth something. I will not give you any investment advice in this book other than some general priorities that you might consider. Mostly you need to pray about God's priorities for *you!* Each of us is unique, and God has a different plan for each of us. Once you get out of debt and make some heart changes in your giving, I would suggest initiating some balanced savings and investments. By *balanced* I mean not hoarding.

1. If you have a 401k fund that is matched by employer dollars, it is good stewardship to gain that "free" match money. I would start there.

2. Consider starting a Save-to-Spend account if you have not already been able to do so. This will help with unforeseen expenses, vacations, gifts, etc.

3. Consider saving some money in a "benevolence" fund that allows you to help others in need at any time.

4. Consider an "emergency" fund of three to six months of income. Many advisers mention that everyone should have this at *all times*. If you are anywhere near the financial condition that I was in, you will no doubt laugh every time you read something like that. If we had waited until we had that six-month stockpile to begin paying off our debts or increasing our giving, we would still be waiting! We did not even consider this until *after* our credit cards and vehicles were paid off.

5. Consider using savings vehicles that benefit you in tax savings. Perhaps initiate educational Individual Retirement Accounts (IRAs) for your children's education. Possibly begin an IRA for you or your spouse if you qualify.

6. Consider other investment vehicles such as mutual funds, bonds, real estate, etc.

This book is not meant to be about investments but a book to get you to a place where you *can invest,* both eternally and for your remaining years on earth. Ensure that you pray about a financial planner/adviser and get wisdom and counsel from more than one person on your selection. Many such people might not have your best interests or goals at heart. (See Appendix B for some links to Christian Financial Planners.)

Start Young, or Start Now!

Obviously, the younger you can begin saving the better. The power of interest is incredible. I have shown you how it works against you. Now take a look at Figure 21-1 to see how the power of interest can work *for you*!

Figure 21-1

The Power of Compound Interest—Three Investment Scenarios

Age	Scenario 1	Scenario 2	Scenario 3
25	$2000	$2000	$0
26	2000	2000	0
27	2000	2000	0
28	2000	2000	0
29	2000	2000	0
30	2000	2000	0
31	2000	2000	0
32	2000	2000	0
33	2000	2000	0
34	0	2000	2000
35	0	2000	2000
36	0	2000	2000
37	0	2000	2000
38	0	2000	2000
39	0	2000	2000
40	0	2000	2000
41	0	2000	2000
42	0	2000	2000
43	0	2000	2000
44	0	2000	2000
45	0	2000	2000
46	0	2000	2000
47	0	2000	2000
48	0	2000	2000
49	0	2000	2000
50	0	2000	2000
51	0	2000	2000
52	0	2000	2000
53	0	2000	2000
54	0	2000	2000
55	0	2000	2000
56	0	2000	2000
57	0	2000	2000
58	0	2000	2000
59	0	2000	2000
60	0	2000	2000
Value at Age 60*	$ 215,493	$ 404,171	$ 188,678

* assumes 8% constant interest rate

In Scenario 1, the individual invests $2000/year beginning at age twenty-five and stops investing for some reason at age thirty-three. Although he invests *nothing additional* from ages thirty-four to sixty, he still has $215,493 at age sixty. Wow! Not bad, for having investing only $18,000 at such a young age—much better than paying credit card or car note interest and having that interest work against you!

In Scenario 2, the individual is able to invest $2000/year beginning at age twenty-five and continues investing $2000/year until age sixty. He will have $404,171 at age sixty! Wow! A total of $72,000 is invested over thirty-five years, and the power of interest turns that into more than $400,000! Now you can see how that mortgage interest horror story works against you! Interest can work for you or against you!

In Scenario 3, the individual begins investing $2000/year at age thirty-four and invests $2000/year for the next twenty-seven years. This individual has the least money of all three scenario's at age sixty although he invested $54,000, which is $36,000 *more* than that in Scenario 1. Why? Because of the power of compound interest! The lesson: *Start young!* Begin the habit of saving. But even if you are not young, it is never too late to start!

"If you would be wealthy, think of saving rather than getting"
—Ben Franklin

Warning!

A gray area is the question about when "investing" becomes "gambling" with God's money. All that I can say is to pray and ask the Lord what He would have you do? I do know that the dangerous trend of "buying on margin" is gambling. It is a concept whereby investors borrow money so that they can invest in the stock market. The stock purchased on margin is used as collateral against the value of the loan. Americans are relying increasingly on borrowed money to pay for their investments in the stock market. Margin debt being carried by U.S. investors has soared 435 percent since 1992. Margin debt was the precursor to a market crash as in 1929, which precipitated the Great Depression, and recent trends are alarming.[5]

Year	Margin debt
1992	$ 37 billion
1994	$ 59 billion
1996	$ 73 billion
1998	$127 billion
2000	$198 billion

A Few Thoughts on Investing

- Budget for savings or investments. If you do not plan it, you will not do it.
- Guard yourself against crossing over into hoarding.
- Be willing to use your investments for a giving purpose if God so desires.
- Never slip into the "it's mine" mind set. It is *all* His!
- Divide your portions—diversify!
- There is no such thing as a "sure thing."
- Invest in your 401k if it has a match.
- Start an automatic savings plan. When you get a raise put the extra away before you spend it. If you do not see it, you will not spend it.
- Use dollar cost averaging. Rather than investing a lump sum, invest monthly so that it evens out the ups and downs.
- Do not use the IRS tax rebate as your forced savings plan. You could use the interest.
- Diversify in not only types of investments but also different banks and mutual funds.
- Plan for death. Most Christians do not have a will. That is *poor* stewardship. The government will take much of your money and it could lead to disunity among your family and friends.
- Consider including churches and ministries in your wills.
- Educate your spouse on finances at least yearly.
- Make a summary list of account numbers, assets (including dollar amounts), banking, investment, debt, and insurance information; the location of your will, your attorney's phone number; and other such information at the end of each year. This exercise will

help you see your financial progress yearly. It will also be of help to your spouse if something devastating occurred.

"Manage your money; don't let your money manage you."

<u>ACTION POINTS</u>

1. How much interest are you paying a year? _____

2. Do you need to make any investment changes?

   _____
   _____
   _____
   _____
   _____
   _____

3. What are your investment priorities?

   _____
   _____
   _____
   _____
   _____
   _____

4. Are you gambling with any of God's money? If you are not sure, you might talk to Him about it.

   _____
   _____
   _____
   _____
   _____

CHAPTER 22

A Family Finance Reformation

I debated long and hard about whether to include this chapter in the book because it is not distinctively about finances. However, if you examine the foundation of the house in Figure 16-1, family is a foundational issue that will affect your life's priorities, your giving, and your finances. How we live and act as a family affects significantly our finances, priorities, and giving. If you are single, I would hope that you would still read this chapter regardless of the title. It might help you gain insights into your upbringing and help you with an investment that you can make in other families' or children's lives.

Family is a powerful word. Depending upon our upbringings and family history, it can conjure either negative or positive feelings and images when it is mentioned. This will not be one of those "neat little box" chapters in which I try to fit you into my family box. We are not the same. We were not raised the same. Our parental influences were different. Our financial situations, marriage situations, and children's ages and situations are totally different. Chew it, and then spit out what will not work for you.

A Father's Influence

We are not the perfect family, but we keep striving to improve. I have made family a priority the last five years. Five years ago, my family life was an afterthought and on some days a distraction and a stumbling block to my accomplishing *my* goals and priorities. I knew deep down that investing in my family with my finances, time, and spirituality were important. However, I had not made it a foundational issue—until God spoke loudly and clearly through my father that other things were more important to me than my family. He challenged me. He laid it on the line. I remember sitting in the car with him after lunch when he asked me if I was willing to give up these other things and put my family first. I wept as I knew the answer. He would not let me get out of the car until I answered the question. I knew the answer was that I was *not* willing to give up my dreams and goals for the sake of my family, and it actually took another two years before I fully obeyed.

I have never forgotten that moment of conviction and knowledge that God was really speaking to me and asking me to do something. After obeying, I realized that the most exciting and peaceful place to be is walking in God's will obediently! I will never turn back! Laying my life down for the sake of my family has been the most rewarding experience of my life. Was it easy? No, no, no! Is it easy now? No! It is a daily battle with the flesh. But the rewards have been so great that I cannot possibly put them into words. It is so true that "Whoever loses his life . . . will find it."[1] It is so much more than stuffy words: *responsibility*, *loyalty*, *faithfulness*, *sacrifice*, *trustworthiness*, *endurance*, and *consistency*. Yes, I finally owned up as a husband and father to the fact that I was not practicing many of these concepts. But I am so much more fulfilled since I began putting my wife and children before myself. The journey of selflessness begins first with God, then with the family with which He has entrusted me, and then with others. God has so honored the laying aside of my personal idols and priorities.

24/7!

I like what Dr. Tony Evans said at a recent Promise Keepers conference: "When you come home, guys, you are coming home to your second job." He did not mean to say that it is drudgery and an obligation but rather that my family is *my* responsibility. I will be accountable for them. I needed to sacrifice daily and put them first. The couch, the newspaper, a good book, Sports Center, a meeting—

none of these things were to be first.

This realization affected me so greatly that I no longer do anything for myself until *after* the children are in bed. My priority is my children and my wife until they have closed their eyes for the evening. It is not always easy, and sometimes I feel myself being tugged toward gratifying myself. But it truly has had a significant impact on our family life.

Writing a History Book

I have come to the realization that I am influencing history with my investment in my children. I cannot personally touch lives in the year 2045, but my children can. I am not put here on earth for myself only, nor for just my generation. God thinks beyond our current generation, and so must I. The best way that I can do that is by influencing the younger generation, and if I do not start with my own family, then I am "worse than an unbeliever."[2] Providing for my own family is so much more than just financial. It is also spiritual, physical, and emotional. It is *time!*

We are so convinced by our culture and the media that we need to chase the "rainbows of *today.*" We need to chase that "elusive happiness." It is all about me, me, me. Not anymore. I give my children at least an hour every day. It is unbroken time. I will not be interrupted. We recently had missionaries in our home for a week. I politely broke away one hour before bedtime and kept with my discipline of spending time with the children. No phone calls are accepted during this time—period! It is *our* time. The family needs consistency, not just a couple of hours of bonding once in a while. Obviously, there are exceptions—a meeting, travel out of town, sickness, etc.—but the exceptions are rare, and on average I hit the target five to six days a week.

Our typical "hour" is a time to read a story, read the Bible, pray, and then some sort of activity or game (hide and seek, a board game, swimming, sports, wrestling, "shouting," loud music and dancing, etc.). The beauty of it all is that I needed to get the discipline started for only a month or so, and now guess who holds me accountable? They do!

"Daddy, aren't we going to read the Bible tonight?"

Our response should be as Jesus' was: "Whoever comes to me I will never drive away."[3]

We really teach most effectively by example—not just in words but in deeds. I am really my children's pastor and teacher.

> *"Men preach by their lives, not by their words."*
> **—E.M. Bounds**

Yes, others make an impact on our children's lives: the youth pastor, the Sunday school teacher, or the school teacher. But the family is the place where the deep influence of significance, importance, self-worth, life purpose, and modeling take place. The faces of pastors and teachers will change over the years. We parents are the ones who are to have a *consistent* impact in our children's lives. We have a responsibility to do our best and to make a significant, long-lasting impact. We are passing the baton. It is a long race, not a sprint. We will stumble sometimes as parents and spouses, but we must dust ourselves off and continue the race. Tomorrow is a new day. Remember the importance of it all. We are influencing our grandchildren and great-grandchildren's future with our actions today! Wow!

> *"Only be careful, and watch yourselves closely so that you do not forget the things your eyes have seen or let them slip from your heart as long as you live. Teach them to your children and to their children after them."*
> **—Deuteronomy 4:9**

> *"[H]e commanded our forefathers to teach their children, so the next generation would know them, even the children yet to be born, and they in turn would tell their children."*
> **—Psalm 78:5–6**

Leaving a Legacy

We do not choose whether we leave a legacy for future generations because we all *will* leave one. The issue is *what kind* of legacy we will leave for the future generations. My responsibility as a parent is to teach them. I can teach them about finances, but I must first teach them about my life priorities and values. Yes, there will be times when I must delegate that authority, but the responsibility is still mine. I cannot possibly spend twenty-four hours a day with my children, but I am the primary caretaker, the investor, and the spiritual provider.

"Love the Lord your God with all your heart and with all your soul and with all your strength. These commandments that I give you today are to be upon your hearts. Impress them on your children. Talk about them when you sit at home and when you walk along the road, when you lie down and when you get up.
—Deuteronomy 6:5–7

"Train up a child in the way he should go, and when he is old he will not turn from it."
—Proverbs 22:6

Is It Worth It?

Although I rebelled for twenty-six years, I had something to which to come back. My parents had built the foundation; their training now bears fruit. It took longer than they wanted, but I am thankful that they followed the Lord's admonition. They will influence generations to come by their stand for godliness and by being living examples. Were they perfect? No, far from it. But their three children are now all following Jesus and living purposeful lives.

If I believe that I am to make an impact on future generations, then my daily decisions and actions must be purposeful about my investment in my family. The reality is that there will be some sacrifice along the way. What types of sacrifice? Time, personal goals, recreation, hobbies, finances, energy, career, etc. Is it worth it? Will it be easy? Does anything of real value and long-lasting results just *happen*? Look at the marriages that are crumbling. Look at the attack on the sanctity of "traditional family" relationships. Investment in your family returns great dividends! It *is* worth it!

"The strength of a nation lies in the home of its people."
—Abraham Lincoln

We were hearing of so many friends' marriages that were on the rocks that we decided to start a "Homebuilders" marriage small group study in our neighborhood. It was a great experience and an opportunity to invest in other marriages. If you have a strong marriage, you are needed as models. You are needed to invest in others. If your church does not have a marriage or family outreach, then I would highly recommend your viewing the material at the Focus on the Family Web site (www.HeritageBuilders.com).

We have been duped into thinking that *one* parent has the responsibility to "teach, train, and raise" the children. The Bible says otherwise.

"Listen, my son, to your **father's** *instruction, and do not forsake your* **mother's** *teaching."*
Proverbs 1:8

"My son, keep your **father's** *commands, and do not forsake your* **mother's** *teaching."*
Proverbs 6:20

Both parents are involved. I delete most forwarded e-mails that do not have a "personal" note included because of the sheer volume of people wanting to pass along a good chuckle, poem, etc. However, I thought that the following item was worth keeping.

The Value of Money
—Anonymous

A man came home from work late again, tired and irritated, to find his five-year-old son waiting for him at the door. "Daddy, may I ask you a question?"

"Yeah, sure, what is it?" replied the man.

"Daddy, how much money do you make an hour?"

"That's none of your business. What makes you ask such a thing?" the man said angrily.

"I just want to know. Please tell me, how much do you make an hour?" pleaded the little boy.

"If you must know, I make $20.00 an hour."

"Oh," the little boy replied, head bowed. Looking up,

he said, "Daddy, may I borrow $10.00 please?"

The father was furious. "If the only reason you wanted to know how much money I make is just so you can borrow some to buy a silly toy or some other nonsense, then you march yourself straight to your room. You don't need any more toys! Go play with the ones you already have. I work long, hard hours everyday and don't have time for this."

The little boy quietly went to his room and shut the door. The man sat down and started to get even madder about the little boy's questioning. How dare he ask such questions only to get some money.

After an hour or so, the man had calmed down and started to think that he might have been a little hard on his son. Maybe there was something that he really needed to buy with that $10.00, and he really didn't ask for money very often. The man went to the door of the little boy's room and opened the door. His son was lying on the bed.

"Are you asleep, Son?" he asked.

"No daddy, I'm awake," replied the boy.

"I've been thinking, maybe I was too hard on you earlier," said the man. "It's been a long day, and I took my aggravation out on you. Here's that $10.00 you asked for."

The little boy sat straight up, beaming. "Oh, thank you, Daddy!" he yelled. Then, reaching under his pillow, he pulled out some more crumpled up bills.

The man, seeing that the boy already had money, started to get angry again. The little boy slowly counted out his money, then looked up at his father.

"Why did you want more money if you already had some?" the father grumbled.

"Because I didn't have enough, but now I do," the little boy replied. "Daddy, I have $20.00 now. Can I buy an hour of your time?"

This story is a good reminder that we can get so caught up in other things that do not have eternal and generational values. Time is slipping through our fingers. I recall the song "Cat's in the Cradle" and am reminded of how swiftly the years pass. It is never too late to invest that twenty-dollars' worth of time with someone you love. We must be sensitive to ending a phone conversation, canceling a girl's night out or a golf outing, putting a book or newspaper aside, turning off the TV, stopping the cleaning or chores so that we can give away some of our love and time. If we have truly surrendered "all" to the Lord, then our time is really not ours anyway!

The challenge is to think of my family and their needs as being *more important* than my own time and needs. This is a *daily* battle! Would I personally enjoy something else *more* than soccer or dance class? Sometimes, but we show our daughter, Emily, that what is important to *her* is important to *us*. We show our love for her by participating in her life. Could I wash and vacuum the car more quickly without my sons? Yes, but I invest in and teach Jacob and Justin, but, most importantly, I spend time with them. I love them by giving them my time. Plus, as a bonus, maybe someday they will wash my car!

Making a Lifetime of Memories

We just finished having my daughter Emily's seventh birthday party. It was a fantastic day, and she and her friends had a blast. As I reflected on the day, I began to add up the cost of the party and started to have a little spender's remorse. As Dana and I talked about this very section of the book, we were both reminded that we did not spend a lot on her actual presents. We purposefully invested in "making a memory." The toy or the fad will go by the wayside, but the memory created will last a lifetime. Emily and her friends making a tie-dyed T-shirt, and eating a snow cone with Mom and Dad serving, and taking pictures will outlast the "stuff."

I try to read at least one or two books on parenting and marriage each year to keep myself sharp and to challenge myself to be a better husband and father. If you did not (or do not) have good role models as parents, such an ongoing education becomes even more critical. If your parents did not model loving, serving, and giving, then you need to study or be around those who do model it. We do not even realize that we are making memories for our children. These memories can be good or bad; they can be traditions or attitudes that will also be carried on for multiple generations.

My memory is lousy. If I don't write something down in my daily planner or journal, I just will not remember it. I have few childhood memories, but I do recall some significant ones: sledding, playing in the leaves, delivering newspapers, camping, attending big family get-togethers at Christmas, painting choir boys at Christmas, acting in the Christmas plays, riding the luggage, playing baseball off the steps, playing tennis baseball with friends, vacationing at Camp-of-the-Woods, driving on vacations, and celebrating Thanksgiving. Dana recalls gardening, fishing, and holiday get-togethers. It is amazing how many of those traditions we are now passing on to our kids. It is also amazing that none of the great memories revolve around "stuff" or "things." All of the memories are family events, outings, or time spent together.

Love = Time

It is not easy making memories. It is work. This past Mother's Day I wanted to do something special for Dana that would be a lasting memory. Because she does so much with family photographs, I thought that she might like a collage of all of the kids over the years. My initial plan was to pay someone to do it, but as I thought about creating a memory, it seemed good to include the children, although they were only six, four, and one. It would be much easier to pay someone, but I thought that I would be cheating my wife and the kids by going the easy route. I was also intimidated by my wife's creativity because my idea of creativity is picking a different interstate highway other than the one we *should* take (and then getting lost or stuck in construction). But we did it! Four trips to the photograph reduction machine and six trips to the "creative scrapbook" store. I had the kids cut out decorations and help with the design. Although it was a lot of work, a rewarding memory, in which the whole family invested of their time and love, now hangs on our wall. It was also pretty fun seeing the look on her face when Dana opened it! She was surprised!

It is beneficial to gain life experiences from others. We can learn from and challenge each other. We have truly done that through our church family in the past few years. Our men's group has really challenged me to get out of my box and try some new things.

"As iron sharpens iron, so one man sharpens another."
—Proverbs 27:17

Mirror Moments

In a recent men's group meeting, we were sharing some of our marriage issues and victories. Keith shared how he often spends two hours on the couch talking with his wife. We all just looked at him with a blank stare. Two hours? That was a mirror moment. I looked in the mirror and did not like what I saw. It challenged me. It sharpened me. It had a positive influence on my marriage. With three young children, I do not think that we had done that since we had child number three!

If we stay isolated in our own little family cocoon, we will struggle with the same issues that our parents did. We need to be stretched and challenged! Go to a marriage seminar. Hang around with someone who has a great family life and a great marriage. Do not be intimidated or jealous. Learn. Harvest. Be sharpened.

SELAH 22-1

Take a few minutes to list some childhood memories—both good and not so good. I ask you to include the "not so good" memories so that you can ensure that you don't pass them on!

Good	Not so good
_____	_____
_____	_____
_____	_____
_____	_____
_____	_____
_____	_____
_____	_____

Dana is incredible at creating great memories. She does fantastic photo albums. She has already created a long list of memories and traditions that will affect generations to come. My mother was also great at this. Some people might not have a long list of memories. If not, it is time to start your own! Following are some of the memories that we are "attempting to make." I list these not to boast but possibly to stimulate some new ideas in you. I have put the word *new* beside those that were *not* passed down to us but that we are creating for the first time in our families. We have "stolen" many of these ideas from other "iron sharpeners." Again, if you are struggling, talk to other people, or get a book from the Christian bookstore.

Figure 22-1
Making our Family Memories

- Monthly "Dad Date Nights" with each of the kids (NEW)
- "Backyard memories"—Swing set, baseball, P.E. class, Slip-n-slide, sprinkler, soccer
- Family Walks & Talks (NEW)
- Family camping
- Family gardening
- Reading/Daddy time—one hour a night (NEW)
- Family Fun Nights (NEW)
- Homeschooling (NEW)
- Annual family trip to see Bluebonnets bloom (NEW)
- Annual family trip to Pumpkin Patch to pick our pumpkins, hayride (NEW)
- Fireworks
- Take kids to participate in Inner City Ministry (NEW)
- Nutcracker trip with Mom at Christmas (NEW)
- Attend a play/musical every year (NEW)
- Attend baseball games with the family
- Family driving vacations
- Field trips—Science place, fly kites (NEW)
- Fabulous birthday parties
- Mother's Day—Breakfast in bed (NEW)
- Warm Christmas atmosphere at home
- Make Metro Christmas stockings for Inner city youth (NEW)
- Saturday—donut day with Dad (NEW)

- Tuesday's—night out with Dad—library, walks, ice cream, etc. (NEW)
- Dad takes off on the kid's birthdays and we do something special (NEW)

Here are other things that we are not yet doing but would like to do:

- a family business,
- hiking/canoeing,
- take kids to Inner City Camp,
- Soup Kitchen at Thanksgiving, and
- a family missions trip.

SELAH 22-2

Take fifteen minutes to list what memories you are currently creating for your family and some new ones upon which you might improve.

Family Museum

You choose the memories that you are putting into your "Family Museum." They do not just happen. I like the following excerpt from Edith Schaeffer's "What is a family?"[4]

> *memories ought to be planned,*
> *memories ought to be chosen,*
>
> *memories ought to be put in the budget,*
> *memories ought to be recognized and given the proper amount of time,*
>
> *memories ought to be protected,*
> *memories ought not be wasted,*
>
> *memories ought to be passed down to the next generation.*

If we wait until we are "older" or "more well off" or have "more time," then the right time will have passed us by. What will last longer, a career or a memory; the evening news or an hour with the kids; a new car or a long walk on the beach? You and your spouse are the president and vice-president of your Family Museum. Will it be full or empty?

Backward?

The American businessman was at the pier of a small coastal Mexican village when a small boat with just one fisherman docked. Inside the small boat were several large yellowfin tuna. The American complimented the Mexican on the quality of his fish and asked how long it took to catch them.

The Mexican replied, "Only a little while."

The American then asked, "Why didn't you stay out longer and catch more fish?"

The Mexican said, "I have enough to support my family's immediate needs."

The American then asked, "But what do you do with the rest of your time?"

The Mexican fisherman said, "I sleep late; fish a little; play with my children; take siesta with my wife, Maria; stroll in the village each evening; and relax with my amigos. I have a full and busy life, señor."

The American scoffed, "I am a Harvard graduate with an MBA and could help you. You should spend more time fishing and with the proceeds buy a bigger boat. With the proceeds from the bigger boat you could buy several boats. Eventually, you would have a fleet of fishing boats. Instead of selling your catch to a middleman, you would sell directly to the processor, eventually opening your own cannery. You would control the product, processing, and distribution. You would need to leave this small coastal fishing village and move to Mexico City, then L.A., and eventually New York City, where you will run your expanding enterprise."

The Mexican fisherman asked, "But, señor, how long

will all this take?"

The American replied, "Fifteen or twenty years."

"But what then, señor?"

The American laughed and said, "That's the best part. When the time is right, you would announce an IPO and sell your company stock to the public and become very rich. You would make millions."

"Millions, señor? Then what?"

The American said, "Then you would retire. Move to a small coastal fishing village where you would sleep late, fish a little, play with your kids, take siesta with your wife, stroll to the village in the evening, where you could relax with your amigos."

We need a balance between the American and the Mexican. Why put off what you can begin today? Do not waste today. Do not continue to rationalize neglecting your family for whatever the reason—"I must provide more," or "I must be fulfilled before I can meet their needs," or "I will have time someday." Begin your family legacy today.

The next section might help give you some practical ideas to do just that. Seize the moment; it will not last long!

Figure 22-2
Family Activities

√ Reading aloud to your kids.

√ Talk to your kids—about their day, their joys and sorrows, their valleys and mountains.

√ Purposefully plan family vacations for the kids to make family memories—weekend camping trip, educational sightseeing, sporting events, etc.

√ Plan a missions trip. We will begin planning our first family missions trip in the next few years.

√ Take long walks.

√ Visit museums and libraries, and take free educational trips.

√ Assemble puzzles and play board games together.

√ Try a new sport together as a family.

√ Work and play together in outdoor activities.

√ Include the kids in and teach them about your hobbies (e.g., collecting, crafts, gardening, etc.).

√ Have a Family Fun Night. We use the great Heritage Builders series (Family Night Tool Chest) from Focus on the Family to assist us in creating a spiritually fun family night.[5]

√ Have date nights. At least once a month, I rotate a "date night" with each of the children so that I can have some quality, one-on-one time with them. We go out for dinner and then talk somewhere and just hang out. We have gone frisbee golfing, to the driving range, out for ice cream to talk, and taken a walk in the woods. We stay away from the malls and movies. This has been one of the most rewarding activities that we stole from someone else!

√ Have an All-Kids Night Out. Every week, usually on Tuesdays, I take all the children out to give Mom a break because she rarely gets a moment of peace.

√ Work together in a ministry involvement. As often as possible, I take one or more of the kids to assist in Dallas Metro's inner city outreach. They learn to get outside of their suburban box and touch lives, meet needs, and be around people of different skin colors, different income levels, and different everything. Get involved with some outreach through your church or city and involve the kids.

√ Turn off the TV. I will not meddle, but I believe that the biggest time waster and killer of quality family time is the television set. More than we care to admit, it limits physical activity, decreases communication, and teaches and influences our lives. In this respect, I've found the following quotation to be irresistible:

"I must say, I find television very educational. The minute someone turns it on, I go to the library and read a good book."
—Groucho Marx

The Family Calendar

The *only* way that we have been successful at making family life a priority is to schedule these activities. That might sound rigid, forced, and unnatural, but it is what works for us. I know perfectly well that I have good intentions, but something always *comes up*. If it is on my calendar, then it is locked in.

"Sorry, guys, I have plans on Tuesday."

"Sorry, Pastor, can we do it on Thursday?"

"Sorry, boss, I have an appointment at 7:00 on Thursday."

If your family is a priority, you must make it a calendar priority. On Sunday nights, my wife and I plot out our week and then look at the next couple of weeks to ensure that we know what is happening in each other's lives. It is also a great communication tool to slow us down when some weeks seem out of control. We do not live and die by "the calendar," just as we do not live and die by "the budget." But it is our roadmap, our plan. Plans change and things come up. To be perfectly honest, I do not make every date night. But if I schedule twenty-six date nights a year and make fifteen of them, then I can guarantee that is probably ten to fifteen more than if I had *not* scheduled them!

"Until"

I do know that sacrificing your family now so that you can have "enough" for retirement or for a "sudden death" is not appropriate. The temptation is to continue with our out-of-whack priorities "until we get another car" or "until we get the living room furnished" or "until we have enough saved for college." There will always be another "until," and it is not possible to go backward.

"At some point in his life there came a shortage of future" —Steve Turner (from the poem "Aging")

I would rather have a financial shortage than a shortage of future with my children and family. We must have our priorities in the proper order. If a job is taking you into dangerous ground with your family or into temptations that are unhealthful, then it is time to reconsider your employment and pray about finding a new job.

SELAH 22-3

Take a few minutes to pray for wisdom regarding the balance of "enough" and "until." Pray about the changes that you need to make and when you need to make them.

Education

"In a nationwide poll of four hundred parents of kids ages two to seventeen by the Center for a New American Dream, 50 percent of parents said that their kids would rather go to the mall than walk in the woods with their family. Sixty-six percent of parents said that their kids define their self-worth in terms of possessions, and that the problem has worsened over time. More than half of all parents admitted to buying a product for their child that they disapproved of because the child wanted the product in order to fit in with their friends. It is little wonder that 87% of parents of children aged two to 17 feel that advertising and marketing aimed at children makes kids too materialistic. According to Arts Education Policy Review, over $2 billion is spent on advertising to kids each year- more than 20 times the amount spent just ten years ago."[6]

The outside influences are great. We have much competition in teaching our children. This should give us incentive to fight for our time with them even more. We as parents have a window of opportunity to influence and teach our children. No perfect teachers, no perfect pastors, and no perfect Christians exist. The home—both father and mother—must play a part in the education of our children. We must compensate for both what is not taught and what is taught incorrectly. If strictness is taught, we need to supplement with creativity. If evolution is taught, we need to teach the truth of creation. If relativism is taught and lived, then we need to teach absolutes and the laws of God. If secularism is taught, we need to give adequate time to teaching God's Word and Christian education. If the children are homeschooled or Christian-school educated, they need to be taught about secularism and educated regarding how others live.

We can never start to teach our children about money management too early. Our teaching occurs mostly through our actions and not our words. Involve the children in any actions that you will take as a result of reading this book. We have many opportunities to teach our children about earning, budgeting, saving, patience, investing, taxes, giving, the value of money, and money saving strategies.

Following are some practical teaching opportunities for your kids.

- Give them allowances and do not allow them to purchase a toy for which they have been begging until they save enough to pay for it.
- Teach them to give to the Lord. We use a bank from Crown Ministries that has three "houses" into which to put money—the church, the bank, and the store. Allow them to give in the offering at church.
- Open a checking and/or savings account for them.
- Offer matching funds for big-ticket items. (For example, when they save $50 for that bike, you can agree to chip in the other $50.)
- Offer a reward for their assisting with the chores and behaving well.
- Have them help clip coupons and use them at the grocery store. Show them how much was saved and equate that with what they could buy with that money.
- Start a vacation jar. Put in coupon savings or a portion of unexpected funds. It will teach them savings.
- Take them to work with you and show them your paycheck.
- Pay them for doing odd jobs.
- Teach them to wait. Do not be controlled by their desires for something *now!* This will instill discipline and self-control in your children at an early age.

Guard against Stuff; Make the Choice!

"Do not follow other gods, the gods of the peoples around you. . . ."[7]
*[T]hen choose for yourselves this day whom you will serve. . . .
But as for me and my household, we will serve the Lord."*[8]

It is difficult for me to answer the issues of how much is too much in your life or what is an appropriate standard of living for you. What is a necessity versus a luxury? Who is right in being frugal in one area while being extravagant in another area? How much should you be giving? How much family time do you need to have a "good family life"? The answers are personal and will vary from family to family. I do know that we each need balance in our family financial lives. I do know that we must focus on the present as well as planning for the future. We must give, and we should save. What is the proper balance? You must pray and hear that answer for yourself.

In Unity

Nothing is more important in financial and family matters than unity between husband and wife. Financial issues and money management problems remain at the top of the list of couples' counseling sessions. Thus, it is extremely important to move ahead in unity—in life priorities, giving priorities, and financial priorities. It is also critical that you be candid.

A survey conducted by *Reader's Digest* reported that 42 percent of men and 36 percent of women have kept something secret from their spouses.[9] And the most common secret is the price that was paid for a purchase. Spousal unity might require more honesty, humility, and asking for forgiveness, and it might require some behavioral changes. Take the following quick test to see where you need to focus.

SELAH 23-4
Financial Unity Test

Score you and your spouse on a scale of from 1 to 5 (5 = "Yes, describes us perfectly"; 4 = "Yes, pretty much describes us"; 3 = "Yes, sometimes describes us"; 2 = "No, rarely or never describes us"; 1 = "Does not describe us at all").

We have separate bank accounts. _____

One of us has credit cards or debts without
the other's knowledge. _____

One of us has investments or other accounts
without the other's knowledge. _____

One of us is not fully supportive of a collection
or hobby of the spouse. _____

One of us makes significant purchases (>$50)
without the other's knowledge. _____

We have fights (discussions) about some of these
"secretive" purchases. _____

One of us makes significant purchases (>$50)
although the spouse objects. _____

Only one spouse knows the budget, expenses, bills,
financial situation. _____

One of us has no idea of the total debts or assets
of the family. _____

Certain debts and bills are "assigned" to each spouse. _____

One spouse refuses to be accountable to the other
regarding financial issues. _____

We disagree about how much "giving" should
be done regularly. _____

TOTAL SCORE _____

Scores: >50—Some long discussions and counseling are necessary.

35–49—Some long discussions and radical change need to occur.

26–35—Certain issues still could affect your marriage. Talk them through.

16–25—You have made some good efforts at unity. It is still worthwhile to talk through the high scores.

1–15—Wow! You are in financial unity! You need to be assisting other couples through your modeling.

The enemy, Satan, would like to drive a wedge into your marriage. Those wedges are independence and secrecy. Some of these issues might force some difficult but necessary discussions. Do not just get angry. Be understanding of the reasons why things are the way they are. Obviously, issues and potentially hurtful past experiences must be understood before emotions rage and unwise decisions are made. This is a good chance to talk it through and pray together about your hurts.

Is 2 > 1?

One of the most difficult topics with which we wrestled early in our marriage was that of whether Dana should stay at home instead of working. This decision has the potential to be a unity breaker and also has the potential of being one of the best or worst decisions that a couple ever makes. I have not heard many of the horror stories, but I can imagine that if some of the couples whom I counseled had decided immediately to go from two incomes to one, it would have devastated them both financially and emotionally. I also knew that we would be challenged financially if we made the decision, but we decided that the sacrifice was worth it. God provided more than what we ever could have asked, and it was one of the most rewarding decisions we have ever made! I can testify that it was a decision that we did not take lightly. I will not provide any counsel or advice on the issue other than to ask you to discuss, pray, and plan if this is a desire of *one* of the spouses. God will honor your desire for unity and your involving Him in the decision process. He will help open doors if you commit to the practical financial disciplines that are discussed in this book.

In addition to the spiritual and emotional side of the decision is its financial impact. It obviously is significant. If this possibility is not an option now because of your debt situation, then what are your plans to get out of debt? When specifically will you get out of debt? What are your long-term and short-term goals? (See Chapters 2 and 3.) When do you (or your spouse) desire to stay at home? Do you have a plan written down to accomplish this goal, or is it just a desire?

Does It Pay?

Although we live in a society with an ever-increasing number of dual-income families, in some cases it might not always be the financial windfall that we think. Many couples are forced to add income to make ends meet, and they are sacrificing their families on the altar of "more." According to the U.S. Census Bureau, in 1940, 43 percent of mothers stayed at home while the father worked full time. As of recently, only 21 percent of mothers with kids ages six to seventeen stayed at home.[10]

Every situation will vary, but some "second incomes" are really not adding that much to the total family income when all expenses are factored in. I encourage you to take a detailed look at your own "actual" expenses from your family situation if you so desire to see if it is really "paying off." Some obvious expenses result from an additional "breadwinner," including transportation, day care, clothing, and potential meals out. Those expenses might or might not tip the scales in the decision process. Obviously, the tradeoffs are not just financial, but the financial aspect is a consideration. (See the example in Figure 22-3.)

Figure 22-3
Dual-Income Example

FINANCIAL PIECE OF THE PIE

Salary #2:	$40,000	
Take-home pay:		$28,000
Day care:	$ 6,000	
Gas/transportation:	$ 2,000	
Lunches/snacks/coffee:	$ 2,000	
Dinners out/no time to cook:	$ 2,000	
Work clothing/dry cleaning	$ 1,500	
Business misc. —stamps, briefcase, planner, etc.	$ 800	
Cell phone usage	$ 500	
Coworkers expenses —birthday, Christmas, showers, etc.	$ 500	
Hair/makeup/beauty	$ 200	
Net pay after expenses:		$12,500

Not bad until you think of it in the light of an employer's coming up to you and offering you a full-time job at a salary of $12,500 a year. Would you take it and miss out on your children's lives?

This might be an extreme example, but please do the math yourself before assuming. You might find that it is really not worth it or that it is worth it only for a season, especially in light of the time lost that might have been invested in your children.

TIME PIECE OF THE PIE

Weekly time away from children:	
On the job	40 hours
Lunches	5 hours
Driving time	2–5 hours
Total weekly time away from children:	47–50 hours
Total remaining "waking time" for children:	10–15 hours

You might also consider that you could use some of that forty-seven to fifty hours to save additional money by clipping coupons, shopping smarter, volunteering more, etc. Please do not interpret this section as a guilt trip. I know that many mothers' hearts bleed because they cannot be home with their children. The intention is to challenge you to pray, involve God and your spouse, and include all variables in the decision process. Ensure that you are calculating the additional expenses of the second income. If this is not an option now, then use those ten to fifteen hours as a precious commodity.

A Family Foundation

Just as we discussed the importance of having a "A Life Foundation" or "Life Purpose," it is also important to have a "Family Foundation." When I decided (with God's and my father's prodding) to refocus on my family priorities, I decided to put our "Family Purpose" on paper. It is much more detailed than my "Life Foundation" (Chapter 2).

Our Family Foundation

1. To love the Lord our God with all of our heart, soul, mind, and strength; to pursue Him with an undivided heart, totally abandoned to God.

2. To love Dana as Christ loved the church; to serve her unselfishly, giving myself up for her, putting her before myself, and listening

to her wholeheartedly; to provide for her physical needs and grow with her spiritually; to have a spirit of complete unity and submission between us as we follow Christ Jesus so that with one heart and mouth we may glorify our Father; to be committed to her as long as I live.

3. To raise our children in the fear and admonition of the Lord, training them to follow Christ wholeheartedly, to honor their father and mother, to be submissive and obedient and to be imitators of Christ so that the world may know that they are His disciples; to educate and train our children in the ways of the Lord so that when they are mature they will not depart from it; to instill biblical values and Christian principles through home-schooling and parent-based education; to spend quality time together as a cohesive unit that leans upon and influences each other rather than being influenced by worldly standards and peers; to prepare our children to influence their world for Jesus Christ and help fulfill the Great Commission.

4. To love the poor and our neighbors as if they were a part of our family, giving, serving, and loving others unconditionally.

5. To be intercessors and communicate daily with God such as to walk in the Spirit, listen, and follow His guidance.

6. To daily read and study the Word of God, hiding it in our hearts, living it, preaching it, teaching and being doers of the Word and not just hearers.

7. To fulfill our calling and to use our gifts as working unto the Lord and not unto men; to please the Lord, not men; to teach, train, encourage, serve, give, evangelize, help, and administrate as the Lord leads and opens doors through our local church and other areas of ministry, always keeping our relationship with Him first, others and family second, and then the ministry; to fulfill our roles in the body of Christ, both within His church and to the lost.

8. To give cheerfully and unselfishly as true stewards and caretak-

ers of God's money, keeping an eternal focus and promoting equality among the body of Christ.

SELAH 22-5

Draft a "Family Foundation" for your own family. In the beginning, it might be only a couple of thoughts or lines, but it should line up with your priorities and life goals.

ACTION POINTS

1. How did you feel when you read the "Value of Money" and "The Mexican Fisherman" stories? Do you see yourself in the mirror at all?

_____

_____

_____

_____

_____

_____

_____

2. Review Figures 22-1 and 22-2. What are a few activities that you are committed to adding or changing that will make your family unit stronger?

_____ _____ _____

_____ _____ _____

_____ _____ _____

_____ _____ _____

_____ _____ _____

3. Review Selah 22-4. What actions are you taking to promote family unity? Have you talked to your spouse about any of these actions yet?

_____

_____

_____

_____

_____

_____

4. Consider writing out some thoughts for a "Family Foundation" referenced in Selah 22-5. My own "Family Foundation" statement holds me accountable as I look at it often.

CHAPTER 23

Revival? Reformation? Judgment? It's Up to You!

Time stood still today for what seemed like eternity as I stood on the corner of Lothian and Fountainbridge, in Edinburgh, Scotland. I had been searching for more than an hour for one of the few Bible-believing and Bible-preaching churches in the great city where John Knox once hung his hat and preached fiery sermons against dead religion, man-centered power structures, and faith by works.

Finally, after circling many blocks and retracing my steps time and time again, I was certain that *I had found a church* as a bus stopped and dozens of well-dressed people of all ages stepped off. I could barely keep up with a group of elderly women! They were walking briskly in their hats, purses, and high heels and with a passionate purpose. I nearly cried as I opened the doors to "church" only to discover that it was a bingo parlor. I stood dejected and in shock as I watched for fifteen minutes as people rushed madly toward their destination, with no apparent thought of what they were missing in life—not church, but a life with Jesus as their passionate purpose.

For another fifteen minutes, I searched in vain for a church of any sort. As I gave up my hunt, I saw people going this way and that way, shopping bags in hand, walking aimlessly. I was numb. *Lord*, I prayed, *is there a remnant, one or two churches maybe?* My heart was heavy. Time froze again as I stood on the corner and questioned the Lord. I sipped my lukewarm coffee as a toddler darted in front of me, running defiantly from his parents. Rebelliously, he yelled, "I WILL NOT!" and continued his run from his parents, not caring or even realizing the pain and hurt it was causing them.

The spiritual parallels of this scene crossed my mind. A lukewarm country, a lukewarm church, and an independent people grieve the heart of God. I was reminded of how blessed we are to have Bible-believing churches on nearly every corner in America. My heart warmed as I thought of my local church and the living, breathing fellowship of believers that we have but that we so easily take for granted.

I continued my journey back to the hotel. My spirit leapt as I came upon a sign that read "6:30—Service on Healing." As I walked through the expansive cemetery toward the massive structure, I was surrounded by tombstones larger than I. These were monuments to men dead and gone. I circled the church twice but could find no entrance! The building and its stained glass were intimidating to me, and the lack of an easy entrance left me wondering if this is how God intended it.

I never did find a place of worship that night, but it was a fruitful night of soulsearching for me. It was a night of grieving for what used to be and an expectation of what could be. I believe that God desires more than anything to pour out His Spirit on this country and the world. As I have studied revivalists and reformers of old, I have been stirred with hope for our land. I believe that we need reviving more than ever. Just as there are many interpretations of the word *blessing*, so there are many definitions of the word *revival*. I am not referring to a three- or four-day series of meetings but rather

- a renewed and restored interest in Jesus Christ,
- a rousing and a stirring up of spiritual matters in individuals.

Both of these things will lead to *results* that include repentance, salvation of souls, increased church attendance, increased Bible reading and prayer, increased awareness of the Holy Spirit's presence, changed lifestyles and priorities, a laying down of idols and materialism, etc.

Sometimes it is more obvious to some people than to others that our country needs a revival. Is it that time for America? Are we really at a crossroads? Have we crossed the line from blessing and reached the precipice of judgment? Are we poised for a massive spiritual revival? You will find as many different answers from spiritual leaders in our country as you will find questions.

Historical Hope

I recently read a story from American history that brought me hope for our land. In the middle of the nineteenth century, at a time of prosperity, people were seeking riches rather than God. The churches were losing people, and worldliness was creeping in.[1] Many Christians were praying that the love of money would be broken in people's lives. Samuel Prime's book *The Power of Prayer* provided some explanation about the move to pray. He wrote,

> As a nation, we were becoming rapidly demoralized by our worldliness, our ambition, our vanity, and our vices. The true, the great end for which we believe this nation was raised up, was being lost sight of. The very foundations were moving. We needed this "great awakening" to bring us to our senses, to rouse up the national conscience, to arrest the national decay, and bring us back to a high tone of moral health.[2]

In September 1857, Jeremiah Lanphier, a forty-eight-year-old businessman-turned-lay city missionary, rented a hall on Fulton Street in New York City. He began a prayer meeting that met every Wednesday at noon. Six men assembled for that first prayer meeting on September 23. Two days later, the Bank of Philadelphia failed. In early October, the small but growing number of people meeting to pray decided to meet daily. On October 10, the stock market crashed. "On October 14," Lanphier wrote, "the extensive banking system of the United States collapsed, a far-reaching disaster bringing ruin to hundreds of thousands of people in New York, Philadelphia, Boston, and the industrial centers of the nation." [3]

Some banks refused to redeem their promissory notes; others suspended operations altogether, including eighteen of New York City's leading banks. The panic caused rich men to go broke, literally, overnight. Some felt that the bank panic was divine judgment against a nation that had made money its god. The situation in the United States was a valley that they had never before seen. America was awash in economic, political, and spiritual turmoil. Banks were failing, railroads were bankrupt, factories were closing, and unemployment was increasing.

The financial panic triggered a spiritual hunger. When your food is taken from you, you get hungry. Within two months, two lecture rooms were full of men praying with Jeremiah Lanphier. According to Winkie Pratney, within six months more than ten thousand businessmen were meeting in similar meetings across America, confessing sins, being converted and praying for revival.

In February 1858, the *New York Herald* and the *New York Tribune* gave extensive coverage to the prayer meeting revival. An entire issue was devoted to the revival in April 1858, and news of the event spread quickly by telegraph. Prayer meetings were organized in the cities by lay people and were interdenominational. Apparently, this revival was the first to begin in America that spread worldwide. Ireland and Scotland were soon to follow. The revival spread to Wales, England, and beyond. Unlike the earlier Great Awakenings (George Whitefield, Jonathan Edwards, Charles Finney, Peter Cartwright, and others), this one was an absent the great names connected with a revival. But the results of the revival affected many great Christians who would later become leaders, including D.L. Moody, William Booth, C.H. Spurgeon, and A.B. Simpson.[4]

D.L. Moody began his ministry during this revival, yet he was never ordained. Although he founded a Bible college and pastored churches, he always remained a layman. C.H. Spurgeon, commenting on this great moving of the Spirit, said, "In the City of New York at this present moment, there is not, I believe one single hour of the day where Christians are not gathered together for prayer." The prayer meeting had become one of the institutions of the city.[5]

When Finney returned to Boston the following winter, the interest in revival was under way as he wrote,

This was in the winter of 1857 and 1858; and it will be

remembered that it was at this time that a great revival prevailed throughout the land in such a tremendous manner, that for some weeks it was estimated that not less than 50,000 conversions occurred per week. [6]

Even the secular media reported on this revival. In a two-column editorial on March 20, the *New York Times* said the following about the revival:

> The great wave of religious excitement which is now sweeping over this nation, is one of the most remarkable movements since the Reformation. . . . Churches are crowded; bank-directors' rooms become oratories; schoolhouses are turned into chapels; converts are numbered by the scores of thousands. In this City, we have beheld a sight which not the most enthusiastic fanatic for church-observances could ever have hoped to look upon;—we have seen in a business quarter of the City, in the busiest hours, assemblies of merchants, clerks and working-men, to the number of some 5,000, gathered day after day for a simple and solemn worship. Similar assemblies we find in other portions of the City; a theatre is turned into a chapel; churches of all sects are open and crowded by day and night. It is most impressive to think that over this great land tens and fifties of thousands of men and women are putting to themselves at this time in a simple, serious way, the greatest question that can ever come before the human mind—"What shall we do to be saved from sin?"[7]

Although secular historians today barely remember that revival of 1857–1858, it was arguably the greatest of the three Great Awakenings experienced in the United States of America.

"In history, when people got right with God about money, then revival happened. In the U.S., we won't have revival until people come clean about money and align ourselves and our affections with God's priorities. And people won't come clean unless the church tells them the truth."
—Al Taylor

SELAH 23-1

Reflect for a few minutes. Does a relationship in general exist between finances and revival? How about in your life?

If . . . Then . . . But. . . .

Sometimes it is during days of struggle and hopelessness that people realize that they need our God. No longer can they rely on the "seen" things—the bank account, the career, the power, the material things, the vices, and the empty relationships. They realize that they need someone bigger than themselves and their circumstances. Will it come to that again? I do not know. Do I wish it upon us? Absolutely not, but God says that He disciplines those whom He loves. If it will take God's discipline to keep 100 million people from the flames in hell, would it be worth it?

God did say "if." "If my people, who are called by my name, will humble themselves and pray and seek my face, and turn from their wicked ways, then will I hear from heaven and will forgive their sin and will heal their land."[8]

Sometimes we stop reading when it is convenient. Not only is there an *if/then* statement in this passage but also it proceeds to discuss a *but/then* statement: "But if you turn away and forsake the decrees and commands I have given you and go off to serve other gods and worship them, then I will uproot Israel [God's people] from my land, which I have given them, and will reject this temple . . . . I will make it a byword and an object of ridicule among all peoples."[9]

We love to hear about the blessings, but the story does not always end there. Just as there are *if/then* statements in 2 Chronicles 7, the Bible is full of them (see Leviticus 26, Deuteronomy 28, Isaiah 3, Jeremiah 7, Jeremiah 25, and Jeremiah 44.) Rewards for obedience are discussed—rain, crops, harvest, safety, all of the food you want, peace, and favor—but punishment for disobedience is also included—disease, defeated by enemies, enemies eat your seed, bread supply cut off, and fearful hearts.

Let us be honest. We do not like to read about such things. I know that I would rather say, "Tell us pleasant things," as the book of Isaiah states. [10] Unfortunately, the Bible mentions that we need to be reproved, rebuked, and exhorted and not just have our itching ears scratched.

Does this mean that we need to thunder judgment and hell from the pulpit *every* Sunday? No. That is not my Father. Does this mean that we need to be reproved or rebuked or challenged *occasionally*? Yes, I know that I need that.

Dad and Judge

We know that God is the same yesterday, today, and forever. We know that He loves us. But we also know that a good Father or a just Judge cannot just "bless, bless, bless" or "wink at sin." He disciplines those whom He loves. [11] A father's role involves love and mercy, but it also includes discipline.

What kind of a father would I be if I did not discipline my children? Is it fair to them to ignore their rebellion and sin? Is it tough to discipline them? It is for me. I do it with a heavy heart. Justice is not always fun to administer, but it is necessary. A judge's duty is to be fair and just. [12] What kind of judge would I be if I let a murderer off with no punishment just because I did not want to be mean or just because I wanted to give him another chance? Would that be fair to the victim or the other "potential" victims? No, but God is a loving, merciful God. In fact, He is slow to anger. [13]

But God also must be just. I am thankful about that "slow to anger" part, but He does get angry. Jesus was angered often by the Pharisees. He threw the moneychangers out of the temple. He rebuked His followers. Yes, He spoke the truth in love, but we do not know his tone of voice or voice inflections by reading the Word. We do know that God's anger burns against the disobedient and for those countries that have forsaken him (Sodom and Gomorrah and the people of Noah's time are among the many examples). [14]

An Island of Prosperity

I quite often ask, "How long will God wait for America?" We

have been so fortunate in contrast to both those countries that we discussed earlier that have so little and the many countries that have had major collapses in the last decade. Consider, for example, the following:

- South Korea—market down 80 percent, some currencies down 70 percent
- Japan—real estate drops in excess of 80 percent
- Russia—defaults on debt, food shortages

Many countries have had significant declines in their Gross Domestic Product since the late 1990s:

❖ Indonesia	73%
❖ Korea	43%
❖ Thailand	40%
❖ Malaysia	31%
❖ Japan	11%
❖ Hong Kong	3%

"I know of no country, indeed, where the love of money has taken stronger hold on the affections of men."
—Alexis de Tocqueville

We continue to live on an island of prosperity. We are so blessed! However, having too much mercy, too much grace, and too much blessing is like one's eating too many sweets and not enough meat and vegetables. They are so much easier to eat, but they are not creating a healthy individual. Our appetite for "things" has continued to grow, and the "blessing overflow" has crowded out the things of God.

A Slippery Path

We have removed God from many schools and courts. Twenty-two percent of all pregnancies end in abortion. Homosexuality and pornography are attacking at all sides. Our television screens and movie theaters ridicule and blaspheme Christ and biblical family values. We have increased violence in our inner cities and among our youth. And the list goes on. Even the events of September 11, 2001, although significant, humbled us only temporarily. God's mercy is running long. How long can it last?

We can know the future by studying the past. We have had both revival and judgment in our past, but can you have both simultaneously? It happened in 1857. In fact, the revival resulted from financial panic or potential judgment. Although I cannot pretend to know God's intentions or ways, I do believe that God desires a spiritual revival more than any pastor, spiritual leader, or hungry Christian does. But if the means getting to that point are discipline and judgment, then I believe that He will use them to protect His children and to keep the lost from perishing. If we continue on our slippery path of compromise, materialism, and idolatry, judgment might not be far off. Could it occur through a financial collapse, as it did in 1857? It is possible. David Wilkerson's book *America's Last Call*[15] details some of his thoughts and biblical parallels that are quite striking.

Let us pray for our country. Pray that

❖ America will see revival;
❖ God will use you and me;
❖ we will be moved to *action*;
❖ the lost will repent;
❖ Christians will repent of compromise, materialism, and idolatry;
❖ Christians will humble themselves;
❖ we will all seek God's face;
❖ we will all set our life and financial priorities in order; and
❖ the lost will be drawn to Jesus.

"God does nothing but by prayer, and everything with it."
—John Wesley

"Beware in your prayers, above everything else, of limiting God, not only by unbelief, but by fancying that you know what He can do. Expect unexpected things above all that we ask or think."
—Andrew Murray

SELAH 23-2

Take some time to pray for our country.

We must pray. We must expect. But we also must *act*. God was gracious and compassionate with Jonah, but Jonah was more concerned for his own well being, seeking the shade of the vine, while more than 120,000 souls in Nineveh needed Jesus (Jonah 4). On my office wall is a picture of the lives at stake. The picture is described in the following article written by General William Booth and paraphrased by Keith Green before his death. William Booth (1829–1912) and his wife Catherine founded the Salvation Army in 1865 in their home country, England. His passion for the lost, especially those whom the established church considered "irredeemable," was legendary. His whole life can be summarized in his own words: "Go for souls—and go for the worst!"

Who Cares?

by General William Booth
Paraphrased by Keith Green[16]

On one of my recent journeys, as I gazed from the coach window, I was led into a train of thought concerning the conditions of the multitudes around me. They were living carelessly in the most open and shameless rebellion against God, without a thought for their eternal welfare. As I looked out the window, I seemed to see them all— millions of people all around me—given up to their drink and their pleasure, their dancing and their music, their business and their anxieties, their politics and their troubles. Ignorant—willfully ignorant in many cases—and in other instances knowing all about the truth and not caring at all. But all of them, the whole mass of them, sweeping on and up in their blasphemies and devilries to the throne of God. While my mind was thus engaged, I had a vision.

I saw a dark and stormy ocean. Over it the black clouds hung heavily; through them every now and then vivid lightning flashed and loud thunder rolled, while the winds moaned, and the waves rose and foamed, towered and broke, only to rise and foam, tower and break again. In that ocean I thought I saw myriad's of poor human beings plunging and floating, shouting and shrieking, cursing and struggling and drowning; and as they cursed and screamed, they rose and shrieked again, and then some sank to rise no more. And I saw out of this dark, angry ocean, a mighty rock that rose up with its summit towering high above the black clouds that overhung the stormy sea. And all around the base of this rock I saw a vast platform. Onto this platform, I saw with delight a number of the poor struggling, drowning wretches continually climbing out of the angry ocean. And I saw that a few of those, who were already safe on the platform, were helping the poor creatures still in the angry waters to reach the place of safety.

On looking more closely, I found a number of those who had been rescued, industriously working and scheming by ladders, ropes, boats, and other means more effective, to deliver the poor strugglers out of this sea. Here and there were some who actually jumped into the water, regardless of all the consequences, in their passion to "rescue the perishing." And I hardly know which gladdened me most—the sight of the poor drowning people climbing onto the rocks, reaching the place of safety, or the devotion and self-sacrifice of those whose whole beings were wrapped up in the effort for their deliverance.

As I looked on, I saw that the occupants of that platform were quite a mixed company. That is, they were divided into different "sets" or classes, and they occupied themselves with different pleasures and employments. But only a very few of them seemed to make it their business to get the people out of the sea. But what puzzled me most was the fact that though all of them had been rescued at one time or another from the ocean, nearly everyone seemed to have forgotten all about it. Anyway, it seemed the memory of its darkness and danger no longer troubled them at all. And what seemed equally strange and perplexing to me was that these people did not even seem to have any care—that is, any agonizing care—about the poor perishing ones who were struggling and drowning right before their very eyes . . . many of whom were their own husbands and wives, brothers and sisters, and even their own children.

Now this astonishing unconcern could not have been the result of ignorance or lack of knowledge, because they lived right there in full sight of it all and even talked about it sometimes. Many even went regularly to hear lectures and sermons in which the awful state of these poor drowning creatures was described.

I have already said that the occupants of this platform were engaged in different pursuits and pastimes. Some of them were absorbed night and day in trading and business in order to make gain, storing up their savings in boxes, safes, and the like. Many spent their time in amusing themselves with growing flowers on the side of the rock, others in painting pieces of cloth, or in playing music, or in dressing themselves up in different styles and walking about to be admired. Some occupied themselves chiefly in eating and drinking, others were taken up with arguing about the poor drowning creatures that had already been rescued. But the thing to me that seemed the most amazing was that those on the platform to whom He called, who heard His voice and felt they ought to obey it—at least they said they did—those who confessed to love Him much and were in full sympathy with Him in the task He had undertaken—who worshipped Him or who professed to do so—were so taken up with their trades and professions, their money saving and pleasures, their families and circles, their religions and arguments about it, and their preparation for going to the mainland, that they did not listen to the cry that came to them from this Wonderful Being who had Himself gone down into the sea. Anyway, if they heard it, they did not heed it. They did not care. And so the multitude went on right before them struggling and shrieking and drowning in the darkness.

And then I saw something that seemed to me even more strange than anything that had gone on before in this strange vision. I saw that some of these people on the platform whom this Wonderful Being had called to, wanting them to come and help Him in His difficult task of saving these perishing creatures, were always praying and crying out to Him to come to them! Some wanted Him to come and stay with them, and spend His time and strength in making them happier. Others wanted Him to come and take away various doubts and misgivings they had concerning the truth of some letters which He had written them. Some wanted Him to come and make them feel more secure on the rock—so secure that they would be quite sure that they should never slip off again into the ocean. Numbers of others wanted Him to make them feel quite certain that they would really get off the rock and onto the mainland someday; because as a matter of fact, it was well known that some had walked so carelessly as to lose their footing and had fallen back again into the stormy waters. So these people used to meet and get up as high on the rock as they could, and looking toward the mainland (where they thought the Great Being was) they would cry out, "Come to us! Come, help us!" And all the while He was down (by His Spirit) among the poor struggling, drowning creatures in the angry deep, with His arms around them trying to drag them out, and looking up oh! so longingly, but all in vain to those on the rock, crying to them with His voice all hoarse from calling, "Come to Me! Come and help Me!"

And then I understood it all. It was plain enough. That sea

was the ocean of life—the sea of real, actual human existence. That lightning was the gleaming of piercing truth coming from Jehovah's throne. That thunder was the distant echoing of the wrath of God. Those multitudes of people shrieking, struggling, and agonizing in the stormy sea were the thousands and thousands of poor harlots and harlot-makers, of drunkards and drunkard-makers, of thieves, liars, blasphemers, and ungodly people of every kindred, tongue, and nation. Oh, what a black sea it was! And oh, what multitudes of rich and poor, ignorant and educated were there. They were all so unalike in their outward circumstances and conditions, yet all alike in one thing—all sinners before God—all held by, and holding onto, some iniquity, fascinated by some idol, the slaves of some devilish lust, and ruled by the foul fiend from the bottomless pit!

"All alike in one thing?" No, all alike in two things. Not only the same in their wickedness, but unless rescued, the same in their sinning, sinking . . . down, down, down . . . to the same terrible doom. That great sheltering rock represented Calvary, the place where Jesus had died for them. And the people on it were those who had been rescued. The way they used their energies, gifts, and time represented the occupations and amusements of those who professed to be saved from sin and hell - followers of the Lord Jesus Christ. The handful of fierce, determined ones, who were risking their own lives in saving the perishing, were true soldiers of the cross of Jesus. That Mighty Being who was calling to them from the midst of the angry waters was the Son of God, "the same yesterday, today, and forever," who is still struggling and interceding to save the dying multitudes about us from this terrible doom of damnation, and whose voice can be heard above the music, machinery, and noise of life, calling on the rescued to come and help Him save the world.

My friends in Christ, you are rescued from the waters. You are on the rock. He is in the dark sea calling on you to come to Him and help Him. Will you go? Look for yourselves. The surging sea of life crowded with perishing multitudes rolls up to the very spot on which you stand. Leaving the vision, I now come to speak of the fact—a fact that is as real as the Bible, as real as the Christ who hung upon the cross, as real as the judgment day will be, and as real as the heaven and hell that will follow it.

Look! Don't be deceived by appearances—men and things are not what they seem. All who are not on the rock are in the sea! Look at them from the standpoint of the great white throne, and what a sight you have! Jesus Christ, the Son of God is, through His Spirit, in the midst of this dying multitude, struggling to save them. And He is calling on you to jump into the sea—to go right away to His side and help Him in the holy strife. Will you jump? That is, will you go to His feet and place yourself absolutely at His disposal?

A young Christian once came to me and told me that for some time she had been giving the Lord her profession and prayers and money, but now she wanted to give Him her life. She wanted to go right into the fight. In other words, she wanted to go to His assistance in the sea. As when a man from the shore, seeing another struggling in the water, takes off those outer garments that would hinder his efforts and leaps to the rescue, so will you who still linger on the bank, thinking and singing and praying about the poor perishing souls, lay aside your shame, your pride, your cares about other people's opinions, your love of ease, and all the selfish loves that have kept you back for so long, and rush to the rescue of this multitude of dying men and women?

Does the surging sea look dark and dangerous? Unquestionably it is so. There is no doubt that the leap for you, as for everyone who takes it means difficulty and scorn and suffering. For you it may mean more than this.

It may mean death. He who beckons you from the sea, however, knows what it will mean—and knowing, He still calls to you and bids you come. You must do it! You cannot hold back. You have enjoyed yourself in Christianity long enough. You have had pleasant feelings, pleasant songs, pleasant meetings, pleasant prospects. There has been much of human happiness, much clapping of hands and shouting of praises—very much of heaven on earth. Now then, go to God and tell Him you are prepared as much as necessary to turn your back upon it all, and that you are willing to spend the rest of your days struggling in the midst of these perishing multitudes, whatever it may cost you. You must do it. With the light that has now broken in upon your mind, and the call that is now sounding in your ears, and the beckoning hands that are now before your eyes, you have no alternative. To go down among the perishing crowds is your duty. Your happiness from now on will consist in sharing their misery, your ease in sharing their pain, your crown in helping them to bear their cross, and your heaven in going into the very jaws of hell to rescue them. Now, what will you do?

SELAH 23-3

What are your honest thoughts after reading this account? Take some time to get real with Jesus. Don't rush.

I remember being challenged as a new believer by the Keith Green song "Asleep in the Light."

Do you see, do you see, all the people sinking down?

Don't you care, don't you care, are you gonna let them drown?
Open up, open up, and give yourself away,
You've seen the need, you hear the cry, so how can you delay,

Don't close your eyes, don't pretend the job's done. . .[17]

We are so blessed and must use that with which the Lord has blessed us. We cannot forget the souls. We cannot forget the Cross.

Pray Now! Act Now!

It is time to pray. It is time to act. It is so much more than finances. We need proper perspective and proper priorities in our lives to "ease the squeeze" in both our lives and the lives of others. We must get serious about our foundations. Revival will start with our personal prayer lives and our walk with Jesus. We must lay down our priorities and our lives.

E.M. Bounds reported that John Wesley often spent all night wrestling in prayer:

Many times he gathered his company together, and prayed all night.

Charles and John Wesley, with Whitfield sat up till after midnight singing and praying.

About 3:00 in the morning as we were continuing instant in prayer, the power of God came mightily upon us, so that many cried out for exceeding joy, and many fell to the ground.

We continued in ministering the Word and in prayer and praise till morning.

He typically arose at 4:00 every morning to be alone with God in prayer, usually praying until 7:00.[18]

Men such as Rees Howells "continued their prayer-work for some eight hours a day."[19]

Should we be discouraged or feel condemned by our prayerlessness? No, but we should be challenged, and it should move us to action. God wants to help us move the mountains in our lives, but we must have faith, pray, and act!

"Only God can move mountains, but faith and prayer move God."
—E.M. Bounds

"None can believe how powerful prayer is, and what it is able to effect, but those who have learned it by experience. It is a great matter when in extreme need to take hold on prayer. I know, whenever I have prayed earnestly, that I have been amply heard, and have obtained more than I pray for. God indeed sometimes delayed, but at last He came.
—Martin Luther

Time of reflection

Thank you for taking time to read this book. As a last Selah, I would ask you to consider a prayer with those "next steps" upon which you really need to act and on which you really need God's help. He stands watching and waiting.

Our youth pastor shared a picture that God had shown him of a child lost in a crowd of thousands of people. At first, the child did not realize that he was lost. Finally, however, the child realized his condition and began to acknowledge his need for his father. His father actually sought out the child to rescue him. We, too, must realize our condition and the fact that we have a Father who is waiting to rescue us! Following are a few final questions of honest reflection to be answered only between you and God.

1. Does He own you totally?
2. Have you surrendered all to Him?
3. Do you have any idols that you need to lay down?
4. Have you confessed your sin and asked for a new heart?
5. Have you asked Him to take out your wicked, stony heart and put in a new heart?
6. Do you need to repent of any sins? (What about the following examples?)
   - Materialism
   - Hoarding
   - Selfishness
   - Disobedience
   - Lack of discipline
   - Lack of patience
   - Lack of self-control
   - Lack of focus on missions and souls
   - Lack of a proper mix of the eternal and the temporal
   - An improper heart condition in giving
   - A lack of giving
   - Desire for power, position, or pleasure
   - A lust for money

Take a minute and have a talk with God on some of these issues. God desires to unchain you and make you totally and completely *free!* His desire is to walk beside you in your abandonment to Him and give you peace, joy, contentment, freedom, unity, joy, faith, and blessing as His child. Give Him your all. He has already given you His!

As you have hopefully learned from this book, God's desire is for us to be free financially. Financial freedom is not an overnight fix; it requires a major overhaul in our life planning, our giving planning, and our financial planning. May God bless you as you move forward!

I conclude this book by repeating a quotation from the Introduction:

"The great aim of education is not knowledge, but action."
—Herbert Spencer

We need head knowledge, but we also need revelation and heart knowledge. And we also need *action!* I have poured my heart and soul into this book. I pray that it will not be just knowledge obtained but rather will "spur you to action." My goal was not to pass on wisdom or knowledge just for the sake of doing so, but rather that there might be a demonstration of the Spirit's power in your life and finances.

1 Corinthians 2:1–5!

Please write or e-mail me to share your testimony and so that God can be glorified!

<u>ACTION POINTS</u>

1. What do you think is the relationship between finances and revival? Between prayer and revival? Between obedience and revival?

_____

_____

_____

_____

_____

_____

2. What do you think is the relationship between finances and judgment? Between prayer and judgment? Between obedience and judgment?

_____

_____

_____

_____

_____

_____

_____

3. What is your role in revival?

_____

_____

_____

_____

_____

_____

4. Write or e-mail me with your testimony of how this book blessed you.

CHAPTER 24

Summary: The Keys to Your Financial Future— Taking the Next Steps

As you well know, I try to avoid a formula or "seven steps." Because I have read many books, I am quite aware that it is difficult to summarize a book's key points, let alone decide how I can then apply those points to my life. Highlighting and/or keeping a journal is of great help to me personally. When I read an influential book, I try to review and summarize in one or two pages the key points that struck me personally.

To assist in jogging your memory, I have summarized the key areas and action points of this book. Some of them will be applicable to you; some of them will not. Some of them you will have already conquered; others will challenge you. Using the following list, identify specific actions that will assist you in "easing the squeeze" in your life, your giving, and your finances.

NO MORE SELAHs—IT'S TIME FOR *ACTION!*

Developing a Life Plan

√ List the individuals who have influenced your life greatly. Call one who has had a major impact and thank them (Chapter 1).

√ Develop a Life Foundation/Life Purpose (Chapter 2).

√ Generate a "report card" that addresses your priorities and goals (Chapter 2):
- spiritual, financial, family, ministerial, vocational, and physical.

√ Complete a "blessings list" that summarizes all of God's blessings in your life (Chapter 2).

√ Make some changes to simplify your life (Chapter 3).

√ Plan a getaway to help you develop your Life Plan (Chapter 3).

√ List your needs, wants, and desires (Chapter 4).

√ Identify practical ways to exercise self-control (Chapter 4).

√ Ensure that your foundation is on solid ground (Chapter 5).

√ Work on your financial warning signs (Chapter 6).

√ Commit to no new debt (Chapter 7).

√ Search your soul to determine why you are in debt (Chapter 7).

√ Determine the temperature on your "financial freedom thermometer." Reevaluate it in six months (Chapter 7).

Developing a Giving Plan

√ Consider your heart condition (Chapter 8).

√ Conduct a study on biblical giving (Appendix A).

√ Determine if you are walking in active obedience in your giving (Chapter 9).

√ Consider your "blessing readiness" and review how God has blessed you (Chapter 10).

√ Ponder why you give (Chapter 10).

√ Assess how much you are giving and if it is what God wants you to give (Chapter 11).

√ Articulate your giving goal, and determine whether you have tested God (Chapter 12).

√ Pray for your pastor, and consider how you can bless Him (Chapter 12).

—Bless your pastor in a specific way (e.g., time, talents, love, listening, finances).
√ Consider what you can do to make your church a better "feeder" (Chapter 12).
√ Consider giving to someone or a ministry to whom you have not given before (Chapter 12).
√ Contemplate and pray about whether you are hoarding (Chapter 13).
√ Get involved with world missions (Chapter 13).
√ Consider your temporal versus eternal investment balances (Chapter 14).
√ Consider self-denial and sacrificial giving and their role in your life (Chapter 15).

Developing a Financial Plan

√ Consider the stability of your financial house (Figure 16-1).
√ Determine if you are financially free (Chapter 16).
√ Complete the "Daily Spend Sheet" for sixty days (Chapter 16).
√ Complete the "Debt Hit List" (Chapter 17).
√ Establish your goals for debt payoff (Chapter 18).
√ Use the D.E.B.T. test when considering a major purchase (Chapter 18).
√ Complete the "Big-Ticket List" (Chapter 18).
√ Complete the "Cash-Control List" (Chapter 18).
√ Complete the "Save-to-Spend List" (Chapter 18).
√ Complete a budget (Chapter 19).
√ Make some changes that have a positive impact on your budget (Chapter 19).
√ Evaluate how you are doing against your budget (the Scorecard, Chapter 19).
√ Try the "cash envelope system" for a month (Chapter 19).
√ Complete your own "Freedom Factor Lightning Bolt List" (Chapter 20).
√ Make some "little" changes that will make a big positive impact on your finances (Chapter 20).
√ Consider your investment priorities and make appropriate changes (Chapter 21).
√ Articulate what you are doing to affect the financial "slavery"

situation (Chapter 21).

√ Make some changes that will have a positive impact on your family memory book (Chapter 22).

√ Begin some new family activities (Chapter 22).

√ Make some changes to increase family unity (Chapter 22).

√ Write a "Family Foundation" (Chapter 22).

√ Determine your role in revival (Chapter 23).

Keys to Success

The following lists provide keys that will unlock the success padlock.

Life Keys

➤ Become abandoned to God (Matt. 22:37).

➤ Surrender *all* to Jesus Christ.

➤ Focus on foundational priorities (e.g., family, fulfilling purpose, faith).

➤ Simplify your life to shore up foundational priorities.

➤ Set goals!

➤ Practice contentment, and stop "pursuing" stuff.

➤ James 1:5: Do not do it on your own.

Giving Keys

➤ Focus on your heart condition.

➤ Begin giving.

➤ Set goals for increased giving.

➤ Serve others above yourself.

➤ Practice an eternal, not a temporal, perspective. Read Ecclesiastes once a year.

➢ Give cheerfully and generously.

➢ Give *outside* your walls (e.g., missions, ministries, the poor, coworkers, family).

➢ Give *inside* your walls (e.g., storehouse, widows, single mothers, ministers).

Financial Keys

➢ Commit to no new debt.

➢ Have a cash focus near term until your debt is under control.

➢ Set long-term goals, and track your progress.

➢ Maintain good records; have accountability.

➢ Maintain household unity and commitment (Rom. 15:5–7).

➢ Guard against family dissension.

➢ Be honest, confess your past, and grant forgiveness to others.

➢ Practice self-control.

➢ Start with the "Daily Spend Sheet."

➢ Finish with a budget.

➢ Be accountable to someone.

➢ Live within your means (budget).

➢ Be faithful and patient.

➢ Use the tools and spreadsheets (or purchase some financial software).

➢ Identify and implement some "Freedom Factor Lightning Bolts."

➢ Mix faith and action—pray and *do!*

➢ Just do it!

➢ Do not be overwhelmed; move slowly rather than not at all.

Godly Wisdom

➢ Eagerness for money might lead to your wandering from the faith.

➢ Wealth is worthless in eternity.

➢ We were born naked, and we will leave this life naked. We

cannot carry anything with us.

➢ If we love wealth, we are never satisfied and will never have enough.

➢ True, eternal treasures are found only in heaven.

➢ We have nothing if we gain everything temporal but lose our soul.

➢ We must deny ourselves and follow Jesus.

➢ We cannot be a slave to both God and money.

➢ We are not to have idols.

➢ Give and it will be given unto you.

➢ Learn to be content.

Be Wary of Shortcuts

The disease of "quick-fix" bankruptcy is sweeping our nation in record numbers. As a Christian, my recommendation is to avoid bankruptcy by all means. We must be responsible for your actions.

Avoid "easy riches." The ant works hard and gathers money little by little. Avoid the flyer, the mailer, the late-night infomercial, the get-rich-quick conference, and the latest multilevel- marketing scheme, although they might be tempting. The wolf can come dressed in sheep's clothing, and I have seen leaders fall because of it. The Bible says that eagerness for wealth leads to a wandering from the truth. How long did it take Joseph to save for the years of famine? Seven years! Deep changes and progress rarely occur overnight. Tree roots are not visible. Progress might seem slow, but you *are* progressing. God's arm is not too short; He will help you!

Take the Time/Make the Time

Just as some people are born leaders, some people are born planners. I was a decent planner in everything but my finances. If *I* can become a successful planner with *my* money, so can you, but it takes work. We are willing to work on our golf games, our wardrobes, our educations, and the upkeep of our yards and personal appearance, none of which is easy; yet, we find a way.

I like Bill Wilson's (Metro Sidewalk Sunday School) realistic assessment of life: "We make time in life to do exactly what we *want*." Ah, the profundity of the simplicity. It is too true! We do what we *want* to, not always what we *should* do or *need* to do. We like the easy way. Who doesn't? Paul could have taken the easy way and stayed hidden away instead of facing the trials and persecutions that were part of God's purpose. But then he never would have had the eternal impact that he did.

A good strategy will include looking to the past, the present, and the future. Try entering the destination on your travel software without identifying the departure location. It is just as silly to set goals without first knowing exactly where you are. Then you need to know the route to get there. You can travel by plane, train, or automobile. But you have to know the details: the gate, departure time, highways, etc. We like the goal but usually do not spend the time analyzing where we are today to see if those goals are realistic. I would like to get from Texas to Florida in thirty minutes, but technology limits me. So do our incomes, expenses, and debts. Goals should be realistic yet challenging and attainable. If a financial planner offers you an "easy plan" for success or freedom, a red flag should go up. Yes, it is what we want to hear, but this parallels the itching ears mentality. We like it fast and easy. We want it now! That sounds kind of like some of our younger children, doesn't it? Do not be impatient. God is for you, not against you!

Ease the Squeeze!

How Biblical Is It?
A Chronology of Giving

1500–1400 B. C.

Genesis 4:3—Cain brought fruits of the soil; Abel brought fat portions of the firstborn of his flock

Genesis 22:2, 8—Burnt offerings (animal, lamb)

Genesis 22:1–10—Abraham offered Isaac

Genesis 28:22—Jacob gave a tenth

Exodus 29:18–28—Burnt offering (ram), sin offering (bull), wave offering (ram by fire), fellowship offering

Exodus 29:38—Offer on the altar regularly

Exodus 29:40—A tenth of fine flour, a drink offering, a grain offering

Exodus 30:12–15—Atonement offering (used money for services)

Exodus 35:20–29—Offering for work of tent and furnishings

Exodus 36:1–3—Offering for construction, offering of labor (themselves and their skills)

Leviticus 1:3–17—Burnt offering

Leviticus 2:1–16—Grain offering

Leviticus 3:1–17—Fellowship offering

Leviticus 4—Sin offering

Leviticus 5:14–6:7; 7:1–7—Guilt offering

Leviticus 7:37—Ordination offering

Leviticus 22:18, 21—Freewill offering
Leviticus 27:30—A tenth of the produce and the livestock
Numbers 15—Burnt offerings, sacrifice offerings, freewill offerings, festival offerings
Numbers 18:26—Tithe
Deuteronomy 12:17—Tithe (grain, wine, oil, herds, flocks, freewill offering)
Deuteronomy 14:22–29—A tenth of all of your fields, third year tithe (fatherless, aliens, widows)

Late Tenth Century B. C.
1 Samuel 13:9—Burnt offerings

560–550 B. C.
2 Kings 12:9–10—People gave money for the repair of the temple, paid to workmen; guilt and sin offerings for priests.

450–420 B. C.
1 Chronicles 21:26—Burnt offerings
2 Chronicles 7:1—Burnt offerings
2 Chronicles 31:5–19—Firstfruits (grain, wine, oil, fields, produce, tithe of everything)
2 Chronicles 35:7—Passover offerings

Tenth to Fifth Centuries B. C.
Psalms 116:17—Thank offerings

700–680 B. C.
Isaiah 53:10—Guilt offerings

715–710 B. C.
Hosea 6:6—I desire mercy, not sacrifice (holy, steadfast, loyal love)

430-420 BC
Malachi 3:8- Tithes and offerings

A. D.
Matthew 5:23—Offer gift at the altar
Mark 12:33—Love is greater than burnt offerings and sacrifices

Mark 12:41—Putting money into the treasury
Romans 8:3—God offered his Son (sin offering)
Romans 12:1—Offer our bodies as living sacrifices
1 Corinthians 16:2—Set aside a sum of money in keeping with his income, saving it up
Ephesians 5:2—Gave himself up for us as a fragrant offering and sacrifice to God
Philippians 2:17—I am being poured out like a drink offering
Philippians 4:15–18—Gifts were sent. Paul received aid, payment, gifts, a fragrant offering, an acceptable sacrifice, pleasing to God.
2 Timothy 4:6—I [Paul] am being poured out like a drink offering (This was Paul's last letter, written as a prisoner, deserted, treated like a criminal. His ministry was over, and he was near death!)
Hebrews 7:8—Tithe is translated as a percentage
Hebrews 7:27—Jesus offered *Himself*
Hebrews 10:5, 8—Sacrifice and offering you did not desire, but a body you prepared for me. With burnt offerings and sin offerings you were *not* pleased. Here I am. I have come to do your will.
1 Peter 2:5—Offering spiritual sacrifices (building your own spiritual home, holy priesthood)

The interesting thing about this brief chronology on giving is that this giving is *not just money!* We can give in different ways at different times for different purposes. You cannot put giving in a neat little "Tithe, tithe, tithe" box. God is bigger than that.

APPENDIX B

Key Websites and Contacts

Check out www.financialfoundationbuilders.com for updates to this list.

Savings Tools & Consumer Protection & Education

www.Asec.org- American Savings Education Council- Savings tools

www.Ftc.gov/bcp/menu-credit.htm- Federal Trade Commission- Consumer Protection & Credit

Mwhodges.home.att.net/debt.htm- National Debt Data

Mwhodges.home.att.net/nat-debt/debt-nat.htm-   Grandfather National Debt Report

Home.att.net/~mwhodges/index.htm

www.Federalbudget.com- National debt awareness center

www.Publicdebt.treas.gov/opd/opdpenny.htm- Public Debt to the penny

www.Publicdebt.treas.gov/opd/opd.htm#history- Bureau of the Public Debt online, Debt History

www.Stls.frb.org/fred- Federal Reserve Economic Data

www.Ssa.gov- Social Security online- benefit planners, retirement planners

Financial Planning and Calculators/Tools

www.Crown.org- Crown Ministries and Christian Financial Concepts- Online tools, Budget Guide, Credit Card & Mortgage calculators, Local church tools and resources

www.Money.com- Money magazine online- planning, retirement, debt

www.Homestore.com- House and Home network- Find, Buy, Move

www.Christianfpi.org- Christian Financial Planners

www.Napfa.com- National Association of Personal Financial Advisors

www.Fpanet.org- Financial Planning Association

www.Financialengines.com- Financial and Goal Planning tools

www.Troweprice.com/retirement/retire.html- Retirement planning worksheet

www.Quicken.com/retirement- Planning tools

www.Ihatefinancialplanning.com- Multiple Financial tools

www.Savewealth.com- Miscellaneous planning tools

www.Cardweb.com/cardtrak/surveys.html- Low rate/fee credit cards

www.Bankrate.com- Best rates on auto loans, CD's, Checking, Home, etc.

www.Timevalue.com/Tools.htm- many financial calculators

www.Smartmoney.com/pf/- Personal Finance Issues

Discount Airfare/Travel

www.Orbitz.com- Flight search

www.Hotwire.com- Roundtrip hotfares

www.Cheaptickets.com- Travel store- Flights & hotels

www.Smarterliving.com- Travel bargains

www.Lowestfare.com- Low fare specials

www.Expedia.com

www.Priceline.com- name your own price- flights, hotels, rental cars

www.Etn.nl/hotfares.htm- Discount airfare and cruises

www.Cruise.com- Discount cruises

www.Travelocity.com- Farefinder

www.Sidestep.com- Travel deals

www.Farechase.com- Comparison shop for travel
www.AA.com- Netsaver specials
www.Digitalcity.com/Travel.com- Travel bargains
www.Bestfares.com
www.Airfare.com
www.Travel.AmericanExpress.com/travel

Discount Hotels/Lodging

www.Hotwire.com- Hotel discounts & savings
www.Roomsaver.com- Motel coupons and discount
www.Hoteldiscount.com- Discounted hotel rooms
www.Quikbook.com- Hotel deals
www.180096hotel.com- Hotel discounts
www.Travelscape.com- Air and Hotel discounts
www.Destinationcoupons.com- Travel discounts
www.Freecampgrounds.com- Free RV campgrounds
www.Priceline.com- name your own price- flights, hotels, rental
  cars

Savings/Coupons

www.Entertainment.com-Discount Entertainment Club coupon
  book and card
www.Save.com- Online coupon network
www.Flamingoworld.com- Discounts for Internet shopping
www.Valuepage.com- 1001 free things, coupons, etc.
www.Coolsavings.com- coupon service
www.Dealpilot.com- comparison shop- compare prices for same
  product at different stores
www.Mysimon.com- comparison shop
www.Pricingcentral.com- comparison shop
www.Searchboss.com- comparison shop
www.Dealtime.com- comparison shop
www.Bizrate.com
www.Smartshop.com
www.Shopnow.com
www.Thefrugalshopper.com- magazine discounts
www.Ebay.com- online auction/marketplace

www.Half.com- Buy and sell used books, movies, music, games

Ministries

www.Gfa.org- Gospel For Asia- Reaching the unreached people groups

www.Metrodfw.org- Metro Ministries (Dallas)- Reaching the inner cities of Dallas

www.Metroministries.com- Metro Ministries International

www.Compassion.com- Compassion International

www.Christianity.com/feedthechildren- Feed the Children

www.Persecution.com- Voice of the Martyr's

www.Crown.org- Ministry site of Crown & Christian Financial concepts

www.Heritagebuilders.com/what- A Family ministry of Focus on the Family

www.FinancialFoundationBuilders.com- Financial Freedom & Biblical Giving seminars (my website)

www.WorldChallenge.org- A ministry of Times Square Church & David Wilkerson

APPENDIX C

Financial Worksheets

See www.financialfoundationbuilders.com for the most updated version of the tools

Daily Spend Sheet

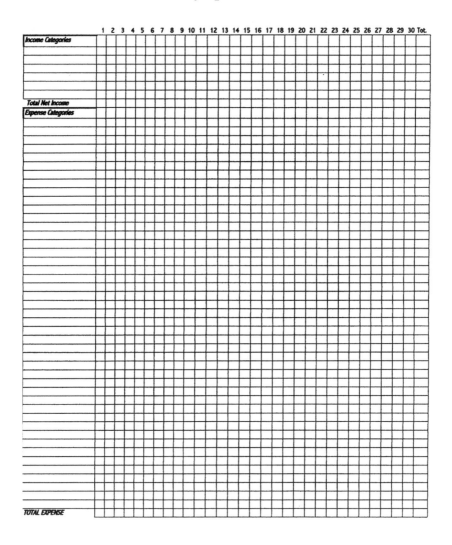

Debt Hit List

DEBT	Total Owed	Min. Pmt.	Payoff Priority	Payoff Target	Reward	bal.	bal.	bal.	3-mo Goal	bal.	bal.	bal.	6-mo. Goal	1-yr. Goal	3-yr Goal
Total Debt															

Big Ticket List

Priority Item	Month	Cost

Expenditure totals

Monthly savings required   (divide by no. months)

Cash Only Control List

	Date	Date	Date	Date	Date	Date
Cash Only Account						
TOTAL CASH ACCT's						

Save to Spend List

	Date	Date	Date	Date	Date	Date
Save to Spend Balances						
TOTAL SAVE TO SPEND						

Save to Spend Account Activity

ACCOUNT: _____   Amount/check: _____

DATE	TRANSACTION DESCRIPTION	DEPOSIT	WITHDRAW	BALANCE

Budget

	Date	Date	Date	Date	Date	Date	Date	Date
INCOME CATEGORIES								
INCOME BEFORE TAXES								
Income tax								
INCOME AFTER TAXES								

S=Save to Spend, C=Cash	Date	Date	Date	Date	Date	Date	Date	Date
EXPENSE CATEGORIES								
TOTAL EXPENSE								
INCOME LESS EXPENSE								

	Date	Date	Date	Date	Date	Date	Date	Date
DEBT BALANCES								
TOTAL DEBT								

The Budget Scorecard

INCOME CATEGORIES	BUDGET	ACTUAL	+ / -
INCOME BEFORE TAXES			
Income tax			
INCOME AFTER TAXES			

EXPENSE CATEGORIES	BUDGET	ACTUAL	+ / -
TOTAL EXPENSE			
INCOME LESS EXPENSE			

DEBT BALANCES	GOAL	ACTUAL	+ / -
TOTAL DEBT			

C = cash, S = Save to Spend

Endnotes

Acknowledgements

1. Dennis Peterson Editing and Writing Services, 7909 Tressa Circle, Powell TN 37849, 865-947-0496, http://go.to/editing, DLPEdit@aol.com.

An Opening Word

1. Lynn Brenner, "What We Need to Know About," *Parade Magazine*, April 18, 1999.
2. John and Sylvia Ronsvalle, *Behind the Stained Glass Windows—Money Dynamics in the Church* (Grand Rapids, Mich.: Baker Books, 1996).
3. John Engen, "Getting the Credit Monkey Off," *Family Money*, July/August 2000.
4. Dr. Henry R. Sefton, *John Knox—An Account of the Development of His Spirituality* (Edinburgh, Scotland: Saint Andrew Press, 1993).

Chapter 1—Modern-Day Pharaoh

1. Isaiah 55:9.
2. Numbers 11:23.
3. Music and lyrics by Helen H. Lemmel, (London : Singspiration, 1922). (Entered public domain in 1997.)
4. Proverbs 22:6.
5. Dennis Rainey, *One Home at a Time* (Wheaton, Ill.: Tyndale House Publishers, 1997).
6. John and Sylvia Ronsvalle, *Behind the Stained Glass Windows—Money Dynamics in the Church* (Grand Rapids, Mich.: Baker Books, 1996).
7. Matthew 7:24–27.
8. Acts 4:13.
9. Matthew 7:24-27.

10. Wayne Watson, *God in a Box, A Beautiful Place* (Nashville: DaySpring, 1993).
11. Deuteronomy 31:6.

Chapter 2—Foundational Blueprints

1. 1 Timothy 1:16.
2. Romans 7:15.
3. James 5:16.
4. Matthew 23:25–28.
5. James 5:16.
6. Acts 17:6.
7. Richard J. Foster, *Celebration of Disciplines* (New York: HarperCollins Publishers, 1998).
8. Philippians 3:10.
9. Philippians 3:14.
10. Barna Research Online, www.barna.org, Venture, Calif. (April 29, 1997, "Angels are In—Devil and Holy Spirit are out.")
11. Proverbs 27:12.

Chapter 3—Choices and Priorities

1. Proverbs 14:15; 16:9; 20:24; Jeremiah 10:23.
2. Arthur Wallis, *God's Chosen Fast* (Eastbourne, Sussex, England: Kingsway Publications, Ltd., 1997).
3. Bill Bright, *The Coming Revival, America's Call to Fast, Pray and Seek God's Face* (Orlando, Fla.: New Life Publications, 1995).
4. Norman Grubb, *Rees Howells, Intercessor* (Fort Washington, Pa.: Christian Literature Crusade, 1952).
5. E. M. Bounds, *The Complete Works of E. M. Bounds on Prayer* (Grand Rapids: Baker Book House, 1990).
6. Proverbs 3:5–6.
7. Watchman Nee, *Love Not the World* (Fort Washington, PA: Christian Literature Crusade, 1969)
8. John 15:5.
9. Richard A. Swenson, *Margin* (Colorado Springs, Colo.: NavPress, 1992). Available www.navpress.com. Used by permission.
10. Galatians 5:22–23.
11. Richard A. Swenson, *Margin* (Colorado Springs, Colo.: NavPress, 1992). Available www.navpress.com. Used by permission.
12. Ibid.

Chapter 4—A Time to Diet and a Time to Get Mad!

1. Richard A. Swenson, *Margin* (Colorado Springs, Colo.: NavPress, 1992). Available www.navpress.com. Used by permission.

2. 1 Timothy 6:10.
3. "Health & Science Wire Report," *Dallas Morning News,* December 15, 2000.
4. *Statistics Related to Overweight and Obesity*, available www.niddk.nih.gov/health/nutrit/pubs/statobes.htm, NIDDK Weight Control Information Network, retrieved March 15, 2002, Am J Clin Nutr., 1992; 55:503-507s
5. John Kenneth Galbraith, *The Affluent Society* (Houghton Mifflin Co., 1998).
6. Deuteronomy 8:18.
7. William D. Perreault Jr. and E. Jerome McCarthy, *Basic Marketing—A Global-Managerial Approach* (United States of America : Richard D. Irwin, Time Mirror Higher Education Group, Inc., 1996).
8. William D. Perreault Jr. and E. Jerome McCarthy, *Basic Marketing—A Global-Managerial Approach* (United States of America : Richard D. Irwin, Time Mirror Higher Education Group, Inc., 1996*). Coens Annual Spending totals 2000,* available www.adage.com/page.cms?pageID=454, QuikFind ID# AAM92F, published June 11, 2001.
9. William D. Perreault Jr. and E. Jerome McCarthy, *Basic Marketing—A Global-Managerial Approach* (United States of America : Richard D. Irwin, Time Mirror Higher Education Group, Inc., 1996).
10. *Tips for Parenting Cowards*, available www.newdream.org/campaign/kids/, retrieved April 2, 2002.
11. Robert Tamura, Department of Economics, Clemson University*, Labor Market Analysis on Living Standards,* available http://people.clemson.edu/~rtamura/401/data/living.pdf, retrieved March 15, 2002.
12. John Gertner, "What Is Wealth?" *Money Magazine*, December 2000.
13. Barna Research Online, www.barna.org, Venture, Calif. (*Perceptions about Money.* Research Archive "Money"), retrieved March 15, 2002.
14. Ibid.
15. Richard J. Foster, *Celebration of Disciplines* (New York: HarperCollins Publishers, 1998).
16. Matthew 9:12.

Chapter 5—My Financial Foundation . . . and Then Some

1. Tedd Tripp, *Shepherding a Child's Heart* (Wapwallopen, Pa.: Shepherd Press, 1995).
2. Proverbs 3:5-6.
4. Hebrews 9:27.

Chapter 6—Cocaine and the Plastic Plunge

1. Larry Burkett, *The Complete Guide to Managing Your Money* (New York: Inspirational Press, 1996).
2. Mark 10:27.
3. Jeremiah 32:17.
4. *Card Learn Frequently Asked Questions*, available www.cardweb.com/

cardlearn/faqs/2001/june/averagehousehold.amp, retrieved February 26, 2002.

5. Jason Fields & Lynne M. Casper, U. S. Census Bureau, Department of Commerce, *America's Families and Living Arrangements, Population Characteristics, 2000,* 104.7 million households according to www.census.gov/prod/2001pubs/p.20-537.pdf, issued June 2001.

6. *The Federal Reserve Board Statistical Release,* available www.federalreserve.gov/releases/g19/current, retrieved March 7, 2002.

7. Available www.Cardweb.com, retrieved June 30, 2001, P. O. Box 1700, Freederick, MD 21702, 301-631-9100, cardmail@cardweb.com.

8. Ibid.

9. *Distribution of U.S. Payment Cards Report,* available www.Cardweb.com, retrieved March 15, 2002.

10. Available www.Cardweb.com, retrieved November 19, 2001.

11. Available www.Cardweb.com, retrieved November 21, 2001.

12. *Historical Table of U.S. Bank Credit Card Loans,* available www.Cardweb.com, retrieved March 15, 2002

13. *Average U.S. Credit Card Debt per Household,* available www.Cardweb.com, retrieved March 15, 2002.

14. "Study Shows Student Credit Card Debt Rising," available www.NellieMae.com, retrieved February 13, 2001.

15. Christine Dugas, Debt Smothers Young Americans, *USA Today*, February 13, 2001.

16. John Engen, "Getting the Credit Monkey Off," *Family Money*, July /August 2000.

17. Grady Cash, "Financial Wellness: Will it be your next health promotion program?" Center for National Well Being Survey, 1996, available www.healthy.net/library/articles/cash/center/worksite.htm, retrieved April 3, 2002, permission granted.

18. Colossians 3:5.

19. Luke 12:15.

20. Romans 12:2.

Chapter 7—Tricks, Traps, and Monsters

1. Matthew 4:9.

2. 1 Timothy 6:9–10.

3. Job 31:24–5, 28.

4. 1 Corinthians 6:9–10.

5. Luke 12:15.

6. Psalm 115:4–7.

7. 2 Corinthians 6:10.

8. Philippians 4:11–13.

9. Hebrews 13:5.

10. Matthew 16:24–26.

11. Colossians 3:5–6.

12. Romans 12:2.
13. Luke 12:33.
14. Matthew 6:25–34.
15. John Gallagher, "The Debt Set: Consumers are carrying $1.6 Trillion in Credit, *Detroit Free Press*, December 26, 2001. Available www.freep.com/money/business/debt26_20011226.htm.
16. *Personal Income and Its Disposition*, Bureau of Economic Analysis, GDP news release, February 28, 2002.
17. Tax Foundation, available www.taxfoundation.org/prtfdhistory.html, retrieved April 13, 2001.
18. John Gallagher, "The Debt Set."
19. *U.S. Bankruptcy Filing Statistics*, American Bankruptcy Institute, available www.abiworld.org/stats, and www.federalreserve.gov/releases/g19/Current, retrieved March 15, 2002.
20. Available at Bureau of Public Debt Website, www.publicdebt.treas.gov/opd/opdpenny.htm, retrieved March 29, 2002.
21. *U.S. Bankruptcy Filing Statistics*, March 15, 2002.
22. Ibid.
23. "Senate Passes Bankruptcy Bill," available www.policyalmanac.org/economic/consumer.shtml, retrieved March 15, 2001.
24. Larry Burkett, *The Complete Guide to Managing Your Money* (New York: Inspirational Press, 1996)
25. Steve Brown, "Bigger Homes Still the American Way," *Dallas Morning News*, February 15, 2002.
26. Available at Bureau of Public Debt Website, www.publicdeb.treas.gov/opd/opdpenny.htm, retrieved April 19, 2002.
27. Ibid.
28. Michael Hodges, "Grandfather Economic Report, available www.Mwhodges.home.att.net/debt.htm, retrieved March 14, 2002.
29. *FY2003 Budget of the U.S. Government, Analytical Perspectives*, Office of Management and Budget, available www. Access.gpo.gov/usbudget/, pp. 269, 395.
30. *U.S. Treasury Domestic Finance Report, Major Foreign Holders of Treasury Securities*, available www.treas.gov/domfin/foreign.htm, November 30, 2001 (retrieved February 27, 2002).
31. Scott Burns, "Winding up the National Debt Clock", *Dallas Morning News,* December 12, 2000.
32. Robert Preidt, "Credit card debt may be hazardous to your health," *Dallas Morning News*, May 6, 2000.
33. *Personal Income and Its Disposition,* GDP news release, Bureau of Economic Analysis, available www.bea.doc.gov/briefrm/tables/ebr6.htm, retrieved February 28, 2002.
34. Timothy Lamer, "Is there no tommorrow?," *World Magazine*, August 7, 1999, available www.worldmag.com/world/issue/08-07-99/cover_1.asp.
35. Ibid.

Chapter 8—Do You Have a Heart Condition?

1. George Barna, *Perceptions about Money*, available www.barna.org (research archive "Money"), retrieved March 15, 2002.
2. 2 Corinthians 2:17.
3. Jeremiah 29:13.
4. Psalm 86:11.
5. 1 Corinthians 7:35.
6. Ezekiel 11:13–25.
7. Romans 6:14.
8. Matthew 23:23.
9. 2 Corinthians 8:1–12.
10. 2 Corinthians 9:7.

Chapter 9—That Tough Word!

1. Psalm 119:105.
2. Hebrews 4:12.
3. 1 Corinthians 3:2; Hebrews 5:12.
4. Philippians 3:10.
5. Isaiah 1:19.
6. Proverbs 22:3; 1 John 3:17–18.
7. Genesis 12:1.
8. Tedd Tripp, *Shepherding a Child's Heart* (Wapwallopen, Pa.: Shepherd Press, 1995).
9. 2 Corinthians 9:2.
10. James 2:17–24.
11. Matthew 11:19.
12. 2 Corinthians 8:11.
13. Isaiah 1:11.

Chapter 10—The Results of Giving: Blessing!

No reference citations.

Chapter 11—That Controversial Question: How Much Should I Give?

1. John and Sylvia Ronsvalle, *Behind the Stained Glass Windows—Money Dynamics in the Church* (Grand Rapids: Baker Book House, 1996)
2. Gustav Niebuhr, "Evangelicals putting less in the plate.", *Dallas Morning News*, December 13, 1997.
3. John and Sylvia Ronsvalle, U.S. Per Capita Income/per Member Giving as a Percent of Income, Empty Tomb Research, available www.emptytomb.com/fig1.html, retrieved November 22, 2000.
4. George Barna, "Churches Lose Financial Ground in 2000," *The Barna Update*, June 5, 2001.

5. Luke 12:48.
6. Romans 6:14.
7. Hebrews 10:5–6.
8. Genesis 14:20.
9. Luke 19:8.
10. Mark 12:43–44.
11. Matt Redman, I Will Offer Up My Life © KINGSWAY THANKYOU MUSIC. All rights reserved. Used by permission.
12. Acts 11:29.
13. 2 Corinthians 8:2–3.
14. 1 Corinthians 16:1–2.
15. Luke 6:38.
16. Philippians 4:19.
17. Exodus 25:1–2.

Chapter 12—Who Gets My Money? Going once, Going Twice. . . .

1. Genesis 41:56; Deuteronomy 28:8; 1 Chronicles 27:25; 2 Chronicles 32:28; Psalm 33:7; Jeremiah 50:26; Malachi 3:10; Luke 12:24.
2. Malachi 3:10.
3. 1 Kings 7:51; Nehemiah 10:38; 13:12.
4. George Barna. Evangelicals are the most generous givers, but fewer than 10% of born again Christians give 10% to their church. Tithers are rare, available www.barna.org , Ventura, Calif., April 5, 2000.
5. Numbers 18:21, 28.
6. Acts 10:4.
7. Matthew 6:3–4.
8. Proverbs 28:27.
9. Matthew 19:21. (See also Luke 12:33; Deuteronomy 15:4.)
10. Galatians 2:10.
11. Proverbs 19:17.
12. Luke 14:13.
13. 2 Corinthians 8:13–15.
14. Deuteronomy 14:28–29.
15. Proverbs 25:21–22.
16. Acts 20:34–35.
17. Matthew 10:42.
18. Acts 2:45.
19. Luke 6:24–25.
20. Luke 16:15.

Chapter 13—A Land of Rich Young Rulers?

1. George Barna, Self Descriptions (2000) Research Archive "Money," available www.barna.org, retrieved March 15, 2002.
2. Proverbs 6:6–8; 30:25.

3. Proverbs 21:20.
4. Matthew 25:27.
5. Proverbs 13:22.
6. James 5:3–5.
7. International Literary Explorer, UNESCO World Education Report 1998. available www.litserverliteracy.upenn.edu/explorer/countriesselect.html, retrieved March 15, 2002.
8. Carmen DeNavas-Walt, Robert W. Cleveland, Marc I. Roemer, *Money Income in the United States, Current Population Reports*, U.S. Census Bureau, Issued September, 2001.
   available www.census.gov/prod/2001pubs/p60-213.pdf .
9. *The State of the World Population 2001, Determining the Impact of Human Activity*, available www.worldpopulationgrowth.org, retrieved March 15, 2002.
10. Ibid.
11. Ibid.
12. *The State of the World Population 1999, 6 Billion, A Time for Choices*, available www.worldpopulationgrowth.org , retrieved March 15, 2002.
13. Ibid.
14. Ibid.
15. Ibid.
16. Ibid.
17. *Least Reached People's Joshua Project List*, November 12, 2001 status, available www.Joshuaproject.net/statusoriginal.html, retrieved March 16, 2002.
18. *Consumer Expenditure Survey, 2000*, U.S. Department of Labor, Bureau of Labor Statistics, retrieved April 4, 2002. Used data for Husband and Wife consumer unit with average annual income of $53,232.
19. Ibid.
20. Ibid.
21. Ibid.
22. Ibid.
23. Ibid.
24. *Holiday Credit Card Use to Rise by 7%*, November 19, 2001, available www.cardweb.com (Frederick, Maryland).
25. *Internet Gambling Research Briefing, MIT Sloan School of Management*, available www.web.mit.edu/ecom/www/Project98/G8/contents.htm, March 19, 1998.
26. *U.S. Pet Industry Sales to Cross $33.5 billion by 2005*, available www.veterinarysavings.com/pressrelease.com, report RGA-034Y, Business Communications Company Inc., 25 Van Zant Street, Norwalk, CT 06855, Telephone: (203) 853-4266, ext. 309, Email: Publisher@bccresearch.com, retrieved April 4, 2002.
27. *1998 Sales and Market Share*, Marketview 2000, available www.cosmetic-market.com/page8smscat98.html, retrieved April 4, 2002.
28. *Worldwide BoxOffice U.S. Annual Box Office Statistics,* as of April 3, 2002,

available www.worldboxoffice.com, retrieved April 4, 2002.

29. *Lifestyle Table,* available www.emptytomb.org/lifestylenew.html, retrieved April 4, 2002, data from U.S. Census Bureau, Statisticsal Abstract of the United States: 2000, pg. 758.

30. *Lifestyle Table,* available www.emptytomb.org/lifestylenew.html, retrieved April 4, 2002, "Born Into Slavery," AP article, Champaign-Urbana News Gazette, July 22, 2001, B-1.

31. *Lifestyle Table,* available www.emptytomb.org/lifestylenew.html, retrieved April 4, 2002, "Vending Machines Turning High-Tech," AP article, Champaign-Urbana *News Gazette*, April 1, 2001, C-2.

32. *Lifestyle Table,* available www.emptytomb.org/lifestylenew.html, retrieved April 4, 2002, John A. Siewert and Dotsey Welliver, eds. *Mission Handbook, U.S. and Canadian Ministries Overseas 2001-2003*, 18th ed. (Wheaton, Ill.: Evangelism and Missions Information Service, 2001), p. 45.

33. *Least Reached People's Joshua Project List*, November 12, 2001 status, available www.Joshuaproject.net/statusoriginal.html, retrieved March 16, 2002.

34. *About the Bible, National Bible Association*, United Bible Societies Scripture Language Report (New York, NY: National Bible Association, 1999). Available www.nationalbible.org/atb/featuares/atbubstran00.htm, retrieved March 16, 2002.

35. *The State of the World's Children 2002, Statistical Tables p.12-15,* United Nations Children's Fund, available www.unicef.org/pubsgen, retrieved April 4, 2002.

36. Ibid.

37. *Facts that Substantiate the World's Widening Rich-Poor Gap*, Mennonite Central Committee, December 20, 1990, available www.mccorg/respub/occasional/1316.html, retrieved April 4, 2002.

38. Ibid.

39. Ibid.

40. Ronald J. Sider, *Rich Christians in an Age Of Hunger* (Dallas, Tex.: Word Publishing, 1990).

41. *World Need and Giving Potential*, available www.emptytomb.org/potential.htm, retrieved April 4, 2002.

42. Ibid.

43. *What America's Users Spend on Illegal Drugs, 1988–1998*, available www.whitehousedrugpolicy.gov, December 2000, retrieved February 27, 2002.

44. *Reporting Public Charities in the U.S. by Type, Circa, 1999* (National Center for Charitable Statistics, June 2001). Available www.nccs.urban.org/factsht.htm, retrieved March 5, 2002.

45. *Poverty 2001, Poverty Thresholds for 2001* (Washington, D.C.: U.S. Census Bureau, January 22, 2002). Available www.census.gov/hhes/poverty/threshld/thresh01.htm, retrieved February 27, 2002.

46. Greg Long, *"The Sacrifice"*, Now (Nashville, TN: Word Records, 2001) Used by Permission.

47. Matthew 10:8.
48. Deuteronomy 15:7.
49. Luke 3:11.
50. Frances J. Roberts, *On the Highroad of Surrender* (King's Farspan, 1973).

Chapter 14—Keeping It all in Perspective—Temporal vs. Eternal

1. Matthew 6:19–21.
2. Ecclesiastes 5:10, 13, 15.
3. Luke 12:15–21.
4. Luke 12:33–34.
5. Proverbs 23:5.
6. Matthew 25:21.
7. Luke 16:11.
8. Romans 8:5–8; Philippians 3:19-20; Colossians 3:1–2.

Chapter 15—The Spiritual vs. the Practical

1. Proverbs 6:6, 8.
2. Proverbs 30:25.
3. Proverbs 21:20.
4. 1 Corinthians 16:2.
5. 2 Corinthians 8:3.
6. Genesis 12:1ff.

Chapter 16—The Path to Financial Freedom

No reference citations.

Chapter 17—Digging out of Debt

No reference citations.

Chapter 18—Determining Your Destiny

1. Steve Farkas, *Miles to Go: A Status Report on Americans' Plans for Retirement,* (New York, NY: May 20, 1997) available www.publicagenda.org/aboutpa/aboutpa3g.htm, retrieved April 2, 2002.
2. *Credit Cards: Blessing or Curse?* PBS, Online Newshour Forum, Financial Adviser Dave Ramsey response, May 30, 1997, retrieved April 4, 2002, available www.pbs.org/newshour/forum/may97/credit5.html .
3. Maria Halkias, Payback Time, Credit Cards Leave Holiday Hangover, Dallas Morning News, January 21, 1999.

Chapter 19—The Dreaded "B" Word

No reference citations.

Chapter 20—Freedom in a Flash

1. Entertainment Card, available www.entertainment.com, 1-800-374-4464, P.O. Box 5061, Troy, MI 48007-5061.
2. Ibid.

Chapter 21—The Eighth Wonder of the World

1. Mark Lino, Center for Nutrition Policy and Promotion, *Expenditures on Children by Families: 2000 Annual Report* (Washington, D. C.: U.S. Department of Agriculture, Miscellaneous Publication Number 1528-2000, May 2001. Available www.usda.gov/cnpp, retrieved April 4, 2002.
2. *Consumer Expenditure Survey, 2000*, U.S. Department of Labor, Bureau of Labor Statistics, retrieved April 4, 2002. Used data for Husband and Wife consumer unit with average annual income of $53,232.
3. Heidi Knapp Rinella, *Money Management- Climbing Out of Debt*, Las Vegas Review Journal, April 17, 2001
4. Jane Seaberry, "As home equity loan's rise, credit card borrowing follows," *Dallas Morning News*, February 22, 1999.
5. New York Stock Exchange, *NYSE Customer's Debt Margin*, available www.nyse.com/marketinfo/nysestatistics.html, retrieved April 4, 2002.

Chapter 22—A Family Finance Reformation

1. Matthew 10:39.
2. 1 Timothy 5:8.
3. John 6:37.
4. Edith Schaeffer, *What Is a Family?* (Grand Rapids: Raven's Ridge Books, 1975).
5. Jim Wiedemann, Kurt Bruner, *An Introduction to Family Nights: Creating Lasting Impressions for the Next Generation* (Colorado Springs: ChariotVictor Publishing, 1997), available www.Heritagebuilders.com.
6. *87% Of Parents Say That Advertising and Marketing Aimed at Children Makes Kids Too Materialistic*, Center for a New American Dream, Takoma Park, MD, available www.newdream.org/campaign/kids/press-release.html, retrieved April 4, 2002.
7. Deuteronomy 6:14.
8. Joshua 24:15.
9. Teresa Gubbins, "Survey Tells the Honest Truth," *Dallas Morning News*, August 4, 2001, 1C.
10. "Proportion of Working Mothers with Babies Decreases," *Daily Policy Digest,* Women in the Economy, National Center for Policy Analysis, avail-

able www.ncpa.org/iss/wie/pd1101901c.html, retrieved October 19, 2001.

Chapter 23—Revival? Reformation? Judgment? It's Up to You!

1. Christian History Institute, *The Great Awakening of 1857–1858*, available www.smithworks.org/stephen/revival/1857.html and www.members.truepath. com/hf/nyprayer.htm, retrieved June 21, 2001.
2. Ibid.
3. J. Edwin Orr, *The Great Awakening of 1857-1858*, available www. smithworks.org/stephen/revival/1857.html, retrieved June 21, 2001.
4. Christian History Institute, *World-Wide Revival Born out of a New York Prayer Meeting*, available www.members.truepath.com/hf/nyprayer.htm, retrieved June 21, 2001.
5. David Smithers, ed. and comp., *Why Did the Fire Fall in 1857?* (The Watchword, 2001). Available www.watchword.org/smithers/ww40c.html, retrieved June 6, 2001.
6. Christian History Institute, *The Great Awakening of 1857–1858*, available www.smithworks.org/stephen/revival/1857.html, retrieved June 21, 2001.
7. Ibid.
8. 2 Chronicles 7:14.
9. 2 Chronicles 7:19–20.
10. Isaiah 30:10.
11. Hebrews 12:6.
12. Psalms 9:8, 16.
13. Numbers 14:18.
14. Genesis 6, Genesis 13:13, Genesis 19, Leviticus 26:14-46, Deuteronomy 28:15-68, Isaiah 3, Jeremiah 7, Jeremiah 25, Jeremiah 24, 2 Kings 22:13, 16-17.
15. David Wilkerson, *America's Last Call: On the Brink of a Financial Holocaust* (Lindale: Wilkerson Trust Publications, 1998).
16. This Article was reprinted from The Last Days Magazine. If you would like additional copies of it in tract form, please write to Last Days Ministries at Box 40, Lindale, TX 75771-0040 and ask for #020.
17. Melody Green and David Hazard, No Compromise. The Life Story of Keith Green (Chatsworth: Sparrow Press, 1989).
18. E. M. Bounds, *The Complete Works of E. M. Bounds on Prayer* (Grand Rapids: Baker Book House, 1990), pp. 10, 211, 212.
19. Norman Grubb, *Rees Howells, Intercessor* (Fort Washington, Pa.: Christian Literature Crusade, 1952), p. 46.

Author Biography

The author married his wife Dana in 1993. They have been blessed with three children: Emily (1994), Jacob (1996), and Justin (2000). They currently reside in McKinney, Texas. Doug, the only "non-native" Texan in the Hagedorn family, was born near Detroit and was raised in Grand Rapids, Michigan. He received his B.A. degree in Business Administration at Michigan State University (1987) and his M.B.A. degree in Business Management at University of Dallas (1991). He is currently completing course-work at Tyndale Theological Seminary. He is a member of the Lead Faculty for LeTourneau University (since1996), has served as the Treasurer and Finance Committee Chairman for Dallas Metro Ministries since 1994, and is active in his local church as Treasurer, Sunday school teacher, and small group leader (since1999). He is currently employed at Raytheon Corporation (since1987). He has conducted Financial Foundation Builders seminars in churches since 1997 (references available upon request) and is also available for Biblical Giving teaching sessions. The author was born again in 1991 and is a Promise Keeper.

Financial Foundation Builders Seminars

Seminar Format

➢ A colorful, graphical, lively, informative presentation (using PowerPoint or overhead transparencies)
➢ Workbook provided
➢ NO SALES PITCHES or "INVESTMENT OPPORTUNITIES"
➢ Presented on the basis of a love offering
➢ Nondenominational emphasis
➢ *Ease the Squeeze* available

Seminar-Length Opportunities

Plan A: 2 to 4 hours on a Sunday evening or a weekday evening
Plan B: 4 to 8 hours on a Friday evening and a Saturday morning
Plan C: 4 to 8 hours in a Saturday or a Sunday workshop
Plan D: 4 to 8 hour Saturday session with 30 minutes Sunday morning
Plan D: Two night sessions, 1 to 3 hours each
Plan E: 30-minute to 1-hour teaching(s) on Sunday morning (see biblical giving teachings)
Plan F: Tie-in "Christmas on a Budget" Seminar (my wife) with any of the preceding plans
                 - Creating Family Traditions and Stress-Free Holidays
Plan G: You name it!

Seminar Objectives

♦ To provide solid /biblical approaches to money management,

finances, and giving.
♦ To help individuals develop a Life Plan (mission for living), a Financial Plan, and a Giving Plan.
♦ To emphasize strongly stewardship, giving, and missions.
♦ To share my personal testimony of how I achieved complete financial freedom (debt-free, giving).
♦ To present biblical teachings on materialism, self-control, obedience, discipline, and spiritual/financial parallels.
♦ To help individuals regain control of their finances.
♦ To demonstrate how to develop personal and family goals—for finances and for life.
♦ To demonstrate how to set up a realistic, structured budget to help individuals get out of debt (tools and worksheets provided).
♦ To provide an opportunity for an evangelistic outreach to the community that meets a real need.
♦ To arm Christians with tools to achieve financial freedom and to assist others in doing the same.
♦ To see a significant increase in local church and missions giving.
♦ To increase marital and family unity.
♦ To ground youth in financial principles and to encourage planning early in life.
♦ To see those people who are in debt become totally and completely debt free.
♦ To provide pastors; church boards; and leadership, finance, and benevolence committees with tools for financial requests and followup.
♦ To meet a practical, critical need within the church.
♦ To offer money-saving ideas and educational Web sites.
♦ To provide an opportunity for the Holy Spirit to deal with greed, materialism, selfishness, and idolatry.
♦ To glorify Jesus Christ!

Financial Foundation Builders
"Biblical Giving Teachings"

The author has taught on the following topics:

- ➢ Giving—A Heart Condition
- ➢ Hoarding vs. Giving—The Great Tug of War
- ➢ The Storehouse
- ➢ The "Trap"—Materialism and Idolatry
- ➢ Obedience in Giving
- ➢ Tithing or Voluntary Giving? Which Is It?
- ➢ Basics of Giving—What? To Whom? Why?
- ➢ The Results of Giving (Blessings).
- ➢ Giving—"A Practical Side and a Spiritual Side"
- ➢ Giving—"A Guaranteed Eternal Investment"
- ➢ Equality—"Reaching our World" (missions emphasis)
- ➢ An Undivided Heart
- ➢ Generosity and Cheerful Giving

Information/Order Form

Please send more information:

_____ Please send a brochure with more information on "Financial Freedom/Biblical Money Management Seminars" or "Biblical Giving" teachings.

_____ Please send a Sample "Biblical Giving" Teaching tape.

_____ Please send more information regarding "e-coaching" (budgeting & financial help and coaching via e-mail).

Please send additional copies of "Ease the Squeeze"

_____ I would like to order _____ additional copies of Ease the Squeeze ($20 includes shipping). Please make check or money order to "FFB" and send to the address below.

_____ Please send a complimentary copy of "Revolution in Third World Missions" (1 Free copy with purchase).

Send Testimonies, requests for information or book orders to:

**Financial Foundation Builders
c/o Doug Hagedorn
P.O. Box 3143
McKinney, TX 75070**

e-mail: doug@financialfoundationbuilders.com

Financial Foundation Builders

BUDGETING·STEWARDSHIP·GROWTH

---

www.financialfoundationbuilders.com
972-529-1366 or 1-866-66BUILD

Information/Order Form

Please send more information:

_____ Please send a brochure with more information on "Financial Freedom/Biblical Money Management Seminars" or "Biblical Giving" teachings.

_____ Please send a Sample "Biblical Giving" Teaching tape.

_____ Please send more information regarding "e-coaching" (budgeting & financial help and coaching via e-mail).

Please send additional copies of "Ease the Squeeze"

_____ I would like to order _____ additional copies of Ease the Squeeze ($20 includes shipping). Please make check or money order to "FFB" and send to the address below.

_____ Please send a complimentary copy of "Revolution in Third World Missions" (1 Free copy with purchase).

Send Testimonies, requests for information or book orders to:

Financial Foundation Builders
c/o Doug Hagedorn
P.O. Box 3143
McKinney, TX 75070

e-mail: doug@financialfoundationbuilders.com